Pan's Daughter

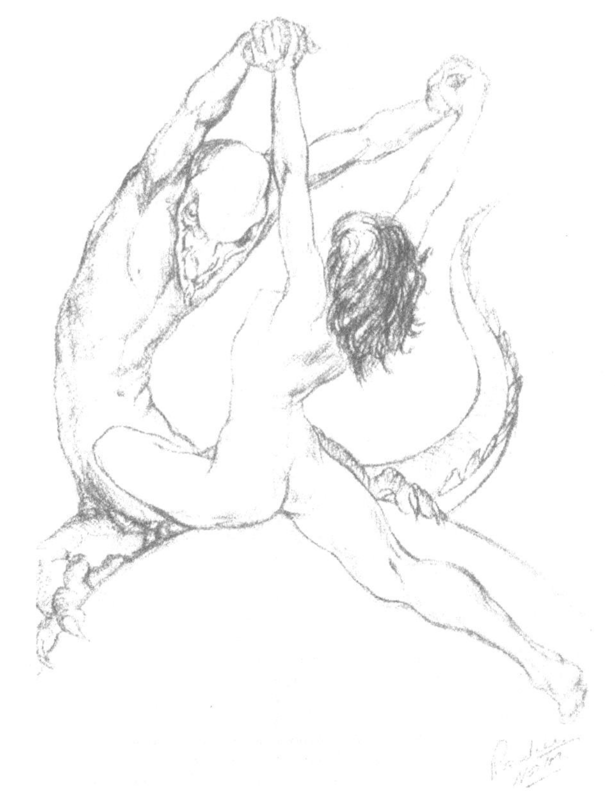

Pan's Daughter

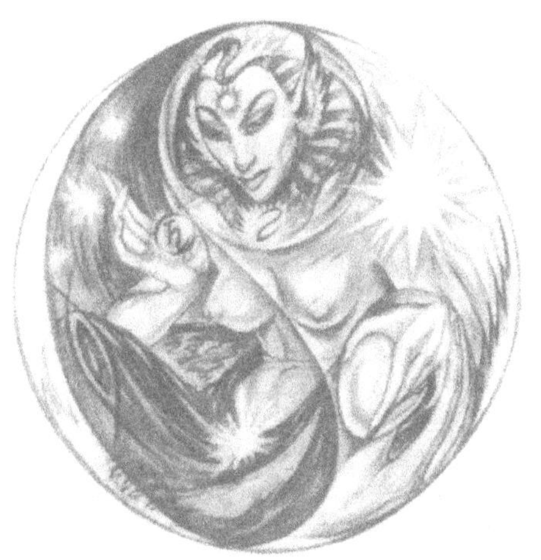

The Magical World of Rosaleen Norton

Revised and expanded edition

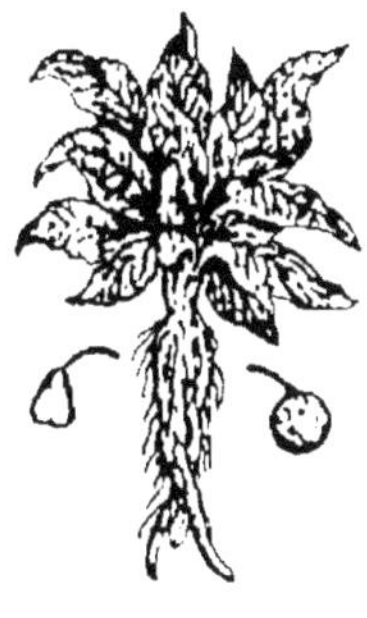

Nevill Drury Ph.D

This paperback edition 2016
1st Edition Hardback 2013

Published by
Mandrake of Oxford
PO Box 250
OXFORD
OX1 1AP (UK)

Contents

This book is dedicated to Rosaleen's sister Cecily and also to Wally Glover Snr and Jock McKenna – all of whom have passed away since publication of the first edition of this book. Without their kind assistance, the threads of this story could never have been woven together

Acknowledgements

I would like to acknowledge the assistance of the three people who made this biography possible – Rosaleen Norton's sister Cecily, Wally Glover and Jock McKenna. Since the first publication of this book in Australia in 1988 all three have died.

Originally wary of allowing a biography to be written at all, Cecily finally warmed to the idea when I promised to research the book carefully and present the details of Rosaleen's life in a factual and unsensational way.

Wally proved to be a source of wonderful and fascinating information, both with regard to his early years with Rosaleen and her lover, Gavin Greenlees, and also in his accounts of events following Norton's death in 1979. But it was Wally's friend Jock McKenna who provided perhaps the greatest favour of all – by lending me material from his extensive Rosaleen Norton scrapbooks and newspaper jottings dating back to the 1940s. Jock had met Rosaleen Norton in Kings Cross in 1944, while visiting with adventurer Tex Clarke, and he had been impressed by her kindness and personal warmth. As a result, he kept extensive news clippings of her subsequent career and these were, of course, a marvellous resource. Without Jock's collection, Wally's delightful reminiscences, and Cecily's support, this book could never have been written.

Others who helped me with information include Jim Russell, who read and corrected the material on *Smith's Weekly*, and Dr Marguerite Johnson who shared details of the magical correspondence between Rosaleen Norton and Eugene Goossens while I was researching my Ph.D at the University of Newcastle. I am also indebted indirectly to Mrs Y.

Raphael-Oeser who sent details of Rosaleen Norton's 1949 psychological evaluation at the University of Melbourne to Wally Glover. This material – which included a lengthy interview with psychologist L. J. Murphy – provided fascinating insights into Norton's trance techniques and her attitudes to sexuality.

Introduction

During the 1950s Norton was well known in Australia as 'the Witch of Kings Cross' and was portrayed in the popular media as a colourful and 'wicked' bohemian figure from Sydney's red-light district. Her provocative 'pagan' art, exhibited first at the University of Melbourne Library in 1949 and later in the Apollyon and Kashmir coffee-shops in Sydney's Kings Cross, plunged her into legal controversy, and her 1952 publication, *The Art of Rosaleen Norton*, was banned when it was released in Australia on the basis that it contained allegedly obscene material. Norton was involved in a number of court hearings and was widely criticised in the media for engaging in bizarre sexual practices with her lover, the poet Gavin Greenlees. She was also associated with the scandal that eventually engulfed the professional career of renowned musical conductor and composer, Sir Eugene Goossens, who arrived in Australia in 1947 and later became a member of Norton's magical coven in Kings Cross.

Most people knew Rosaleen Norton simply as 'Roie'. The Roie I remember was slight in build, with dark and rather untidy curly hair, quick darting eyes and mysterious arched eyebrows. During the 1950s she had become famous – perhaps one should say notorious – as an eccentric and bohemian practitioner of witchcraft. She wore flamboyant blouses, puffed on an engraved cigarette holder, and produced bizarre fantasy paintings which had a distinct touch of the pagan and demonic about them.

This was of course a time when a rather prudish and puritanical mentality prevailed in Australia and society in general was by no means as culturally diverse or as tolerant as it is today. The public at large was astounded by Rosaleen's risqué paintings and drawings which depicted naked hermaphroditic beings, phalluses transforming into serpents, and passionate encounters with black panthers. And while Norman Lindsay's work was halfway to becoming respectable – a type of tempered voyeurism made it possible to admire the naked frolics depicted in his paintings and drawings and call them 'art' – it was by no means as easy for Rosaleen to be accepted. As she herself would say, Lindsay's figures were creatures of the day and had frivolous, happy natures, whereas her compositions invariably focused on figures of the night – phantasms from the darker recesses of the soul.

Roie originally presented herself as a trance artist. From an early age she had a remarkable capacity to explore the visionary depths of her subconscious mind, and the archetypal beings she encountered on those occasions became the focus of her art. It was only later that Roie was labelled a witch, was described as such in the popular press, and began to develop the persona which accompanied that description. As this process gathered momentum, Roie in turn became intent on trying to demonstrate that she had been *born* a witch. After all, she had somewhat pointed ears, small blue markings on her left knee, and also a long strand of flesh which hung from underneath her armpit to her waist – a variant on the extra nipple sometimes ascribed to witches in the Middle Ages. However, I feel that much of this was simply the development of her mystique. From her earliest childhood, Roie wanted to be different. She revelled in being the odd one out, purporting to despise her schoolmates. She argued continuously with her mother. She 'hated' authority figures like headmistresses, policemen, politicians and priests. She had no time at all

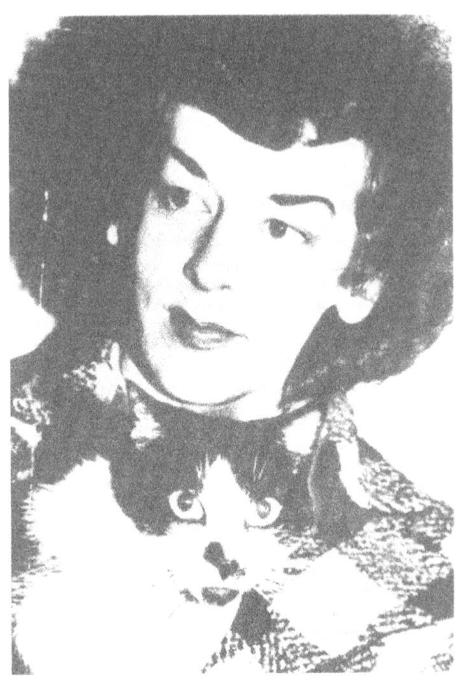

ROSALEEN AND HER PET CAT, PHOTOGRAPHED IN THE 1950S

for organised religion, and the gods she embraced – a cluster of ancient gods centred around Pan – were, of course, pagan to the hilt. She regarded Pan as the God of Infinite Being. Traditionally Pan is known as the god of flocks and shepherds in ancient Greece. Depicted as half-man, half-goat, he played a pipe with seven reeds and was considered the lord of Nature and all forms of wildlife. He was also rather lecherous, having numerous love affairs with the nymphs – especially Echo, Syrinx and Pithys.

Pan was undoubtedly a rather unusual god for a young woman to be worshipping in Australia. But then Roie was different. And she was different in an age when it was quite a lot harder to be different than it is now. She was bohemian, bisexual, outspoken, rebellious and thoroughly independent in an era when most young ladies growing up on Sydney's North Shore would be thinking simply of staying home, happily married with a husband and children. Roie was not afraid to say what she thought, draw her pagan images on city pavements, or flaunt her occult beliefs in the pages of the tabloids. To most people who read about her in newspapers and magazines she was simply outrageous. Norton was invariably depicted in the popular media as a pagan rebel and portrayed in such ungracious terms as 'the notorious, Pan-worshipping Witch of Kings Cross…a person known to the police through two prosecutions for obscenity'.[1] Most of her mainstream print media coverage was generated by popular gossip-driven magazines like *The Australasian Post*, *People*, *Truth* and *Squire* that inclined towards sensationalist articles, and tabloid newspapers like *The Daily Telegraph*, *The Daily Mirror* and *Sun*. But all of this salacious media interest in Norton has to be seen in an historical context. During the immediate post-World War Two period Australia was both socially and politically conservative, ruled by the highly traditional prime-minister Sir Robert Menzies, who promoted a harsh stance on censorship. Norton was portrayed in the popular media as a Devil-worshipping harpy, ever eager to flaunt accepted social conventions at a time when the appropriate place for a woman was perceived to be within the home, focusing on domestic concerns and attending to the needs of husband and children. During the 1960s, with its increasing intake of migrants from many European and Asian countries, Australia began the slow process of becoming a genuinely multi-cultural society with a wide range of new religious faiths.[2] However, up until the period immediately after World War Two, Australia was still conventionally Christian. Over 80 per cent of the entire population was Anglican, Presbyterian, Methodist or Roman Catholic.

Because witchcraft has long remained linked to medieval and early modern Western Christian demonology[3] it is hardly surprising that in most media depictions of Norton during the 1950s and 1960s she was portrayed as a renegade from mainstream society, as an anti-Christian Devil worshipper, and as a practitioner of 'black magic'. However, this perception of her was distorted and completely uninformed. In fact, Norton was a pantheist and practising witch who paid homage to a range of ancient pagan deities associated with the primal forces of Nature and the Underworld. The latter included Pan and Hecate, to whom she dedicated her ritual altars. Norton was also involved in sex magic, pursuing various forms of ritual practice influenced in part by the occult teachings of Aleister Crowley.

Although the Australian popular media labelled Norton a Devil worshipper, I do not believe that Norton was a practising Satanist in the literal sense of the word. Even so, it is clear that Norton's inclination was very much toward the 'night' side of magic and much of her occult imagery as a visionary artist is associated with the *Qliphoth*, or dark energies of the Kabbalistic Tree of Life – a central motif in modern magic. Norton's esoteric beliefs, cosmology and visionary art are all closely intertwined – and reflect her unique approach to the magical universe.

* * *

I met Roie towards the end of her life, in 1977. She had already become a recluse but a friend of mine, Barry Salkilld, and I had tracked down a person called Danny who knew her. Danny worked in a jeweller's shop in Kings Cross and we explained to him that we were genuinely interested in magical techniques and practices and wanted to discuss both her personal view of magic and her perceptions of the world at large. The message filtered through and we were granted an interview.

Roie was living then in a rather dark basement flat at the end of a long corridor in an old building in Roslyn Gardens, just down from the Cross in the direction of Rushcutters Bay. She was somewhat frail but still extremely mentally alert, with expressive eyes and a hearty laugh. She even invited us to share an LSD trip with her, but in the gloomy recesses of her basement flat we shuddered to think of the shadowy beings we might unleash through this powerful psychedelic, and we both politely declined. I later found out that Roie periodically used LSD to induce visionary states and that this was all about enhancing her awareness as an artist. She did not, however, use the drug simply for recreation, for she was well aware of its potency.

We talked at that meeting about the gods Roie encountered in trance, about her view that Pan was alive in the 'back-to-Nature' movement supported by the counterculture, and we also discussed her strong personal bond with animals. Roie told us that she believed most animals had much more integrity than human beings and she also felt that cats, especially, could operate both in the world of normal waking consciousness and in the inner psychic world simultaneously. She even remembered a time which may have been a previous incarnation. She believed she had once lived in a past century in a rickety wooden house in a field of yellow grass, somewhere near Beachy Head in Sussex. There

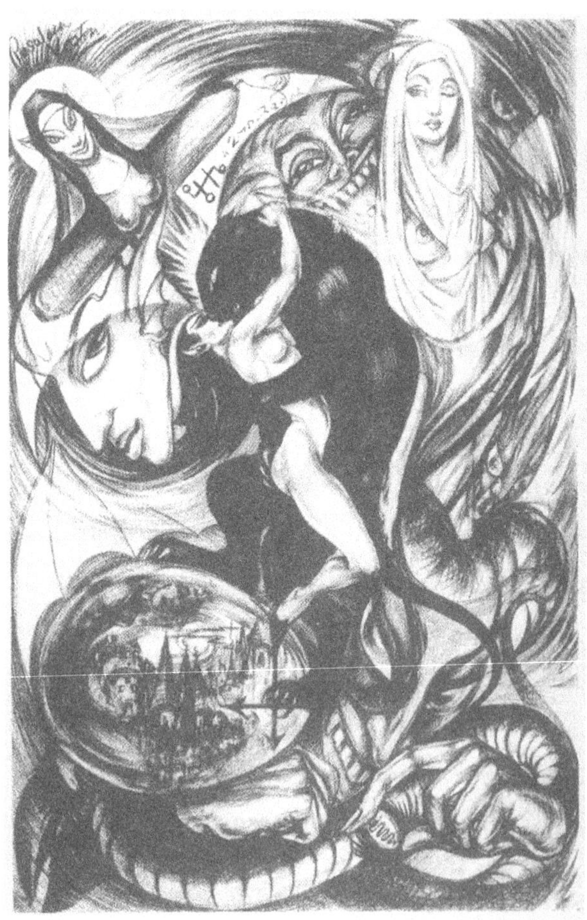

BLACK MAGIC – *A CONTROVERSIAL WORK FROM THE 1950S ASSOCIATED IN THE PUBLIC MIND WITH SATANISM AND DEVIL-WORSHIP*

were several farm animals there – cows, horses and so on – and she herself was a poltergeist, a disembodied spirit. She recalled then when 'normal' people came near the house they were frightened by her presence and could not accept the existence of poltergeists or any other 'supernatural' beings. But the animals accepted her as she was – as part of the natural order.

For Roie this went some way towards explaining her love for her own pet animals, and throughout her life she lived surrounded by creatures of all kinds – from pet lizards and spiders through to mice, turtles and cats. In the Cross, in her dark and very private living room, she still had her animal friends to comfort her, and she related to them more positively than to her human neighbours in the in the daylight world outside. One couldn't help feeling that here in the twilight realm of her Kings Cross basement flat she felt thoroughly at home. She no longer felt any strong desire for regular contact with the external world.

This book is not only about the life and times of Rosaleen Norton, but also describes her rather complex and unusual world view. Her personal beliefs were a strange mix of magic, mythology and fantasy, but derived substantially from mystical experiences which, for her, were completely real. She was no theoretician. Part of her disdain for the public at large, I believe, derived from the fact that she felt she had access to a wondrous visionary universe – while most people lived lives that were narrow, bigoted, and based on fear. Roie was very much an adventurer – a free spirit – and she liked to fly through the worlds opened to her by her imagination.

Roie's art reflected this. It was her main passion, her main reason for living. She had no career ambitions other than to reflect on the forces within her essential being, and to manifest these psychic and magical energies in the only way she knew how. As Roie's sister Cecily later told me, art was the very centre of her life, and Roie took great pride in the brief recognition she received when the English critic and landscape artist John Sackville-West described her in 1970 as one of Australia's finest artists, alongside Norman Lindsay.[4] It was praise from an unexpected quarter, and it heartened Roie considerably because she felt

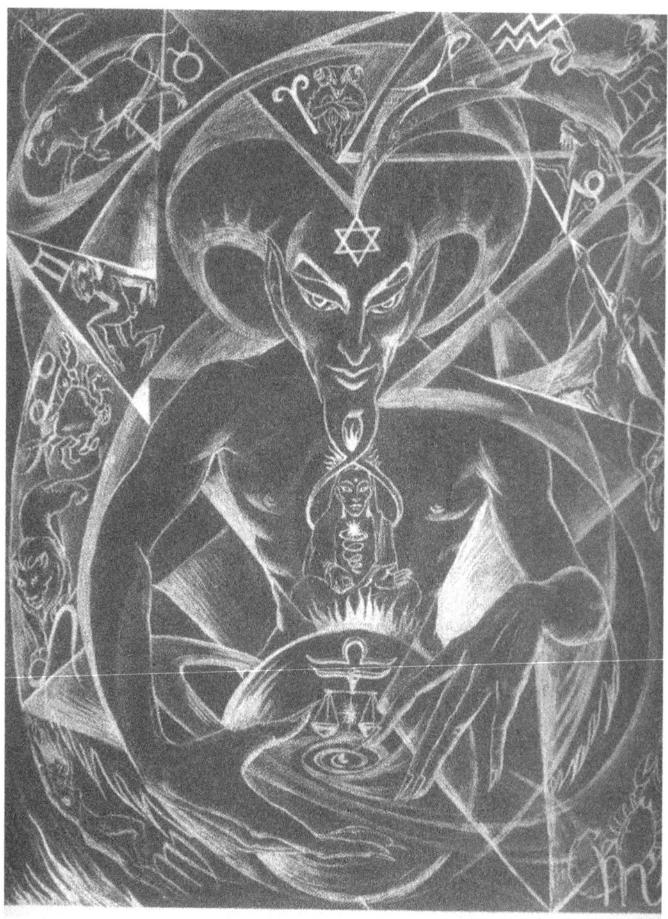

THE MASTER – *ANOTHER ALLEGEDLY 'DIABOLICAL' IMAGE*

that at last someone had understood her art and had responded to it positively. All too often her critics had responded only to her outer veneer – the bizarre and often distorted persona created by the media – and this was not the 'real' Roie at all.

I hope that this book throws some light on her extraordinary life, for we have not seen anyone else quite like her since her death in 1979. She was an amazing person – a woman of strong convictions and unusual beliefs – and quite a deal more complex than the cheap, sensationalistic stories in the tabloids would suggest. As will become obvious, Rosaleen Norton was very much ahead of her time and was widely misunderstood by the public at large. I sincerely hope that this book will go some small way to correcting these lingering misconceptions.

Nevill Drury

1 D. Salter, 'The Strange Case of Sir Eugene and the Witch', *Good Weekend/Sydney Morning Herald*, Sydney, 3 July 1999: 17.
2 C.M. Cusack, 'Tradition and Change: Australian Churches and the Future', *Australian Review of Public Affairs*, University of Sydney 2003:1.
3 M.D. Bailey, 'The Meanings of Magic', *Magic, Ritual and Witchcraft*, University of Pennsylvania Press, Summer 2006: 22.
4 John Sackville-West was a traditional artist who had two works accepted by the Royal Academy in London. As reported in the *Sun Herald* (25 October 1970), he specifically named Norman Lindsay and Rosaleen Norton as 'two of Australia's finest artists'.

In the spiral horns of the Ram,
In the deep ascent of midnight,
In the dance of atoms weaving the planes of matter
is Life.
Life spins on the dream of a planet,
Life leaps in the lithe precision of the cat,
Life flames in the thousandth Name,
Life laughs in the thing that is 'I'.
I live in the green blood of the forest,
I live in the white fire of Powers,
I live in the scarlet blossom of Magic,
I live.

Rosaleen Norton ,
1962

1
'Nothing Beasts'

As if anticipating the spectacular events of her later life, Rosaleen Norton was born during a violent thunderstorm in Dunedin, New Zealand. It was around 4.30 in the morning on 2 October 1917 and, as Rosaleen later related, it was perhaps because of this that she developed an enduring fondness for storms and the night-side of life. 'Storms arouse in me a peculiarly elated, almost drunken sensation,' she reminisced in 1957, 'Night is for me the time when all my perceptions are alert, when I feel most awake and function best; and this idiosyncrasy was a perpetual bone of contention with my mother, since persuading me to go to bed was no easy task – nor was waking me in the mornings.'

An unconventional child from the outset, Rosaleen Miriam Norton was the third of three sisters in an orthodox Protestant family. Her parents were Church of England – 'not deeply religious, but God-fearing' – and were reasonably well-to-do. Rosaleen's English-born father, Albert Thomas Norton, was employed as a master mariner with the New Zealand Steamship Company. He had been at sea since becoming an apprentice deckhand at the age of 16, and much later, in 1940, when Italy entered World War II, he was appointed captain of the *Remo*, an Italian vessel stationed in Melbourne – the *Remo* had been requisitioned as a prize of war. Even in the 1920s he was often at sea for long stretches of time, visiting such locations as Vancouver, San Francisco and the Pacific Islands.

In view of his frequent travels it was thought that Sydney might prove to be a better base than Dunedin. So in June 1925 the Nortons migrated, establishing themselves in Lindfield on Sydney's North Shore. The family home was a solidly built brick house in Wolseley Street, close to the railway line on the western side. The Nortons were quite comfortably off and as Rosaleen's sister Cecily would later recall, the home was happy and comfortable – a place 'full of animals, music and books'. Albert was a warm and friendly man and a cousin of the composer Ralph Vaughan Williams, whom he resembled in physical appearance. But because of his lengthy periods at sea, the day-to-day responsibility for bringing up the children necessarily fell to his wife Beena [Norton], who dedicated herself to the task of being a devoted and responsible mother.

There were three daughters, Cecily [Norton], Phyllis [Norton] and Rosaleen. Cecily and Phyllis were, respectively, twelve and ten years older than Rosaleen and were inclined to pamper and spoil their younger sister. Not surprisingly, young Rosaleen became used to getting her own way and Mrs Norton sometimes found her rather difficult to control. But she doted on her daughter and although Rosaleen may perhaps have felt a little smothered, there is no doubt that deep down Rosaleen was very fond of her. A letter written to her mother while away on holidays began 'Darlingest precious Mummy...' and was decorated with kisses in the margins. But Roie would later describe her mother as a 'conventional, highly emotional woman, far too absorbed in her family' and during an interview with psychologist L.J. Murphy at the University of Melbourne in 1949, she portrayed her mother as 'a very difficult woman, hysterical, emotional and possessive'. Looking back on her youth, Roie held a grudge

ROSALEEN, AGED FIVE

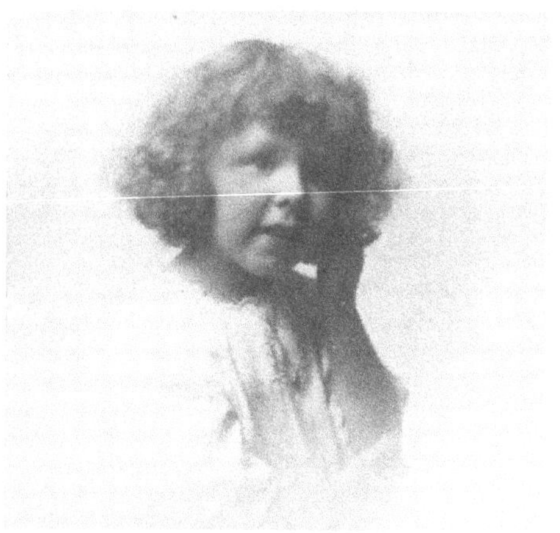

against her mother because, as she put it, 'she wouldn't fight fair'. According to Roie, she would burst into tears, say how much she loved her daughter, and try to urge her to do things mother's way.

Her father, on the other hand, was a figure she respected. Although his visits home were sporadic she had a clear-cut relationship with him which was more to her liking. 'He fought clean,' Rosaleen told the university psychologist. 'If I disobeyed him he would smack me when I was a child and make me do what he wanted me to do without all the emotional upsets that I had with my mother.'

At the time of moving to Lindfield the two older Norton sisters had already left school but young Rosaleen, who had commenced her education in Dunedin at the age of four, was now sent to a private infants' school and then on to the Church of England Girls' School in Chatswood. From the start she had a flair for disobedience. Always a rebellious child, she later recalled:

> I disliked school and I disliked the other children – I hated the way they 'crawled' to the teacher. I used to love making the teachers mad by getting the other children to do naughty things. They used to follow me, but I don't think they liked me. Yet I always took the blame when anything went wrong.[1]

Perhaps exaggerating the tensions of her early childhood, Rosaleen later described her early life as 'a generally wearisome period of senseless shibboleths, prying adults, detestable or depressing children whom I was supposed to like, and parental reproaches'. This led, not surprisingly, to a singular feeling of independence:

> As a child my chief aim was to be left to my own devices, and to this end I staged a hunger strike for the right to have meals

> alone (which I liked to eat on the roof and in other odd places). After a couple of days mother capitulated – apparently not realising that I had access to a well-stocked provision cupboard. Soon after this I acquired a tent which, pitched in the garden, became my sleeping quarters until it fell into tatters three years later. [2]

It was during this escapade in the garden that young Rosaleen developed a special fondness for insects, and especially for spiders – which would later feature in her macabre drawings. Indeed, it was while camped in the garden that she acquired her first pet:

> A big furry night-spider of the orb-weaving type soon took to spinning nightly over the open tent door. I became very fond of this being, whom – regardless of sex – I named Horatius, because she guarded me from invasion single-handed.
>
> Most of my family were terrified of her, so I could stay up until morning if I felt like it, secure from interruption as long as she loomed in her great circular web over my doorway. [3]

For Rosaleen, it was part of the instinctive process of getting closer to Nature, of developing an increasing familiarity with the myriad creatures of bush and garden. As a child Rosaleen always had lots of pets – at different times an assortment of cats, lizards, mice, guinea pigs, a possum, an echidna, a goat, tortoises, dogs and various toads – and she spent hours poring over her biology texts. 'I was fascinated by zoology and entomology' she would later recall, reflecting on her childhood, 'and at 9 or 10 I could have answered a quiz on prehistoric animals with a reasonable chance of winning the jackpot.' In fact, Rosaleen found more solace among animals and insects than among most members of her family:

'Family affection as such never meant anything to me, and although I was very fond of two relatives – my eldest sister [Cecily] and one of my aunts – it was because I regarded them as friends rather than relations.'

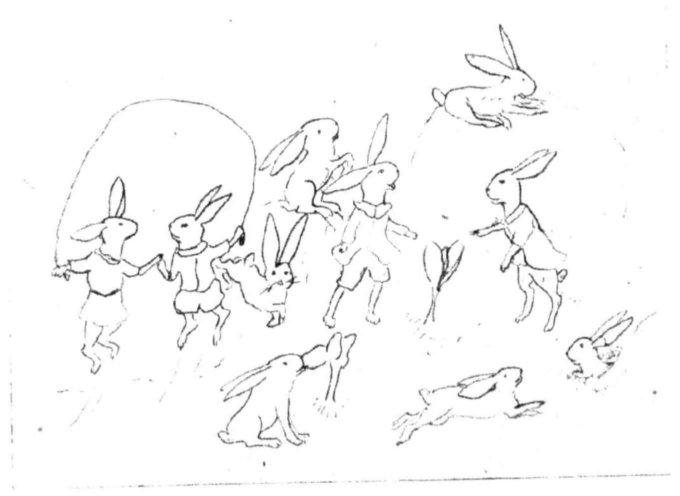

ROSALEEN'S EARLIEST KNOWN ART-WORK, AGED SEVEN

Quite apart from her love of animals and insects, another aspect of her character also manifested at an early age - her propensity for producing nightmarish art. In an account published in *Australasian Post* in January 1957, Rosaleen provided interesting details of her early 'visionary' memories:

> My first drawings, at about 3½, were mainly creatures called 'Nothing Beasts' and 'Flippers' , which I knew very well as presences. The latter looked rather like the conventional sheeted ghosts, and were hostile to me; but they were kept at bay by my friends and protectors, the 'Nothing Beasts', who had animal heads surmounting a mass of octopoid

tentacles, with which they seemed to swim through the ether.

Apropos of apparitions, various psychic manifestations, both subjective and objective, have always been an integral part of my life; consequently I accepted them unquestionably as part of the natural order of things.

Some typical early examples include a ghostly 'lady in a grey dress' who was often standing beside my bed when I was 5 or 6; an apparition of a shining dragon [at 5], which together with other elements in this vision had, as I later discovered, profound symbolic significance for occultists; and a dream of a small weatherboard house surrounded by pepper trees, called 'Railway Cottage', which I located in waking life some three or four months later in Chatswood, a suburb which at the time of the dream I had never visited. My only reaction on actually seeing 'Railway Cottage', in the weatherboard if not exactly the flesh, was a feeling of 'Oh yes, there it is.'

While on the subject of psychism, a recurrent experience of my early years is worth mentioning as I now recognise it as a trance condition similar to those practised in certain forms of Yoga. My name for it was 'Big Things and Little Things', and it always began with a floating state, as though disembodied. Then came a feeling of growing and expanding. Larger and larger I grew, until size became so unthinkable that it ceased to exist, and I encompassed all things and was everywhere.

After a timeless pause again came movement, this time of contraction and shrinking down, down until I had returned to my starting point; but the sense of dwindling still contin-

> ued. Down through successive stages becoming smaller and smaller, until at last I was a point too tiny to exist at all; a nothing that was somehow still sentient. Soon the growing, expanding process was repeated, back to the original size – and so on. It was rhythm suggesting some vast form of breathing.
>
> At seven-years-old two small blue marks very close together appeared on my left knee, and they are there still. I have since learned that two (or sometimes three) blue or red dots together on the skin are among the traditional witch marks.
>
> Although, of course, I didn't know this at the time, I remember noticing them the year we arrived in Australia, and wondering what they were: they seemed important in some way that I couldn't define. [4]

Whether she had already begun to tap her future potential as a witch we can never know, but at the Church of England Girls' School Rosaleen began producing strange drawings for her classmates. These became increasingly bizarre, culminating in an interpretation of Saint Saens' *Danse Macabre*, complete with vampires, ghouls and werewolves. It featured, Rosaleen said later, '...every sort of grotesque horror I could put pencil to, in a great cavern under the earth'.

This drawing was simply too much for her teachers, who for several years had endured her eccentric and disruptive behaviour. Soon afterwards fourteen-year-old Rosaleen was summoned from her class and expelled from her school under a cloud. Her headmistress subsequently wrote to her mother complaining that Rosaleen had a depraved nature which would corrupt the innocence of the other girls and making it clear that it was time for Rosaleen and the Church of England Girls' School to part company.

At first disheartened, but then equal to the challenge, Rosaleen enrolled at East Sydney Technical College. She studied art for two years under the tutelage of the noted sculptor, Rayner Hoff – head of the Art School. Hoff believed that a vivid and uninhibited imagination was needed for artistic development, and Rosaleen had these qualities in abundance. 'He freed me from routine and let me spend my time at figure drawing and composition,' she would later recall, 'and since for the first time I was encouraged to work continuously at my own art form, I became an exemplary student.' [5]

It was while she was attending East Sydney Technical College that Rosaleen also became Australia's first woman pavement artist, although this was to be a very brief career. Roie had a favoured location at the bottom of Rowe Street, near the General Post Office in Martin Place, and at this spot she would draw on the pavement to attract attention from passers-by. On her first morning she earned herself seventeen shillings, one penny – a small fortune.

Part of the appeal of this location was that it was just below the Millions Club, the members of which had a tradition of throwing pennies out of the window for a joke. The idea was that the people below would think pennies were raining from heaven. However, one day while exhibiting her art on the pavement, Roie was hit on the forehead by a falling coin, and as her sister Cecily later told me, 'It dealt her quite a blow. She decided that the site was too dangerous, and did not go back.'

At this stage Roie was still living at home but she had already begun to stimulate her imagination by performing private rituals in her bedroom, using robes, Chinese joss sticks and wine which she had taken from a stock supply hidden by her parents. It was strange time for Roie because a new world was gradually opening for her through her art, and also through exploratory dabbling in magic. And yet she was still not totally free. Rayner Hoff was encouraging her at the College, allowing her to work at her own pace without doing the 'hack work' required of the other students, and yet she was still tied to domestic routines at home. Hanging over her always was the nagging question of what would happen

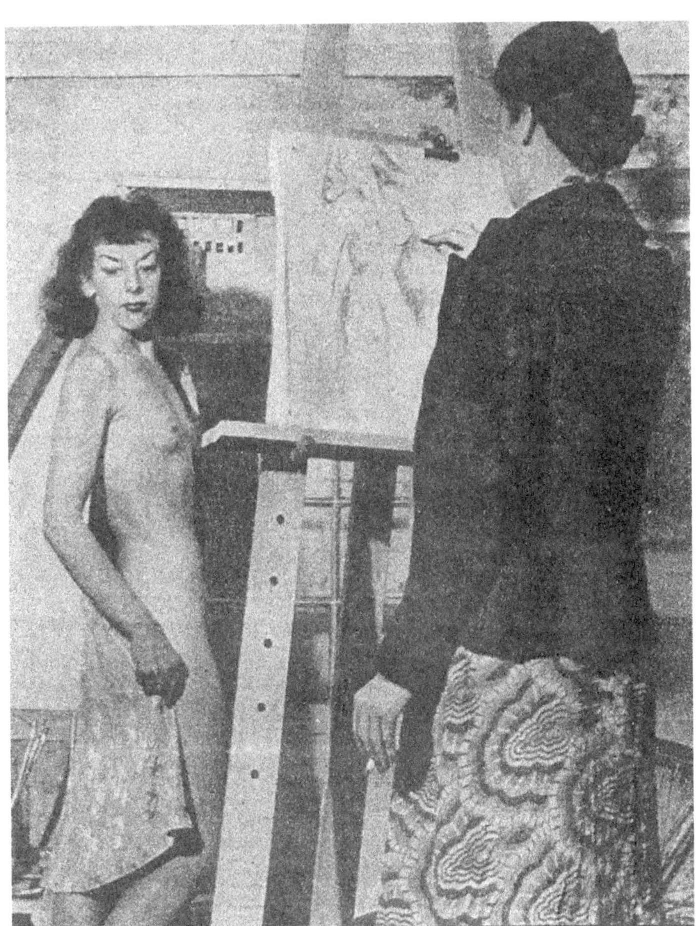

MODELLING IN ART CLASSES

after East Sydney Tech. Could she continue as an artist, could she strike out on her own, or would she need some more conventional means of earning a livelihood ?

ROIE, THE WRITER

Although one thinks of Rosaleen now primarily as a witch and bohemian artist, she also had considerable talents as a writer – albeit of macabre and exotic tales. She had submitted several stories to *Smith's Weekly* when she was only fifteen, and had had them accepted. It occurred to her that perhaps she could become a journalist, even though this would never be her preferred choice of occupation.

When Rosaleen first sent a short story to *Smith's* she had received resounding praise: 'Never have we discovered a juvenile author so gifted as is obviously Rosaleen Norton,' wrote editor Frank Marien – welcome encouragement indeed. In writing, as well as in art, she could give free rein to her imagination.

Her first story concerned a young man who was exploring a strange street by night when he came across a waxworks – admission sixpence. Since he liked waxworks, he decided to patronise the place:

A witch-like woman took his sixpence 'in a grey talon' and led him up rickety, worm-eaten steps...The young man ultimately found himself in a vast room lit by candles as black as pitch. Leering, misshapen forms were all around him, throwing criss-cross shadows on the floor. It was like a picture painted by a decadent genius. Were they only waiting for a signal from their master, the devil, to descend from their wooden pedestals and sport in a hellish saturnalia ? Terrified of the atmosphere, the young man sought to flee, but found that he had been locked in.

Somewhere, a clock struck midnight. A low, clear note of music sounded in the room and that music came from the pipes of a waxen satyr. Carl's brain reeled in an ecstasy of horror. The pieces of the waxworks were descending from their pedestals... the light snuffed out...

Next morning two policemen on patrol heard a shriek. Entering an empty, deserted old place that had once held a waxworks, they found 'the pitiful remains of what had once been a young man... his eyes had the look of one who had seen things mortals should not see.[6]

Rosaleen was then invited to submit another short story, and she sent in a piece titled *The Painted Horror*, a tale even more disturbing than the first.

It described a young artist who, while painting in his garret, noticed his hand being mysteriously guided into painting 'a gigantic, sickening mass of purplish, bloated flesh, looking as if it had risen from a sea of corruption, topped by a squat, leering, half-human head, and great, thick, blood-bedabbled fingers like writhing worms...The vast hulk crouched on the canvas ready to spring.' The mysterious force fed upon the artist's mind and soul and then, one morning, he was discovered on his studio floor 'torn to pieces and chewed'. A policeman who found the bizarre death impossible to solve noted: 'Funny the way a big canvas in his studio had a great hole in it, as if something had jumped right out of it, or through it.' [7]

Frank Marien was intrigued by these stories from the pen of a fifteen-year-old girl, and so he requested yet another tale for publication. This one, titled *Moon Madness*, was a study of a girl who, under the influence of the full moon, murders her sisters as a sacrifice to the marble statue of a young man in an orchard: 'There was one shriek from Corinne as

Vivienne's teeth met in her jugular. A shriek, short and horrible like a trapped rabbit – but there was nobody to hear it…only the thin carven lips of the youth seemed to smile as the warm blood of the sacrifice flowed over his feet.'

Fascinated by Rosaleen's imaginative, if gruesome, skills as a writer, Frank Marien decided that he would offer her a job as a cadet journalist, although he realised that he would have to channel her creative energies into a more palatable form. Since leaving school Rosaleen had become increasingly committed to her lifestyle as an art student and she was not immediately enticed by the offer. Were there any jobs going at *Smith's* as an artist she asked? Marien agreed to meet her to discuss it further. He would have to decide whether the young and precocious talent, Miss Rosaleen Norton, had a future on the staff of one of Australia's most popular newspapers.

1 Interview between L.J. Murphy and Rosaleen Norton, University of Melbourne, 27 August 1949.
2 Rosaleen Norton : 'I was born a Witch', *Australasian Post*, 3 January 1957: 4.
3 Ibid.
4 Ibid: 3.
5 Rosaleen Norton, 'Hitchhiking Witch', *Australasian Post*, 7 February 1957: 10.
6 Quoted in George Blaikie, *Remember Smith's Weekly ?*, Rigby, Adelaide 1975: 89.
7 Ibid: 90

2 From *Smith's Weekly* to *Pertinent*

Smith's Weekly seemed, on the face of it, to be an interesting and attractively unconventional place for Rosaleen to begin her career as a journalist and illustrator. As a broadsheet, it had something of a reputation for being irreverent and audacious and for championing minority causes. It was renowned for its artists, many of whom in their own way would contribute to Australia's social history, and it was famous also for its outspoken, candid comments. Today we would regard many of its editorial perspectives as racist and reactionary.

Smith's Weekly had been founded in 1919 by two journalists, Robert Clyde Packer and Claude McKay, and Englishman Sir James Joynton Smith, the son of a Cockney gasfitter. Published originally as a tuppeny paper, *Smith's* demanded a 'fair go' for the workers, denounced 'Bolshies', the Yellow Peril, quack doctors and prostitutes, and also took a strong line against bureaucrats, inter-racial sexual relationships and white bread – as distinct from wholemeal.

Despite its polemical overtones, however, the broadsheet attracted some of the best known graphic illustrators of the day, including Stan Cross, Syd Miller, George Finey, Cecil Hartt, Jim Russell, Virgil Reilly, Lance Driffield, Charles Hallett and George Donaldson. Later, Norman

Mitchell, Les Dixon, Eric Jolliffe and Emile Mercier would also become associated with it. Over the years the paper became famous for promoting the Digger cause. Indeed, most of its readers were returned servicemen. Its appeal was very much to the jingoism of the day and to that extent its scope was limited to a specific generation of readers. The popularity of *Smith's Weekly* began to wane after World War II and in October 1950 it finally yielded to the imminent onset of television as the medium of news and popular entertainment.

Rosaleen first visited Frank Marien and his staff at *Smith's Weekly* some time in 1934, when she was sixteen years old. Mollie Horseman and Joan Morrison remember that when she peeped around the office door she seemed to be just a child – hardly the same person who would later gain notoriety as the 'witch of Kings Cross'. However, even then she had a fanciful, exotic view of life. She told Mollie Horseman that her idea of a perfect weekend was to relax in a hot bath, eating chocolates and smoking cigarettes.

Following their meeting, Frank Marien hired Rosaleen to be a cadet journalist, largely on the basis of the stories she had sent in. Graphic artist Jim Russell remembers that Norton made quite an impact among the staff right away, but perhaps for the wrong reasons:

> I was working at *Smith's Weekly* then as a senior artist, and one night one of the nude models we used in our sketch club said, 'Remember me?' I said, 'No.' She said, 'Rosaleen Norton. I had white clothes on then.' We became quite friendly, and had coffee and things – as artists did with models – and one day she turns up at the office with artwork, which was quite out of this world... devils and things. Frank Marien, the editor, liked

> her work… thought something may come of it. He sat her in a room next door to me with two other girls. One of them was a Bohemian type like a big horse, and the other was a prim little school ma'am type. Rosie [sic], however, fitted in quite well. There was one, funny, little touch. Rosie didn't wear a blouse. She wore a big scarf with one end tied around her neck and the other around her waist. Now this was OK when she stood up, but when she sat down, and leant over, you could see all of her boobs. All the editorial staff would come in for a bit of a perve, and I told her one-day what was going on. 'If they want to look, that's OK,' she said. 'I've posed for you in the nude. So what the hell?' [1]

Soon, Rosaleen began to insist to Frank Marien that she earn her way as an artist rather than as a journalist. Marien was unsure of her talents in this direction and told her that the sort of drawings needed at the paper were humorous and witty, the main aim being simply to make readers laugh. Rosaleen told him she would have no trouble producing drawings like that.

Unfortunately, she was unable to deliver the goods. The first drawing she offered Marien showed a number of women sitting in a circle on some grass, biting their babies and laughing their heads off. It was hardly the type of humour he had in mind. Another drawing showed two girls outside a tiger's cage at the zoo. One of the girls was glaring at the zoo keeper and remarking to her friend, 'Wouldn't it be a thrill if one of the beasts devoured him!'

This was too much for Frank Marien. It was abundantly clear that Rosaleen's style was both highly idiosyncratic and not a little warped. Over the next few months he tried to get her to work in a more acceptable style, but to no avail – she was quite unable to produce for him the sort of illustrations which were acceptable to his readers. After eight months, she was shown the door and it was clear that she would have to pursue her artistic freedom in other quarters.

Rosaleen now felt that not only would she have to find a more congenial work environment than *Smith's Weekly* but she would also have to leave the family home in Lindfield. Her mother had died a short time before so there was no emotional pressure to stay on at home.

Roie left a note on the mantelpiece for her father and sisters, gathered her main possessions and then headed for the railway station. However she soon realised that her departure had not been properly planned:

> The only thing I had overlooked was money. At the railway station I realised I hadn't a farthing. I couldn't walk into town with two heavy suitcases but I managed to borrow two shillings from the local librarian. That took me in triumph – and a train – to the city.
>
> The next thing was money for a room. Leaving my suitcases at the station, I called at various studios for work as an artist's model. I was accounted a good model; not because of my curves, which were and are inclined to be conspicuous by their absence, but being myself an artist I knew which poses were best to draw.
>
> There was plenty of work, but all some days ahead. Meeting my current boyfriend, I was greeted by the news that he'd lost his job too; however, there was enough to take a room (eight shillings in those days) at a fabulous old building in Gloucester Street – the erstwhile Ship and Mermaid Inn, Sydney's first

pub, which later became the haunt of artists, musicians and drunks.[2]

The inn was also known as 'Beggary Barn' – or less politely as 'Buggary Barn' – and it stood overlooking Circular Quay. Built in 1841, it had been frequented by both Jack London and Joseph Conrad and was ideal 'digs' for an art student and model like Rosaleen. It was here, too, that she first began to read esoteric literature, including works on the mystical Jewish Kabbalah, comparative religion, primitive beliefs and medieval demonology. She also fostered her own developing interest in the Greek god Pan, the half-man, half-god deity who spent most of his time rollicking with young nymphs in the Arcadian meadows. For Rosaleen it was a time of freedom and self-exploration for she had finally cast away the domestic trappings of her conventional upbringing and she now felt that for the first time she could embrace the world at large.

She began to take various part-time jobs as the opportunities arose. During the next few years she worked as a kitchen maid in a hospital, designed toys for a toy manufacturer, sold art union tickets dressed as a jockey, and served as a waitress-cum-assistant in a bohemian nightclub. She also worked as a PMG messenger girl delivering telegrams, and as a model for Norman Lindsay. Lindsay himself considered Rosaleen's drawings to be rough and unsophisticated but there was no doubting his influence on her style. Rosaleen would become famous for exactly the same type of bacchanalian art– pagan revelries, frolicking naked women and satyrs – which had made Norman Lindsay's early line drawings both controversial and notorious. But Rosaleen was still formulating the rudiments of her own style and developing her unique range of nightmarish images.

Sometime during the year of 1935, Rosaleen met a young man called Beresford Conroy at a social gathering in Bellevue Hill. They were both seventeen at the time and quickly became infatuated with each other. Beresford was well-built and handsome, and an early photograph shows the young couple as a happy, smiling twosome. They married on 24 December 1940 and, as Rosaleen put it, 'went on the track', hitch-hiking from Sydney to Melbourne, then north to Brisbane and Cairns.

Back in Sydney the couple moved into an old sandstone stable in Bayswater Road, now the site of a Church of England retirement home. But unfortunately the marriage with Beresford did not last. Inspired by a burst of patriotism with the rapidly escalating tensions of World War II, Beresford enlisted as a commando and went off to serve in New Guinea, leaving his young wife behind in the stable! Roie was not impressed and when he returned from the war she demanded a divorce, although this would not be formally settled until 1951. Beresford and Roie now parted and she went to live in an old stone building called *Merangaroo*, which was just as colourful as Beggary Barn. Built by convicts and located close to the Garrison Church in the Rocks area, it was run by an eccentric landlady called Mrs Carter. It housed all manner of people – bohemian artists, sailors, and even an English secret service agent who on one occasion bailed up a suspected Nazi youth sympathiser for three weeks in his bedroom. It was an exotic and unpredictable place – the sort of eccentric, communal living Roie thoroughly enjoyed. It also stimulated her imagination and made her ponder on the best outlets for her talents.

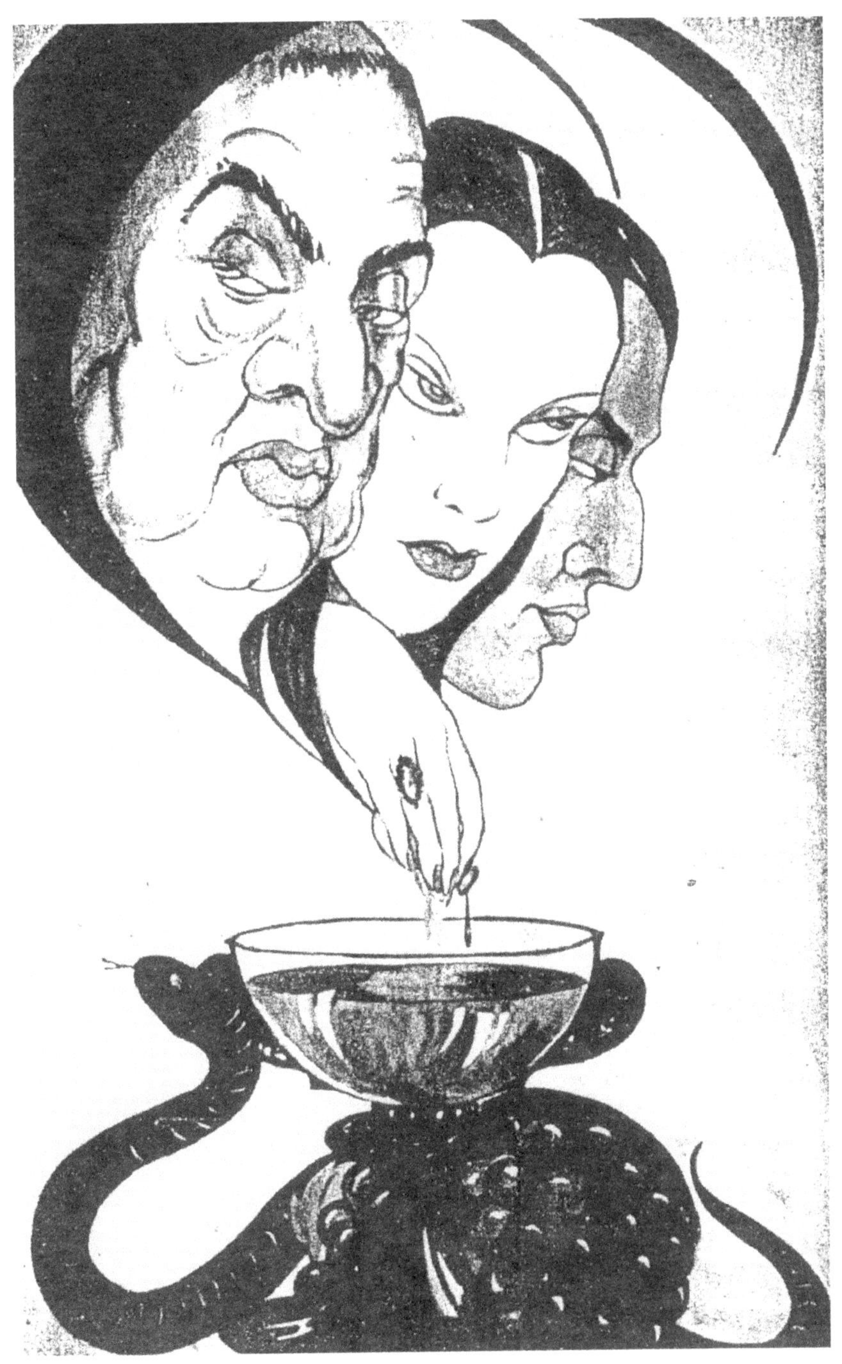

AN EARLY PENCIL STUDY

- THE BORGIAS

Rosaleen soon found herself drifting back to the world of magazines and tabloids. With *Smith's Weekly* now closed to her as an option, she began to search for a suitable outlet for her drawings and writing. She eventually found it in the form of a small magazine called *Pertinent*, a pocket-sized monthly which proclaimed itself to be a blend of 'fiction, fotos and fact'.

At the time of the outbreak of World War II in 1939 there were only two 'little magazines' in existence in Australia. These were *Bohemia*, which occasionally published avant-garde writing, and a journal called *Venture*.

However, in the last few months of 1939, three new magazines came into existence: *The People's Poetry*, *Western Writing* and *Southerly*. They would in due course be followed by several others. It seems that the war years actually stimulated the rise of new magazines. To a large extent this was due to restrictions on imported publications – part of the rationing of 'luxuries' at the time – and people therefore had more money to spend on the local alternatives.

Pertinent was edited by the poet Leon Batt, and the first two issues, published in August and September 1940, retailed for sixpence. Later the price rose to a shilling. *Pertinent* was quite different from *Smith's Weekly* in emphasis, defining its editorial approach succinctly. 'What it does not want,' announced Leon Batt in a trade advertisement, are 'sentimental clichés, conventional drama, chauvinistic patriotism and romantic unrealistics [sic]. Cartoons, ideas for cartoons, and unusual photo-stories are considered, while *Pertinent* is one of the few non-intellectual publications which are interested in poetry.'[3]

Batt went on to say: 'We want simplified articles calculated to

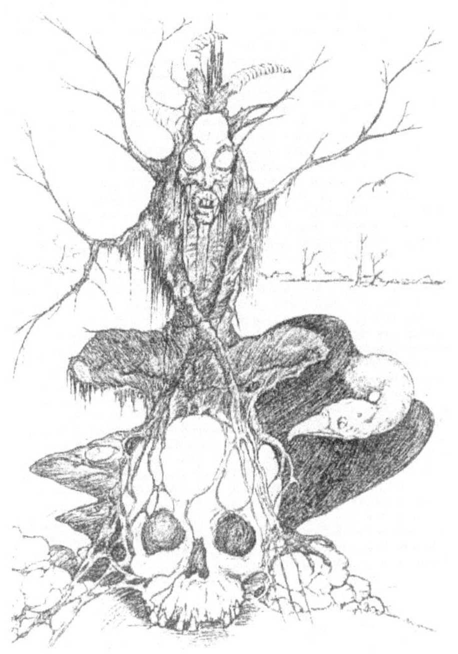

DESOLATION

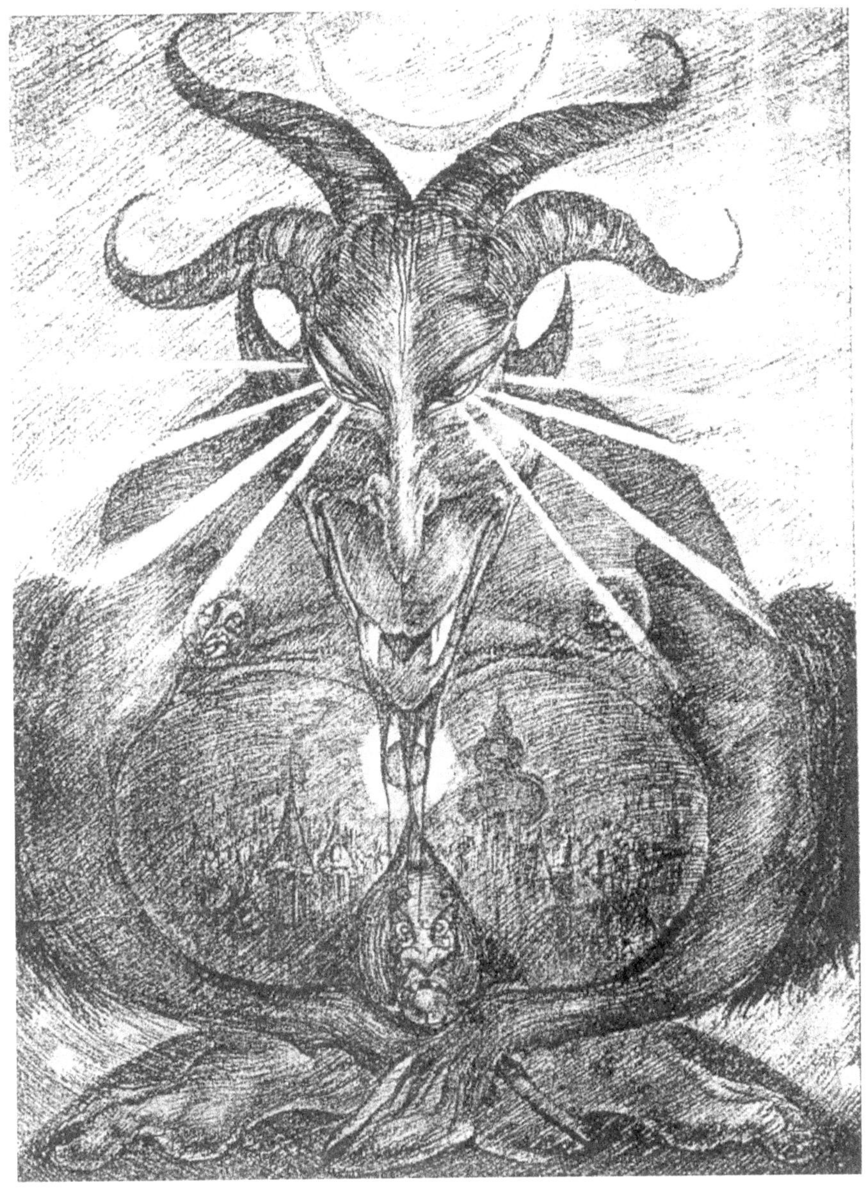

THE GOAT OF MENDES

stimulate Australian cultural achievement; no political bias required. Direct, succinct writing and thinking only. *Pertinent* despises pseudo-intellectuality, and will consider any material which can help, whilst entertaining, Australians to take an added interest in the cultural emancipation of themselves in order that they may become citizens, not only of a subservient country, but of an independent cultural nation.'

It was the free-thinking, innovative approach of *Pertinent* which attracted Rosaleen as a potential contributor. Her first drawings to be accepted for publication in its pages – two fantasy works depicting ghost-like elementals and a pencil study titled *The Borgias* – appeared in issue number three in October 1941. The following issues, in November and December, carried major articles on her work. 'Few, if any, other Australian artists have aroused as much astonishment, as well as technical controversy, as Miss Rosaleen Norton', proclaimed the opening paragraph in the December feature. Almost gloating in the recognition of a major new talent, the article went on to announce: 'Further studies by this most remarkable artist discovery will be published in future issues of *Pertinent*. Originals of such work may [also] be purchased.'

The November article included three visionary drawings: *The Rite of Spring*, showing a bearded centaur; *The Dream*, with its mix of Egyptian and Saturnalian images, and *Sorcery*, featuring a horned version of Merlin wearing a conical tower-like headpiece surrounded by a cluster of leering ghouls and hobgoblins.

The accompanying article acknowledged no author and was probably written by Batt himself. After exploring Rosaleen's pagan influences it went on to proclaim that the artist's work, 'apart from the alleged "unorthodoxy" of theme and outlook, [was] undeniably advanced far beyond the ordinary; it merits more interest and attention than it has been afforded in the past'.

Perhaps this was a sly dig at *Smith's Weekly* and Frank Marien, who clearly had not appreciated Rosaleen's artistic talents. The editor of *Pertinent* obviously believed that he had made a real discovery in Rosaleen Norton:

> '*Pertinent* feels that in Miss Rosaleen Norton, has been found an artist worthy of comparison with some of the best Continental, American and English contemporaries.'[4]

True to its word, the December edition gave the artist further pictorial coverage. The article 'More from the Folios of Miss Rosaleen Norton's Art' opened with a watercolour and pencil rendition of 'The Goat of Mendes', a stylised interpretation of the Devil as a leering goat-headed monster. Also featured were two other spectacular works: *Nightmare* and *Desolation.*

It was a good break for Rosaleen. Recognition and praise were hers at last, albeit in the pages of a minor and somewhat obscure magazine. And whether she suspected it or not, the connection with *Pertinent* would have a lasting impact on her life, for soon the journal would begin publishing the works of a young poet who in later years would become her lover and ally in magic: Gavin Greenlees.

As a poet, Greenlees was certainly a precocious talent, for some of his early poems were published in *Pertinent* in 1943, when he was only thirteen. In this capacity young Gavin was following several well-known figures into the pages of Leon Batt's journal. Other notable writers whose work had been published in the magazine included the colourful 'Queen of Bohemia', Dulcie Deamer, Yvonne Webb, William Hart Smith, Ian Mudie, Kylie Tennant, George Farwell, Marjorie Quinn, Marien Dreyer and Robert Crossland. Now Gavin was to be a regular contributor as well. One of his early submissions, a work titled simply *Poem*, had a quality that was both surreal and whimsical:

After the burst of orange light
After the horrible return of ninepins in the dark.
I court the other land...
O daisies!
O caterpillars hanging in a long protracted wet symphonic note
And the diaphragm of icy stars that nitred run
(The vast electric dark...)
In the depth of the forest, there is a green square
Sustained to courage by the thought that help may arrive.
And in the city square, there is a thermometer
lying, overpowered by Bertha Bliven.
(Poor objects!
You will die as soon as I wake.
Your existence is as brief as a match star
Or a square egg!)
I ventured into the unmapped land.
I glory to discover that the door has been made into a
marigold.
I am the protagonist of Light
A voice talks of the limitless possibilities of the
gramophone
And I see, as if a drop scene,
Many pale flowers fading into the background.

But O, the endless possibilities of Night

Across a dark background, bulked huge,
romantic shapes come thumping -
And I see a flat thumping-board,
To which is tied an electric-light globe.
All these endless possibilities
I see, as the Wolf-man saw the head of the shell
Under the castle...

Another poem, *The Ear*, combines imagery from the world of music and Nature in a manner that is both bizarre and colourful:

I found a funny old ear
The other day
Where the nerve-groups end
In green and pink.
There are most inspiring objects in my grandmother's
fernery!
Large green patches with hurdy-gurdy legs and straps tied
under the chin!
At the window lives an ancient gas-meter
Who thinks metal thoughts at one o'clock in the morning
And, buried deep in the green residue of saxophones
Piled on the cells
Of plants and minerals growing at 5/4 time
A pipe sings.
Sometimes, among the little glades
You see this strange metal ear hopping and singing
His song from an envelope filled with symphonics.
My song streaks.
Nearby a pot-plant zooms and cries.

A bird falls into the reception ear.
How pleasant everything is!

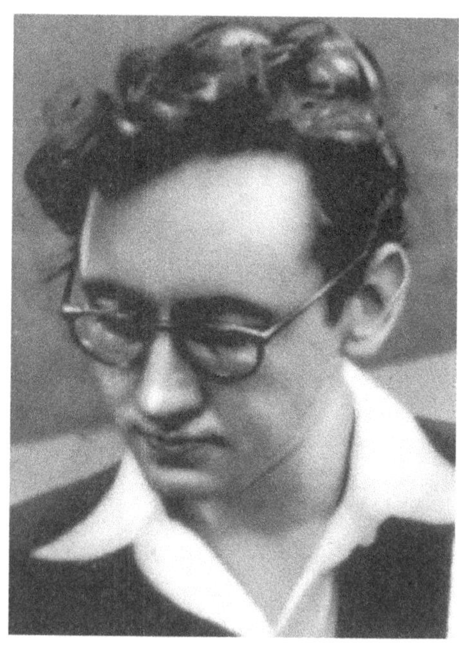

GAVIN GREENLEES

Gavin Greenlees had been born in the Melbourne suburb of Armadale on 15 April 1930. His parents were comfortably middle-class, if not especially affluent. His father, Gavin senior, was a journalist and his mother Gladys a social worker. They certainly imbued their son with a love of literature as he was growing up, and ensured that he had a sound and rigorous education.

Most of Gavin's early life was spent in Elwood – between 1930 and 1938 the Greenlees family lived at five different addresses in the same suburb. Gavin began his education at Elwood Public School, later becoming a pupil at Christian Brothers' College, St Patrick's, Ballarat, and Melbourne High School.

Gavin's talent for poetry manifested at an early age. When he was twelve he won three successive poetry competitions sponsored by the Australian Broadcasting Commission – he even had to provide proof of his age – and several of his works would later appear in the *Australian Weekend Book*. In the early 1940s a number of his poems were also published in the *ABC Weekly* and in *Australia Monthly*, so his appearance in *Pertinent* was clearly no flash in the pan.

Greenlees' earliest intellectual influence was Surrealism, which he discovered when he was twelve. In Rosaleen's personal commentary in *The Art of Rosaleen Norton* – their collaborative work first published in 1952 – Rosaleen wrote that Surrealism 'excited his imagination to such a degree that he became obsessed... Intuition sensed mysterious, unknown realms and the possibility of evoking them...'

It is unlikely that Rosaleen knew Gavin personally during the early years of *Pertinent*, for he was still a schoolboy living in Victoria. But they had certainly met each other by 1949, the year Rosaleen held her controversial art exhibition at the University of Melbourne. Leon Batt's magazine was already drawing them together as part of its *milieu.* A further article on Rosaleen's occult and visionary art appeared in the June 1943 edition, and the same issue contained a poem by Gavin titled *Winter Night Thoughts*. Here again was evidence of the poet's surreal mind at work:

All is dark in the house,
Far out in the street I can hear fireflies buzzing in
telephone boxes,
The electric sparks of the stars hum softly in the
cabbage-patch,
Trams roar distantly into hell...

The new article on Rosaleen was subtitled 'A Vision of the Boundless' and it must have excited the young thirteen-year-old poet as he leafed through its pages. Here Rosaleen was presented as a psychic who could provide a glimpse of 'hidden worlds', a mystic able to penetrate dimensions of consciousness only dimply perceived by ordinary mortals.

Rosaleen had just had a show of paintings at Pakie's Club in Sydney, a popular spot in Elizabeth Street frequented each night by artists, journalists and assorted bohemians. The *Pertinent* article, written by an author identified simply as 'Paul', was a critique of the exhibition.[5]

Paul explained how, when he first looked at Rosaleen's pictures, 'many appeared unpleasant because they [were] presentations of evil.' Indeed, most of the works disgusted him, but he went on to blame himself, and not the artist, for this response. 'If I am to analyse this feeling quite honestly now,' he wrote, 'I find only one explanation: "to the impure all is impure".' There is nothing disgusting about them, not even those which depict horrible, terrifying, even repulsive ideas or images. One and all, the drawings and paintings shown are perfect in drawing and design, and even where they remain somewhat sketchy due to the subjects used, they are well balanced, considered and complete.'

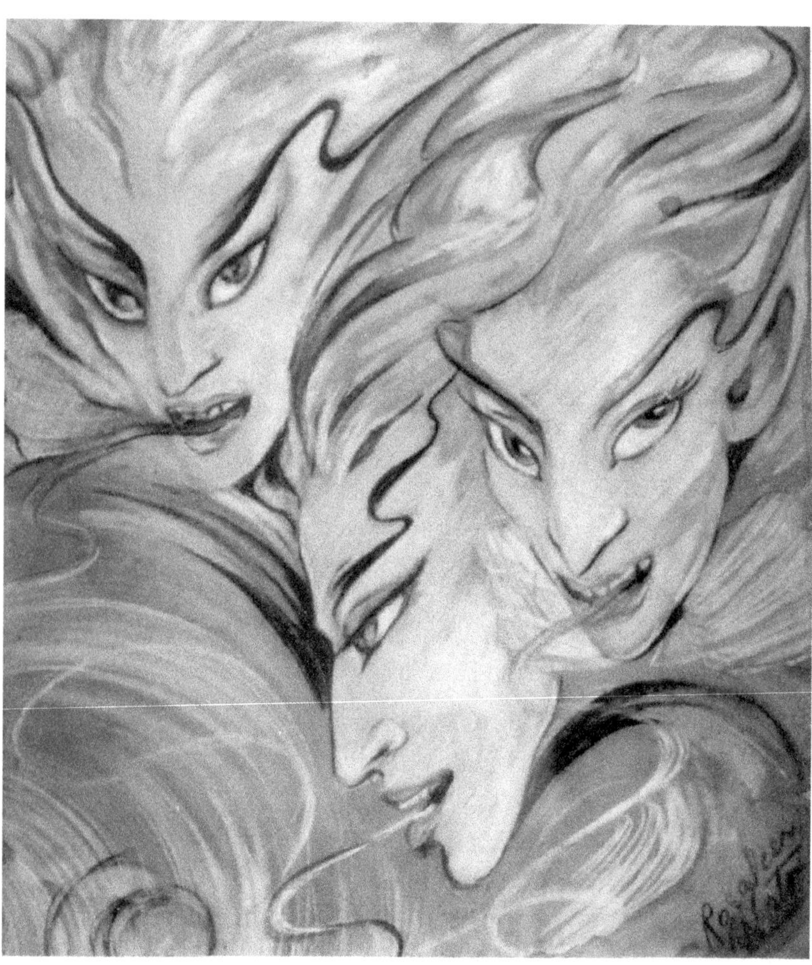

THREE SISTERS

Paul went on to present Rosaleen as a person well versed and interested in 'occult and psychic phenomena'. But most importantly, she was a *practitioner* – a person who knew of these things first-hand. 'From a practice of self-hypnosis,' wrote Paul, 'she had developed a most exceptional ability to actually enter the psychic sphere, to transport her personality to other planes than the physical one, and to sensually perceive that which, to most of us, remains for ever hidden...' [6]

The article was accompanied by three Rosaleen Norton drawings. One, titled *Challenge*, showed a naked woman wrestling with a spider. Another, *Medieval Scene*, portrayed a cluster of jovial monks, magicians, warlocks and court jesters. *Nightmare*, however, was perhaps the most interesting of all, for it showed an archetypal god-form rising up from the naked prostrate body of a woman who was clearly Rosaleen herself. Here was a representation of human consciousness transcending temporal boundaries and penetrating the astral and mythic realms – a clear depiction of trance states manifesting in art. It was to be the precursor of the many visionary illustrations which would later accompany Gavin Greenlees' poems in the limited edition publication *The Art of Rosaleen Norton.*

1 Ned McCann, interview with Jim Russell, June 1998. See 'And Dangerous to Know' published on http://nedmccann.blogspot.com.au/2005/09/blog-post_1126598873608270\86.html, posted 13 September 2005.

2 Rosaleen Norton, 'Hitchhiking Witch', op cit:10.

3 Quoted in a sumary of Australian newspapers and periodicals in *Artist's Market*, circa 1940. *Pertinent's* office was at 431b Kent Street, Sydney.

4 *Pertinent*, November 1941

5 'Paul' was in fact a science fiction writer named David R. Evans. Evans sent a copy of one of Rosaleen's drawings, *Challenge*, to the noted American fantasy collector Forrest J. Ackerman. This drawing, which depicted a naked woman embracing a spider, was published in Ackerman's newsletter and Roie would later claim on the basis of this that her occult art was well known in the United States – a slight exaggeration.

6 *Pertinent*, June 1943: 33.

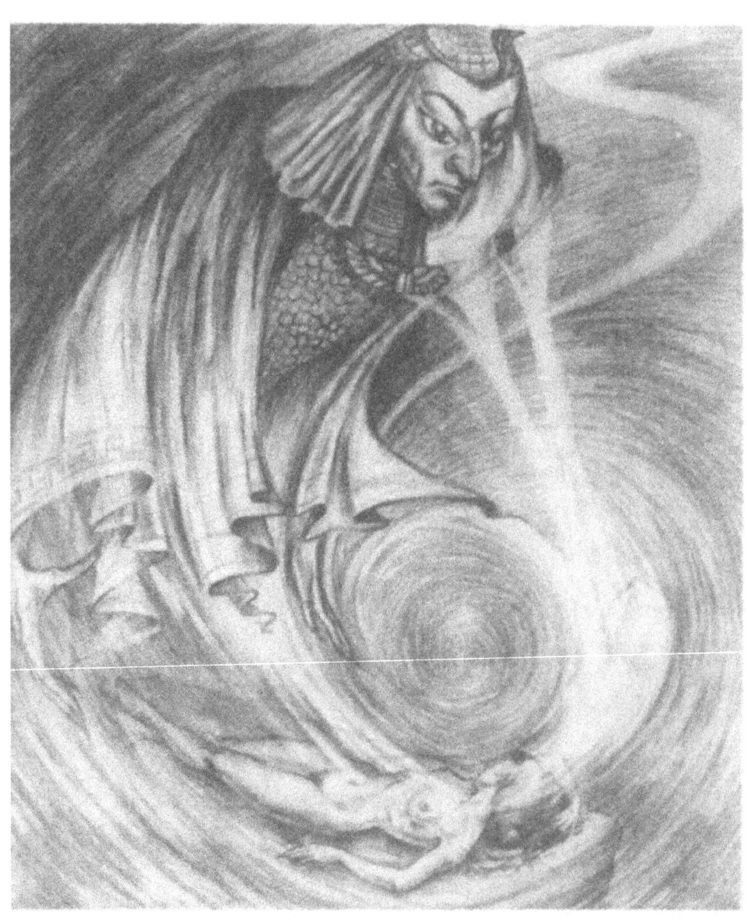

NIGHTMARE

3
Journeys to the World Beyond

Roie had begun to experiment with self-hypnosis in 1940, when she was twenty-three years old. She was already familiar with the writings of Carl Jung and Sigmund Freud and had read widely in the field of witchcraft, occultism, demonology and pantheism. It seemed to her that hypnotic trance states could open the door to a vast and awesome inner mythology which she very much wanted to explore first-hand.

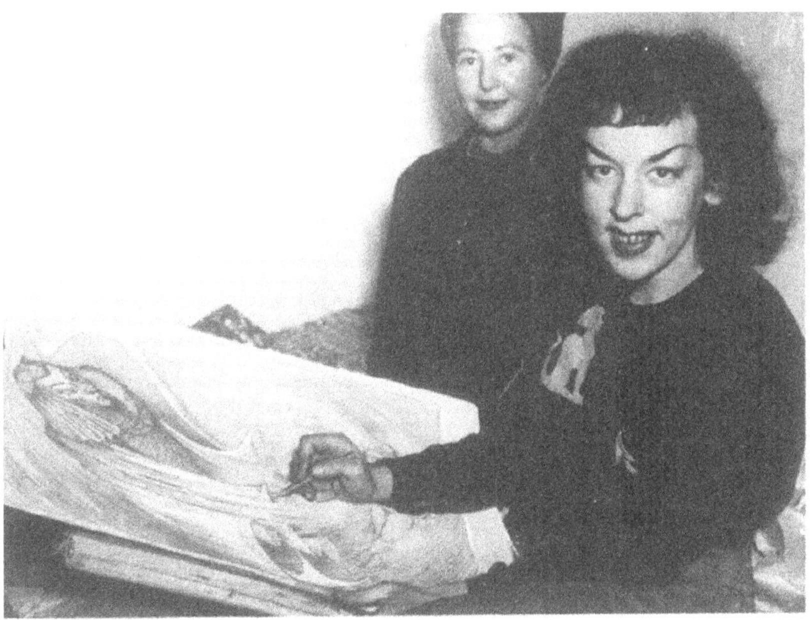

According to an article published in *People* in March 1950, Roie began her experiments by shutting off her normal consciousness in an effort to induce automatic drawing, allowing 'the force' to take her over.

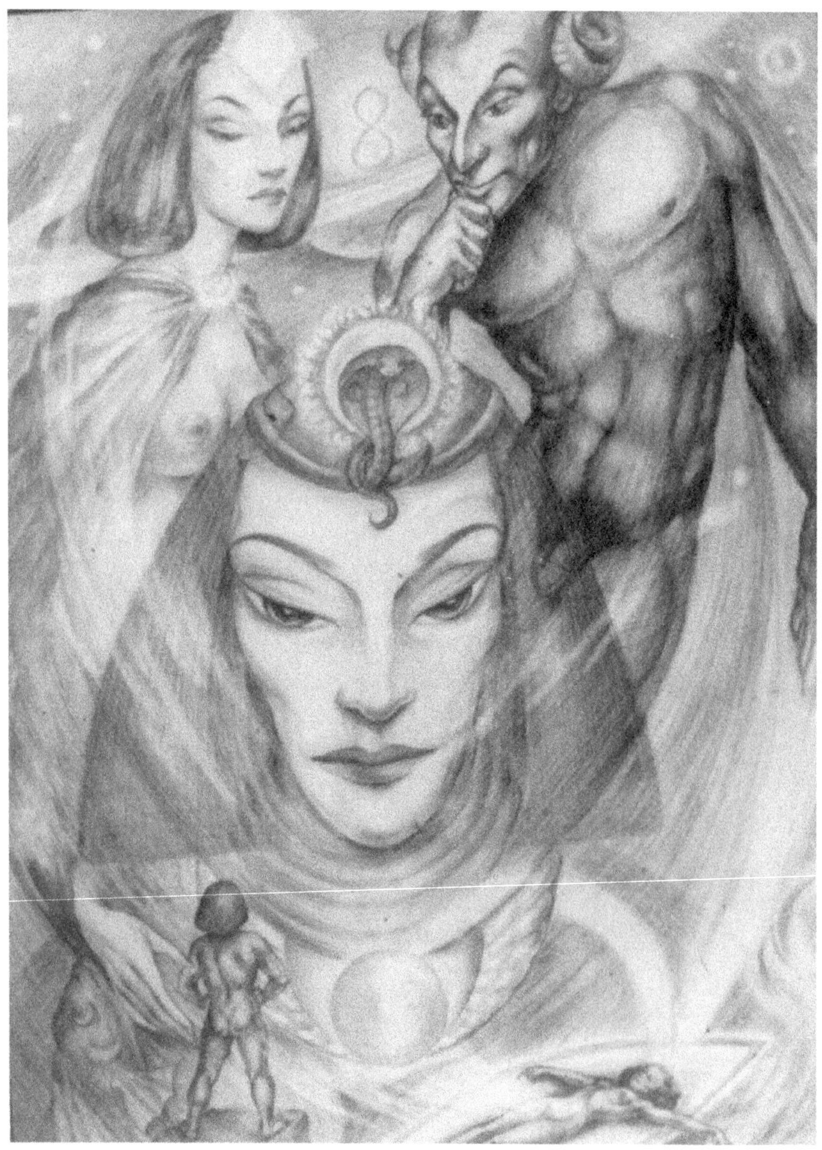

SPHINX AND HER SECRETS

This produced, she said, a number of peculiar and unexpected results and some drawings that were later exhibited. Most interesting of all, her experiments also culminated in a period of extra-sensory perception, together with a prolonged series of symbolic visions.

TRANCE JOURNEYS

Norton's exploration of trance states was central to her creative process as an artist, and some of Norton's artworks from the 1940s reveal specific aspects of her trance technique. Drawings like *Astral Scene* and *The Sphinx*, for example, show Norton's body in a comatose horizontal position with magical 'thought-forms' issuing from her head.[1] In *Astral Scene* a stream of white energy zig-zags into space from Norton's mouth, culminating in a magical *sigil* which seems to split into two magical 'horns' and apparently results in the successful invocation of a horned deity. This deity is described in the accompanying caption as the 'cryptic-faced Aegypan [who] represents Being'

The caption beneath this image, published in *Pix* magazine in July 1943 and evidently written with Norton's input, identifies the zig-zag energy as 'ectoplasm issuing from [Norton's] mouth' and states that this is the 'astral body'– a clear indication that Norton had been influenced by modern spiritualism as well as other aspects of the Western esoteric tradition. Ectoplasm is the ethereal substance which is said to emanate from the bodies of spirit mediums while they are in a state of trance, thereby allowing deceased spirits to manifest themselves visually to the audience assembled in the seance. However, the fact that the mythic figure of the 'cryptic-faced Aegypan' appeared to Norton during this trance journey rather than the spirit-form of an actual, deceased person (which would be the normal expectation during a spiritualistic seance) indicates that Norton was using trance states to project her astral body with magical intent, rather than taking the passive role of a spiritualistic trance medium. In *Sphinx and Her Secrets* the magical intent associated with the act of astral projection is even clearer. The picture is dominated

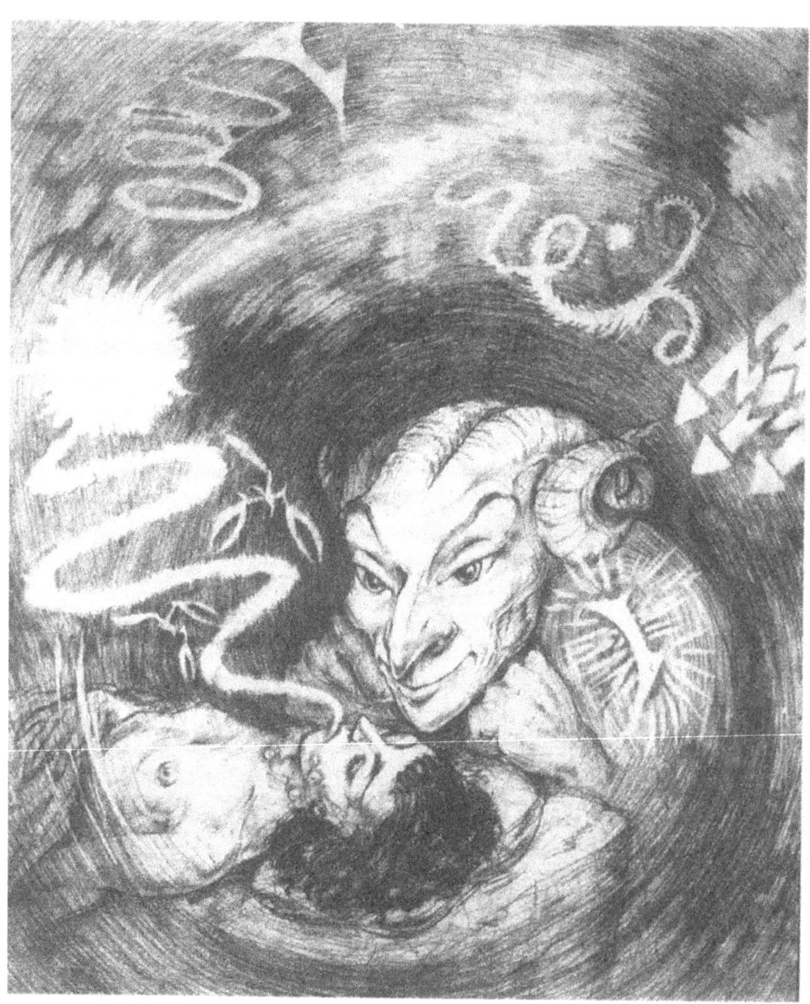

ASTRAL SCENE – *A PENCIL DRAWING FROM THE EARLY 1940S SHOWING ECTOPLASM ISSUING FROM NORTON'S MOUTH AS SHE PROJECTS A MAGICAL SIGIL*

by a central female head adorned with ancient Egyptian head-gear: this figure clearly embodies Norton's conception of a 'female' Sphinx. Two other mythic beings are shown rising up behind her. One is a naked male figure with circular horns – possibly a depiction of Pan; the other is a bare-breasted ancient Goddess wearing a ceremonial robe. The head-gear worn by the central female Sphinx-figure is surmounted by a serpent rising up from a coil – a likely reference to the *Kundalini* serpent – while immediately behind this serpent a solar orb radiates wispy filaments of energy, an allusion to the serpent's 'fiery' nature.

In his 1948 critique of Norton's artworks, 'The Art of Rosaleen Norton', published in *Arna*, Owen M. Broughton writes that the figure of the Sphinx 'has become synonymous with Mystery and is the Guardian of Secrets'.[2] Broughton also draws attention to the fact that the naked figure of Norton, who is shown horizontal in a state of trance, is depicted as lying within the form of a *yoni*, or vulva – a symbol not only of Norton's 'Receptivity to Forces from other planes and Dimensions of Being', as Broughton puts it, but also an indication of Norton's interest in Tantra and Kundalini Yoga.[3] Broughton also notes that 'The central face is the Spirit of the Sphinx which embodies the mystery of Being – which can be applied both to Being in general and to the Self. The two figures behind and merging into the Sphinx represent the ... active and passive principles in Nature and the Male and Female Principles in the Self.'

If Norton believed that she was able to contact the 'active and passive principles in Nature' as god-forms on the astral planes – an ability she emphasised in her statements to Melbourne psychologist L.J. Murphy – she also believed that she had encountered the entity she referred to as the Adversary (Lucifer / Satan) as an embodied, tangible presence. When

I interviewed Norton in her Kings Cross apartment in 1977 she told me that she regarded Lucifer not as 'evil', but as humanity's natural adversary. In Norton's words:

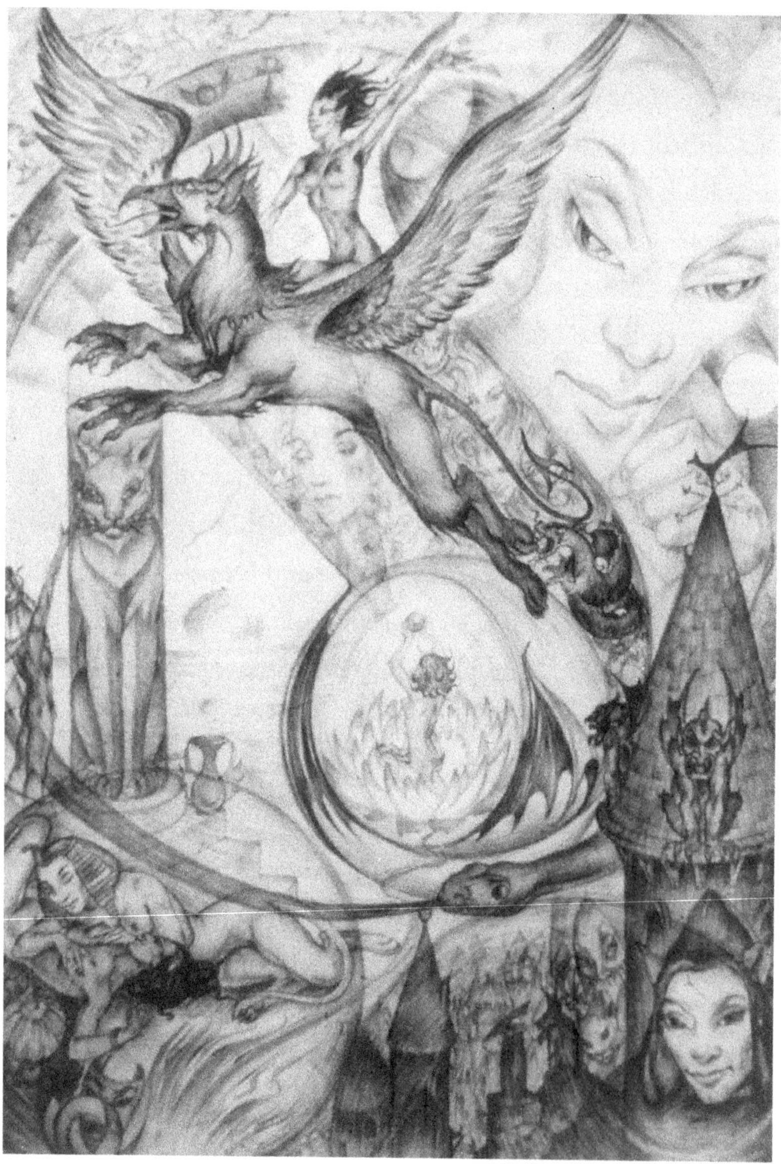

TIMELESS WORLDS

> He binds and limits man when it appears that he is growing too big for his boots. He tries to trick man, not with malicious intent, so much as exposing the limitations of the ego and man's pride in his own existence.[4]

Norton's concept of Lucifer is also referred to in Broughton's 1948 article, mentioned above. Here [Owen M.]Broughton writes that Norton's portrait, *The Adversary*, 'represents the "Opposition Principle" operating throughout Nature – the large figure being the personification of this principle and the small figure depicting Man attempting to challenge an indestructible power...'

Norton told me during the interview that she invoked the gods 'inwardly' and 'intuitively'. Then I raised the issue of a particular magical concept, accepted by many modern occultists, namely that both the 'gods' and the magical universe generally could be regarded as a projection of humanity's own existential reality, My notes from the interview read as follows:

> She says that she has discovered certain of the qualities of these gods in her own temperament and this is a natural catalyst which makes their invocation much easier and more effective. But she does not contain them in the manner of the occult practice of 'assuming the god form',[5] for example. She goes to be with them on the astral planes, and on different occasions it may be that they show different aspects, or facets, of their own magical potency. [6]

Norton's magical trance journeys invariably took place in a secure location. According to her older sister, Cecily, Norton used to come across from Kings Cross to Kirribilli, on the lower North Shore near the

Sydney Harbour Bridge, to undertake some of these trance journeys. Cecily lived in an old block of flats in Kirribilli Avenue with large windows overlooking the harbour. According to Cecily, Norton regarded this apartment as her second home and would often spend time there. There was a special tree in a park nearby and 'Roie used to meditate near it, go into trance, and communicate with the spirit of the tree'. According to my notes from an interview with Cecily in August 1986, she clearly recognised that her sister had a natural ability to enter trance states and other dissociated forms of consciousness, and was keen to assist her in this process. On one occasion, Cecily was present when Norton went into trance states continuously over a five-day period. Cecily left water nearby and understood that her sister's body 'mustn't be disturbed'. Norton confirmed in her autobiographical article 'Witches Want No Recruits', published in January 1957, that her trance journeys could last as long as five days:

> ...some years ago I underwent a deep trance lasting five days. Shortly after this I met a Buddhist monk from Burma, who was an expert on such things. He seemed astounded when I described the contents of this trance, and after questioning me closely on the subject, said that it had undoubtedly been what some Buddhist schools call the 'Trance of Annihilation'.[7]

While any interpretation of Norton's experience of the 'Trance: of Annihilation' must necessarily remain speculative [8] it is nevertheless clear that Norton was capable of entering deep trance states in which she had metaphysical experiences involving encounters with such mythic and magical entities as Pan, Hecate, The Adversary (Lucifer/ Satan), Lilith and the Werplon. Reproducing the 'god-forms' associated with these magical beings became a central feature of Norton's creative art-making process during the 1940 and 1950s.

An additional point of interest is that Norton depicted herself in her drawings as being completely naked while in a state of trance. According to Cecily, this was simply a symbolic device indicating that a 'voyage of the spirit' was taking place. Norton apparently thought it would be far less effective depicting herself wearing clothes, so she showed herself naked for greater visual impact. Obviously, to undertake deep trance journeys over a period of several days without being warm and physically protected would have been very hazardous indeed.

THE L.J. MURPHY INTERVIEW

We may never have known the full details of Rosaleen's explorations of trance states and automatic drawing, however, had it not been for the probing questions of a psychologist, L.J. Murphy. Obviously fascinated by the symbolism of her art, Murphy conducted an extensive interview with Rosaleen shortly after her exhibition of paintings at the University of Melbourne on 27 August 1949. During that session she also provided a very complete statement of her experiments with self-hypnosis. The following text was written by Norton herself, probably following a request from L.J. Murphy. Where capital letters are used within the text I have followed Norton's original style and emphasis. It is reproduced in full here because of its significance as a statement of magical intent.

> I decided to experiment in self-induced trance; the idea being to induce an abnormal state of consciousness and manifest the results, if any, in drawing.[9]

My aim was to delve down into the subconscious and, if possible, through and beyond it.

I had a feeling (intuitional rather than intellectual) that somewhere in the depths of the unconscious, the individual would contain, in essence, the accumulated knowledge of mankind: just as his physical body manifests the aggregate of racial experience in the form of instinct or automatic reaction to stimulus.

In order to contact this hypothetical source, I decided to apply psychic stimulus to the subconscious : stimulus that the conscious reasoning mind might reject, yet which would appeal to the buried instincts as old as man, and would (I hoped) cause psychic 'automatic reflexes' (Religious cults use ritual, incense etc. for the same reason). Consequently, I collected together a variety of things such as aromatic leaves, wine, a lighted fire, a mummified hoof, etc... all potent stimuli to the part of the subconscious that I wished to invoke. I darkened the room, and focusing my eyes upon the hoof I crushed the pungent leaves, drank some wine, and tried to clear my mind of all conscious thought. This was the beginning (and I made many other experiments which were progressively successful).

Following a surge of curious excitement, my brain would become emptied of all conscious thought: my eyes would shut, and I was merely aware that I was drawing on the blank sheet of paper in front of me. The drawings were quite different in form from previous ones, and full of symbols, many of which were previously unknown to my conscious mind, prominent symbols being crescent, fish, ram-headed mask, cornucopia, swastika, 6-pointed star, triple sign, tower etc.

Each of the drawings at this period were compositions having another significance not realised until much later, since they prophesied in symbolic form a future subjective experience for myself. Numerous other things took place which I need not record here: my consciousness, however, was extremely exalted over the entire period – about five months in all.

I seemed, while experiencing a great intensification of intellectual, creative and intuitional faculties, to have become detached in a curiously timeless fashion from the world around me, and yet to be seeing things with a greater clarity and awareness than normally. I was working day and night, having very little sleep or rest, yet a supply of inexhaustible power seemed to flow through me.

One night I felt impelled, quite apart from conscious volition, to perform a kind of ritual of invocation; after which I executed a peculiar waking 'automatic' drawing, the composition of which assumed the form of the symbol

The upper figure is the sign of Thoth – impersonality and balanced force – while the lunar crescent can represent several things, but chiefly (as applied to the individual) receptivity to occult powers; the personality; and, according to the Kabbalists, an emblem of the sphere of magic. I once read of magic defined as 'The science and art of causing supernormal change to occur in conformity with will', which seems a fairly comprehensive description. Events occurred which rendered it impossible to continue these experiments, and conditions returned to normal.

Two years later, I decided to attempt some more investigations, this time with the object of discovering whether life continues after bodily death and, if so, in what form. To this end, I began by attempting to communicate with a dead friend by means of automatic writing. After several unsuccessful attempts, the pencil began to move quite freely, although for some days I obtained only subconscious ramblings and symbolism.

Unexpectedly, however, a great change took place: there was a strong awareness of another presence, and the sensation of the writing altered completely, as though someone apart from myself were guiding my hand. The writing became clear, concise, and altered completely. It altered, in fact, into the handwriting of the friend with whom I was attempting to communicate. Moreover, the answers to my questions became definite and coherent. Soon, and during the following nine or ten months, I gained the rough outlines of a philosophical and metaphysical conception of the Universe and life beyond death which by no stretch of the imagination could I attribute to my normal self, since it embodied knowledge of a type which my studies had never encountered, such as those which dealt with highly abstract propositions entering the realms of higher mathematics. I should make it clear that my previous reading in occult lore had dealt almost exclusively with medieval demonology and witchcraft, this being the side of such matters which chiefly interested me. Inspired by the previous occurrences, I had also studied a certain amount of symbolism, but I had never touched upon either physics, philosophy, or metaphysics, as such. Oddly enough, while actually receiving super-normal information I quite easily comprehended theories which when reviewed later were often difficult to grasp (heightening of faculties).

In this way I also learned something of various other subjects, including the structure of the subconscious mind, comparative symbolism, etc. Meanwhile, without realising it, I was becoming highly sensitised psychically, and soon could communicate

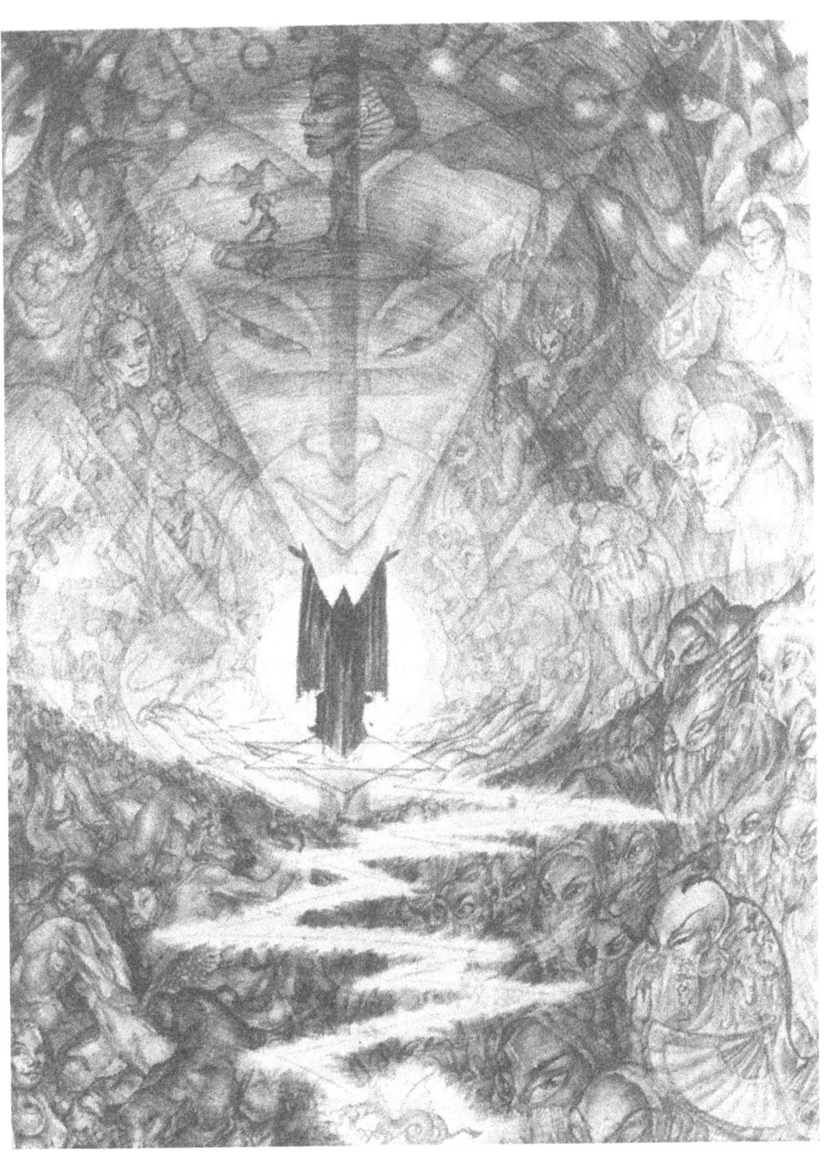

THE DREAM

almost at will, without any effort of concentration. Much of the data was, of course, fragmentary and incomplete owing to the crude method of communication. Other information, particularly that dealing with life on other planes of Being, was misinterpreted owing to lack of standards of comparison on my part: since one can only visualise any image in relation to something in one's own experience, my understanding was necessarily limited. Now, however, I am able to correlate and apply the missing factors to things that were merely hinted at during this period. (I have appended a condensation of the more important questions and answers received during automatic writing.)[10]

Meanwhile, one subject had become paramount in my mind. I had heard that it was possible to achieve transition to a different Realm of existence and live consciously the type of life that is generally experienced after physical death. This became my supreme desire, for a number of reasons. The idea, above all, appealed to me as a type of adventure and exploration more fascinating than any other. There were, too, things that I wished to know which I realised would be impossible without first-hand experience; for I felt that entities who had had the experience of death would have passed into a different and perhaps more advanced state of being, entailing conditions of life which would be almost incomprehensible according to our concepts. As soon as communication was firmly established, therefore, I asked if such a thing were actually possible. The reply was in the affirmative. It seemed that co-operation of will from two planes of Being was necessary for safe accomplishment of the process. I was told, also, that I would have to wait for a few months, presumably to gain the necessary psychic training.

My excitement can be imagined; and during the following months becoming impatient and often sceptical of ever accomplishing any such thing, I made several attempts at separating myself from my body. My conception of the process was a hazy one and very different from actuality, since I imagined that my physical body would temporarily have to die, later to be re-animated on my return.

Once during one of these attempts I succeeded in inducing a type of cataleptic trance. Gradually over the space of about an hour my heart beat became slower and slower – I was very aware of this in a detached fashion – and I could feel my breathing lessening until both heart-beat and breath had

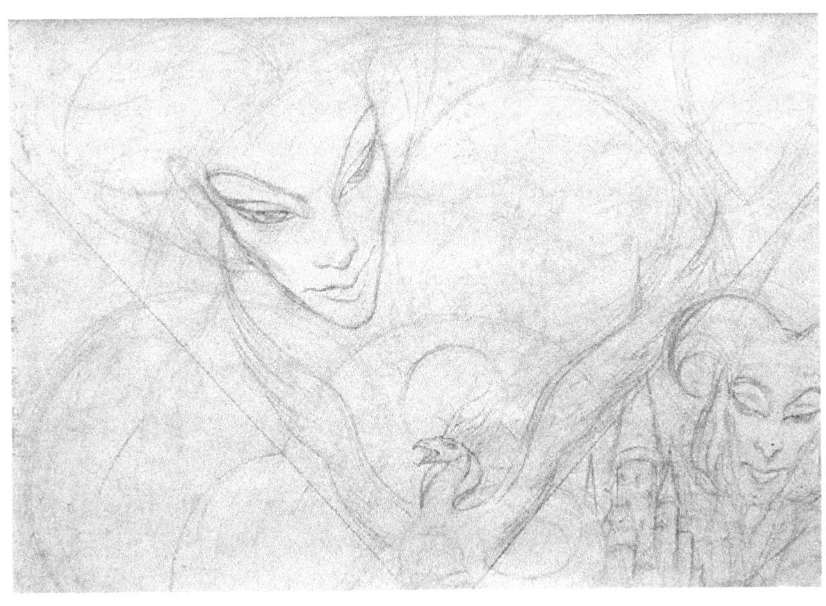

A sketch showing Pan (his horns are barely visible), a griffin and Merlin – a drawing characteristic of Rosaleen's artistic style in the late 1940s and early 1950s

practically ceased; and then an extraordinary sensation ran over my entire body, which I can describe only as 'cessation'. There was an inward hush as though my body's mechanism had come to a pause – and then a light frothing bubbling sensation spread through my veins as though my body were dissolving into foam. I do not know what the result would have been had I not been disturbed. However, at this moment my husband [11] entered the room. Thinking I was ill, he felt my pulse and exclaimed in alarm. The dissolving stopped, there was a sense of shock, and with a slight jerk my breathing started again very slowly. I tried to reassure him, but could not speak at first, as my lips and vocal organs seemed extraneous and difficult to control. It took me another hour to resume normal functioning, after which he told me that my skin had felt icy and slightly damp (I had not been aware of this).

The next step of importance was clairaudience – a clear and coherent form of thought transference which eliminated the cruder medium of automatic writing. The first indication of this occurred under the very prosaic circumstances of washing clothes one afternoon. Possibly for the very reason of lack of conscious concentration my brain was in a receptive condition. I suddenly became strongly aware of another presence. I realised that it was C. (the person with whom I had been communicating) and then unexpectedly, as though my brain were a tuned-in wireless set, I could hear her speaking; which so thrilled me that mentally I positively shouted at her.

'Yes, it really is me,' came the reply. 'I am able to communicate with you directly now.' I was told later that there are numerous cells in the brain which do not normally function. During this conversation I was told, amongst other things, that inter-Plane transition would occur for me in about a month: and so it did, almost to the day.

I doubt if any impression of the actual initial experience could be conveyed in words, so I shall not attempt to describe it, beyond saying that there was a sensation of ecstasy, during which my entire being seemed to dissolve and disintegrate, then gradually re-form into a new whole. The experience was so overwhelming that at first it was difficult to realise what had happened; for simultaneously with this an entire change of consciousness and focus had been effected. My body felt as though it were formed of warm golden light; the physical body had become merely an appendage, and all my sensations were centred in the plasmic body. I had gained new and different senses – and here I must comment upon something concerning which the popular conception of 'discarnate life' is the absolute reverse of reality. Far from being devoid of sense enjoyment, a plasmic body of this type contains the very essence of sensuousness to a degree that renders the physical sensory organs utterly negligible by comparison. As a rough and very inadequate parallel, compare the difference between touching something of delicate texture with naked hands, and with hands encased in heavy leather gloves. 'There' the body is completely a reflection of the mind, so that any type of pleasure, whether emotional or intellectual, engenders as a part of itself a corresponding sensuous enjoyment. (This also applies in the opposite direction so that misery of any description is accompanied by excruciating pain.) Contrary again to the usual idea of such states, sexual sensation still exists in an equivalently more advanced and intensified form.

I have been asked how a purely intellectual activity such as abstract thought could be attended by sensual enjoyment. It is, nevertheless, for instead of feeling interested one 'becomes' an embodiment of Interest itself. It is rather different to explain what I mean by this since a sense or state of Consciousness peculiar to the other realm is concerned. To begin with, 'thought' in those realms is very different from that which is normally understood by the word. There, 'thought' – or rather the energy generated by such – is felt as a tangible thing, a current of living force which assumes palpable and visual form. I had been told, earlier, that 'entities in the Plane assumed form at will'. This is literally true; one actually changes shape very frequently, since the new 'sense' referred to is that which could be described as 'being'. Just as one can see, feel, hear a thing, state or person; and when this occurs one realises and is the very essence of its nature. This sense, if one can call it that, covers a vastly wider field than anything comparable to human life; for in addition to becoming the essence of male, female, or neither, and beings of other orders of Existence, one can 'become' a living embodiment of abstract Ideas of all descriptions.

One of the strangest experiences I had was 'becoming' an embodiment of an Idea of the Universe. This Idea was not anthropomorphised into Entity, as is usually the case with such embodiments. Consequently, although my consciousness existed, there was no consciousness of entity at all. I am not referring to the personal 'I' consciousness, for naturally that alters completely with each form assumed; I have used a capital letter to differentiate between personal ideas and Ideas, which are representations to the consciousness of Group interpretations of Universal facts, according to order of Existence and sub-divisions therein. (By 'other orders of Existence' I mean different classes of Being from Man; highly evolved unhuman intelligences)....

Many of these things, of course, happened much later; however, these examples indicate the complete unity of mind and fluids in the plasmic body, also the sensory tangibility of the thought-force. The manipulation of the latter (to return to my previous statement) in any kind of abstract thinking, is also a sensory skill and actually feeling the keen precision of directed force. In the emotional sphere, there is a different type of awareness. When one feels wonder, serenity, etc., one does not exactly become a representation of these states; rather, there is a sensation of complete unity with that which is causing their manifestation, and yet another sense which is a blending of the familiar five senses into a super-intensified one, plus an indefinable essence.

Another activity could be compared with simultaneously watching and taking part in a play in which all art-forms such as music, drama, ritual, shape, colour and pattern blend into one. These 'plays' were either allegorical or symbolic and generally represented something which had a personal bearing upon my own life in addition to their general significance.

Orthodox occultists occasionally describe the Plane of 'dense' matter as the 'Realm of Form', which to my mind is a complete misnomer. The name should be applied to the realm of which I speak, since things There are seen in their archetypal essence. There, all forms whether abstract or actual appear in their real perfection as part of the very essence of Form itself, which is omnipresent. In speaking of abstract form I refer to System and the pattern of things in general, which interblend in all directions into infinity. As I have remarked elsewhere, the fact of chaos anywhere appears to be only a part of form and system, and as such purely relative.

The realisation of the essential Form of things occurs in various ways... one sees things such as the pattern of a life, for instance, as a complete and perfect thing in itself, yet forming against relationship to other lives part of another wider pattern; which again forms part of another yet larger... and so, ad infinitum. Similarly, with things such as Dimension – Time, Plane and Space – one literally sees the perfect interblending of their relationship to one another and to the Universe as a whole. Here again, the vehicle of realisation of this type of knowledge is greater and more comprehensive than intellectual understanding, although it includes the latter. Many of these Abstract forms appeared as vast animated patterns blending in a kind of geometrical harmony which we felt as well as observed, and into which the consciousness merged. The shapes and manifestations were not those of Euclidean geometry; cosmic mathematics manifesting as an immense art-form is the best analogy I can find.

Concerning 'other types of Existence' and form assumed by such, there are several aspects to be considered. In some of my drawings I have attempted to convey an impression of some of these 'other Realm' shapes and experiences; in some a general and in others a specific impression. With regard to the former, I have used visual forms seen during extra-sensory experiences supplemented where necessary by other, more familiar symbols. Concerning the latter, however, I have endeavoured as far as possible to reproduce accurately the actual visual images only.

Recently, the factual validity of some of these portrayed forms was queried on the grounds that they were apparently 'anthropomorphised'. One of the drawings objected to, for instance, showed a horned being with a comparatively human face – a fawn [sic].[12] Another depicted a being roughly corresponding to one of those known as Djinns. Both of the drawings fall into the latter, or sheerly factual category.

THE GROUNDS OF THE OBJECTION WERE:

1. That, as form follows function in animate nature, a non-human intelligence would not assume a form based upon a human concept, such as the idea of a fawn – which is, superficially, an idealised combination of two phenomena in the natural world. The objection was not to the drawing of a fawn as a symbolic representation of a different state of intelligence, but to my claim of its objective reality.

2. That the concept of such beings was familiar to my personal mind through study of mediaeval demonology etc. and also to the cultural mind of the racial group to which I belong, and that they were therefore more likely to be the result of hallucination or self-deception than actual objective realities (objective on the Astral Plane – not necessarily so on the physical plane). Why, he asked, had I not encountered phenomena familiar to, say, the Zulu Group mind.

All this is a particularly interesting point; for in his grasp of the implications of a type of life essentially different from ours, the sceptic was quite right. Yet in that very difference are embodied the conditions of existence whereby such an apparent irrationality as the objective existence of an 'ectoplasmic' fawn body becomes logically possible. The explanation lies in the nature of the difference between the two Realms (Planes of Being).

The most vital and essential distinction exists more in the way the life manifestation itself functions than in any particular visual form it may assume. On the physical plane, for instance, compare two completely dissimilar forms of life – a plant and a human being. They are totally different in appearance, structure and mode of functioning, yet their material vehicles are both subject to the same Dimensional law. They cannot change form. A plant will undergo only such changes as are normal, ie. inherent in the plant nature, and a man according to those inherent in humanity. They cannot exchange, or vitally change, their physical form outside their respective genus limit, and the life cycles of both follow a broad [sic] similar pattern of birth, growth, maturity, degeneration and death.

In the other Realm, the structure of phenomena is based on other lines. Intelligences are not confined to one form as here; also the consciousness pertaining to each type of form bears a far closer relationship to its material vehicle. The latter, as I have said, being fluid plasmic matter, can and does alter its form to any image appropriate to circumstances. Since, however, the form assumed is a direct reflection of the content or state of consciousness, it is an automatic result of the latter. So, in this Realm also 'form follows function', but in an utterly different way; as function in this sense is synonymous with 'being' or content. Now, what are some of these forms, and how did they originate – such as that of a fawn, for instance? I think I partly answered, or rather, supplied a clue to this in an earlier paragraph (previous section); wherein I defined 'Ideas' as 'Representations' (or embodiments) of group interpretations of Universal facts. Myths and legendary allegories fall into this category.

The myth-making (and image) faculty of the unconscious mind forms a concept of life (relative to the self) which is often embodied as an idealisation – a Being, such as Nature, Phantasy, Power etc. – and which the unconscious mind conceives of as a 'God', or in other words, the motivating powers of Existence relative to himself, as they appear to him. The Symbolic Being is also Self, since it represents the sum of his own experiences and reactions to such; and being therefore a creation of his own Mind, reflects its creator. Yet it is also an embodiment of the forces which have spiritually created or moulded him, and is therefore a personification of God in relation to himself. Generally, the more primitive the mind, the more it anthropomorphises the attributes of its God, since it is less capable of a detached survey.

So with the group: in fact the individual subconscious God-conception generally flows along the group thought channel most appropriate to it, hence all of the Gods of man. Hence also all the demons, spirits, and other representations of forces that have influenced him.

I have spoken of individual mind working upon and moulding plasmic material. Consider the power, then, of this unconscious mass-concentration of human beings, throughout the ages, upon certain idealisations of forms – the God-forms (a generic name for all such forms, including Demons, Faery creatures, 'angels' etc.). This unconscious creative thought concentration has built up images in the aether, moulding raw plasmic matter to the form of these images, and providing vehicles for other intelligences to manifest through, relative to humanity. I do not mean that these intelligences are either confined to any or all of these forms, or that they are the product of human thought, conscious or otherwise. The vehicles, or God-forms, yes, or largely so, but not the intelligences themselves. These vehicles, however, form a useful medium of communication, but naturally their visual form is, to a certain extent, anthropomorphic. Taking the abstract state of consciousness known as 'Humanity' or Human Consciousness (including all Uni-Planal variations) as belonging to one Realm of Being – and the next level of consciousness (ie. Deva consciousness; I have used a Sanscrit [sic] term, failing any English equivalent) as belonging to another Realm of Being, and as such, completely different from state one, the God-forms comprise a link, or half-way state between the two. Human consciousness, then, can move up into these God-forms during trance, or other exceptional conditions; likewise, Deva consciousness can descend into the same form. The inhabiting, or temporary animation of these forms by entities can be likened to an ectoplasmic 'incarnation', during which the entity assumes both the form and the mode of intelligence and perception associated with that form. So then, with the fawn depicted. This, I think, answers the first objection.

Concerning Objection 2: Here again a logical but incomplete conclusion has been reached through not allowing for the missing factors in the case. The statement concerning the 'faun' shape being familiar to myself through both personal and racial associations is quite true. For that reason, it is logical to suppose that I should encounter such 'God-forms' as interest me as an individual., and belong to my racial group, particularly since I had earlier opened a channel of communication to these particular manifestations through study and meditation. Since I had not done this with regard to Zulu culture and beliefs, and having no particular interest in them, no contact was made. This is not surprising, considering that there are endless planes within Planes; consequently in either Realm one only sees those things which are in some way relevant. No-one, for instance, walking along a crowded street sees, or even registers, every face – he only sees those which touch his subjective awareness in some way. He may notice those types of faces which have a personal interest for him, or anyone outstandingly peculiar, or different, from the crowd. If he is interested mainly in the buildings, he will probably notice neither. This automatic selective faculty is equally operative, and necessary, in the other Realm, where one can not only move through planes in space, but also through planes in time. Obviously, one could not see all things at all times, and though consciousness is extended enormously the result would be chaotic, were details in too many different parts of time and space to impinge upon one another simultaneously. This factor of 'relevance' explains why it is practically impossible to prophesy or know what anyone else will see or experience upon the other Plane of Being, despite many books asserting the contrary.

To conclude my discussion of these points, I have commented several times that Forms etc ., having no parallel in life as we know it, are utterly impossible of delineation; consequently I have necessarily selected only such shapes and happenings as

> are to some extent recognisable, for my drawings. (The 'God-forms' probably link up with Jung's 'Archetypes' subjectively, in the Plane of Being.)

This extraordinary account of utilising altered states of consciousness to access the magical universe is one of the most lucid descriptions of its type that I have come across. One needs to remember that this text was written in 1949, long before such topics as meditation, visualisation and 'consciousness expansion' became popular in the late 1960s' counter-culture. What is also of interest here is that when Rosaleen explored the inner planes of magical awareness she discovered that on the 'plasmic level' thoughts themselves could give rise to specific forms, and she was then able to *experience* the forms she visualised. There is also the concept here of an inner-plane conscious intelligence pervading all aspects of the manifest universe – something which magicians in all cultures have utilised as a basis for their activities. In the magical universe, everything is alive and everything is linked energetically within an infinite web of relationships.

Norton's reference to a 'plasmic body' – a body which 'felt as though it were formed of warm golden light' – is reminiscent of numerous accounts found in the parapsychological and transpersonal literature relating to 'out-of-the-body' experiences (OOBEs) and 'near-death experiences' (NDEs) in research that continues to the present day. One of the most vital issues associated with these experiences is the relationship between human consciousness and the brain. For neuroscientists and transpersonal psychologists investigating these altered states of consciousness the issue of whether human consciousness can exist beyond, or outside, the brain is a key concern because it would determine whether the living brain is the actual source of human consciousness or more specifically the vehicle through which consciousness operates. In the latter instance, in a metaphorical sense, the relationship between brain and consciousness could be likened to the electrical impulses received through a television set from an external source of transmission; here the hardware (= brain) is not the actual source of the programme.[13] This scientific dilemma has still not been resolved but the issue itself nevertheless has profound implications for religious concepts of life after death. If the existence of disembodied human consciousness could be scientifically proven it would lend considerable credence to the theoretical possibility of an afterlife, although the actual nature of that afterlife would probably remain a matter of far-ranging religious and metaphysical speculation.[14]

The contemporary Dutch cardiologist Dr Pim van Lommel – a leading medical researcher specialising in the study of near-death experiences (NDEs) – draws on quantum theory to distinguish between what he calls 'phase-space' ('invisible, non-local, higher-dimensional space…where every past and future event is available as a possibility') and 'real-space' which is associated with 'body-linked waking consciousness' and the material, manifest world. Van Lommel believes that in the same way that waves and particles mirror each other in quantum dynamics

> …life creates the transition from phase-space into our manifest real-space…life creates the possibility to receive the fields of consciousness (waves) into the waking consciousness which belongs to our physical body (particles)…there is a permanent interaction between these two aspects of consciousness…

> When we die, our consciousness will no longer have an aspect of particles, but only the eternal aspect of waves [15]

According to Van Lommel the evidence from scientific NDE research suggests that human consciousness is independent of brain function: conscious awareness is received like a wave-transmission by the living brain but does not actually originate within the physical organism itself. Van Lommel believes that consciousness is best understood as being based on fields of information, consisting of waves and... orginates in the phase space...[At] the time of physical death consciousness will continue to be experienced in another dimension, in an invisible and immaterial world, the phase-space, in which all past, present and future is enclosed. [16]

Van Lommel's medical model of life, death and consciousness is pertinent to Rosaleen Norton's experiences of altered states of consciousness because, according to her account, Norton discovered she was able to contact a discarnate human being while in a state of self-induced trance. Norton's cosmology and magical practice similarly depend on her ability to access inner planes of conscious awareness which extend beyond familiar waking consciousness. Like a traditional shaman, accessing mythic realms of awareness while in a state of consciously willed dissociation, Norton was endeavouring to transcend the barrier of physical death through her inner-plane encounters and when she writes about her trance experiences she uses terms like 'ecstasy', 'golden light' and 'inner-plane transition'. She also became aware that in a state of trance-dissociation, 'the body is completely a reflection of the mind' and observes that her consciousness was no longer constrained by physical limitations: 'My body felt as though it were formed of warm golden light; the physical body had become merely an appendage…'

What Rosaleen experienced here is sometimes referred to in the Western esoteric tradition as 'rising in the planes' – the visionary magician 'journeys' upwards through the planes through an act of consciously willed spiritual ascent towards the sacred source of Life itself, perceived variously as the Godhead or Infinite Formlessness. Essentially this process parallels what Van Lommel has described as the return to 'phase-space', where consciousness is experienced as waves (plasmic energy) and the world of particles (physical form) no longer applies. In quantum terms this magical approach could in turn be seen as structuring the transition from conscious awareness at the level of physical reality ('particles') through to transcendence ('waves').

Norton's fascinating inner-plane descriptions clearly indicate that she was also able to explore these metaphysical realms of existence, and they are a valuable contribution to modern occult literature for this reason alone. However, her accounts are unique for another reason as well: in her particular case they led her to formulate a distinctive and somewhat unconventional operative model of the universe. In this model of magical reality Norton describes the way in which mythic entities and metaphysical sentient beings reveal their presence on different planes of existence. In the following section of this chapter I have transposed extracts from Norton's interview with my own commentary.

ROSALEEN NORTON'S CONCEPT OF THE MAGICAL UNIVERSE

One of Norton's earliest findings in relation to what she referred to as 'the other Realm of Being' was that the contents of this domain seemed to be directed by thought itself, almost as if one were consciously entering a dream-world. According to Norton, in the magical realm thoughts become tangible and visible and often assume an anthropomorphic form. Visual images and metaphysical 'entities' also morph from one form into another, subject to conscious or 'willed' intent:

> ...'thought' in those realms is very different from that which is normally understood by the word. There, 'thought' – or rather the energy generated by such – is felt as a tangible thing, a current of living force which assumes palpable and visual form. I had been told, earlier, that 'entities in the Plane assumed form at will'. This is literally true; one actually changes shape very frequently, since the new 'sense' referred to is that which could be described as 'being'. Just as one can see, feel, hear a thing, state or person; and when this occurs one realises and is the very essence of its nature. This sense, if one can call it that, covers a vastly wider field than anything comparable to human life; for in addition to becoming the essence of male, female, or neither, and beings of other orders of Existence, one can 'become' a living embodiment of abstract Ideas of all descriptions.

During a state of trance Norton sometimes experienced sensations of metaphysical abstraction. On these occasions her perceptions were related more to 'essence' than to form:

One of the strangest experiences I had was 'becoming' an embodiment of an Idea of the Universe. This Idea was not anthropomorphised into Entity, as is usually the case with such embodiments. Consequently, although my consciousness existed, there was no consciousness of entity at all. I am not referring to the personal 'I' consciousness, for naturally that alters completely with each form assumed; I have used a capital letter to differentiate between personal ideas and Ideas, which are representations to the consciousness of Group interpretations of Universal facts, according to order of Existence and sub-divisions therein. (By 'other orders of Existence' I mean different classes of Being from Man; highly evolved unhuman intelligences)....

Orthodox occultists occasionally describe the Plane of 'dense' matter as the 'Realm of Form', which to my mind is a complete misnomer. The name should be applied to the realm of which I speak, since things There are seen in their archetypal essence. There, all forms whether abstract or actual appear in their real perfection as part of the very essence of Form itself, which is omnipresent. In speaking of abstract form I refer to System and the pattern of things in general, which interblend in all directions into infinity. As I have remarked elsewhere, the fact of chaos anywhere appears to be only a part of form and system, and as such purely relative.

The realisation of the essential Form of things occurs in various ways... one sees things such as the pattern of a life, for instance, as a complete and perfect thing in itself, yet forming against relationship to other lives part of another wider pattern; which again forms part of another yet larger... and so, ad infinitum. Similarly, with things such as Dimension – Time, Plane and

> Space – one literally sees the perfect interblending of their relationship to one another and to the Universe as a whole. Here again, the vehicle of realisation of this type of knowledge is greater and more comprehensive than intellectual understanding, although it includes the latter. Many of these Abstract forms appeared as vast animated patterns blending in a kind of geometrical harmony which we felt as well as observed, and into which the consciousness merged. The shapes and manifestations were not those of Euclidean geometry; cosmic mathematics manifesting as an immense art-form is the best analogy I can find. [capital letters in Norton's original text]

Here Norton reveals her Gnostic tendencies, perceiving herself 'becoming an embodiment of an Idea of the Universe'. In Gnostic cosmological systems the transcendent Godhead emanates ideas (or archetypes) which in turn manifest gradually into more specific material forms. Norton similarly comes to believe that her trance experiences provide experiential proof that thoughts and emotions can have a tangible impact on the 'plasmic body':

> Many of these things, of course, happened much later; however, these examples indicate the complete unity of mind and fluids in the plasmic body, also the sensory tangibility of the thought-force. The manipulation of the latter (to return to my previous statement) in any kind of abstract thinking, is also a sensory skill and actually feeling the keen precision of directed force. In the emotional sphere, there is a different type of awareness. When one feels wonder, serenity, etc., one does not exactly become a representation of these states; rather, there is a sensation of complete unity with that which is causing their

> manifestation, and yet another sense which is a blending of the familiar five senses into a super-intensified one, plus an indefinable essence.

According to Norton, many of the familiar 'god-forms' and mythic images from the world's various mythological and religious traditions could be regarded as projections of human consciousness. However, this did not make them any less 'real' when experienced in an altered state of consciousness; these powerful mythic images would still have a tangible presence on the magical plane when an individual encountered them in trance via the plasmic body. Norton maintained that *the actual gods or 'intelligences' themselves* could not be constrained by the cultural forms imposed by mythological or religious traditions because these were only human constructs; that is to say, the gods were 'greater' than the 'god-forms' through which they manifested. In this regard Norton emphasized that many metaphysical entities perceived in the trance realm were projections from intelligences whose origins lay far beyond the sphere of human awareness:

> In the other Realm, the structure of phenomena is based on other lines. Intelligences are not confined to one form as here; also the consciousness pertaining to each type of form bears a far closer relationship to its material vehicle. The latter, as I have said, being fluid plasmic matter, can and does alter its form to any image appropriate to circumstances. Since, however, the form assumed is a direct reflection of the content or state of consciousness, it is an automatic result of the latter. So, in this Realm also 'form follows function', but in an utterly different way; as function in this sense is synonymous with 'being' or content....

The myth-making (and image) faculty of the unconscious mind forms a concept of life (relative to the self) which is often embodied as an idealisation – a Being, such as Nature, Phantasy, Power etc. – and which the unconscious mind conceives of as a 'God', or in other words, the motivating powers of Existence relative to himself, as they appear to him. The Symbolic Being is also Self, since it represents the sum of his own experiences and reactions to such; and being therefore a creation of his own Mind, reflects its creator. Yet it is also an embodiment of the forces which have spiritually created or moulded him, and

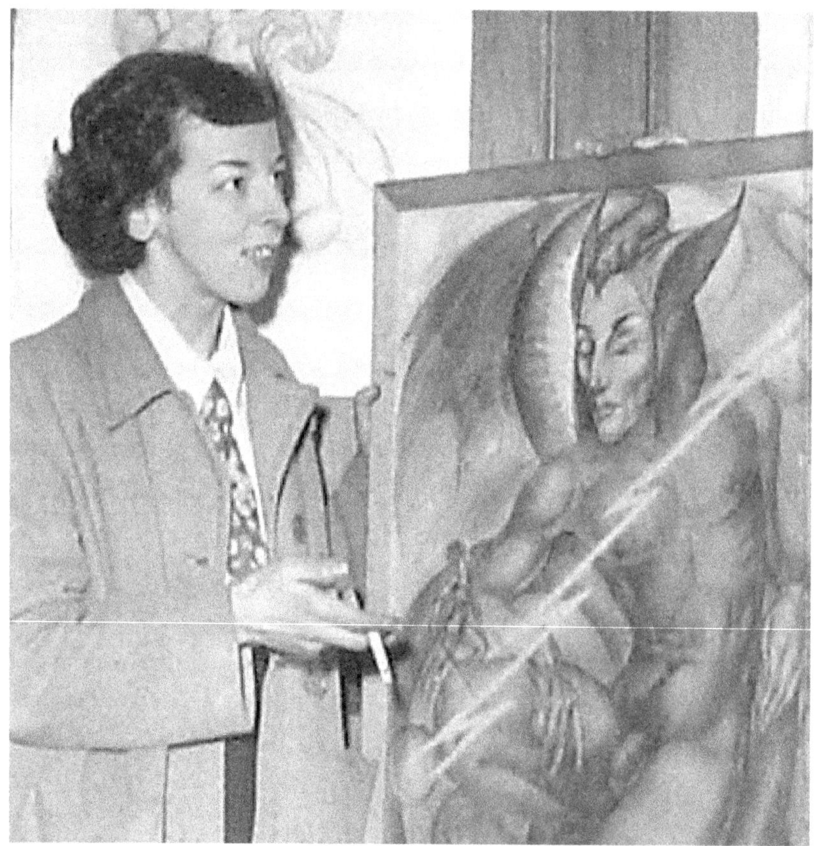

ROSALEEN NORTON AND THE ADVERSARY

> is therefore a personification of God in relation to himself. Generally, the more primitive the mind, the more it anthropomorphizes the attributes of its God, since it is less capable of a detached survey.
>
> So with the group: in fact the individual subconscious God-conception generally flows along the group thought channel most appropriate to it, hence all of the Gods of man. Hence also all the demons, spirits, and other representations of forces that have influenced him.
>
> I have spoken of individual mind working upon and moulding plasmic material. Consider the power, then, of this unconscious mass-concentration of human beings, throughout the ages, upon certain idealisations of forms – the God-forms
>
> (a generic name for all such forms, including Demons, Faery creatures, 'angels' etc.). This unconscious creative thought concentration has built up images in the aether, moulding raw plasmic matter to the form of these images, and providing vehicles for other intelligences to manifest through, relative to humanity. I do not mean that these intelligences are either confined to any or all of these forms, or that they are the product of human thought, conscious or otherwise. The vehicles, or God-forms, yes, or largely so, but not the intelligences themselves. These vehicles, however, form a useful medium of communication, but naturally their visual form is, to a certain extent, anthropomorphic...'

According to Norton, the fluid nature of the astral realm allowed metaphysical entities and intelligences from higher planes of existence to manifest themselves, or 'incarnate', at lower levels of the astral plane and at this time they would appear in anthropomorphic god-forms

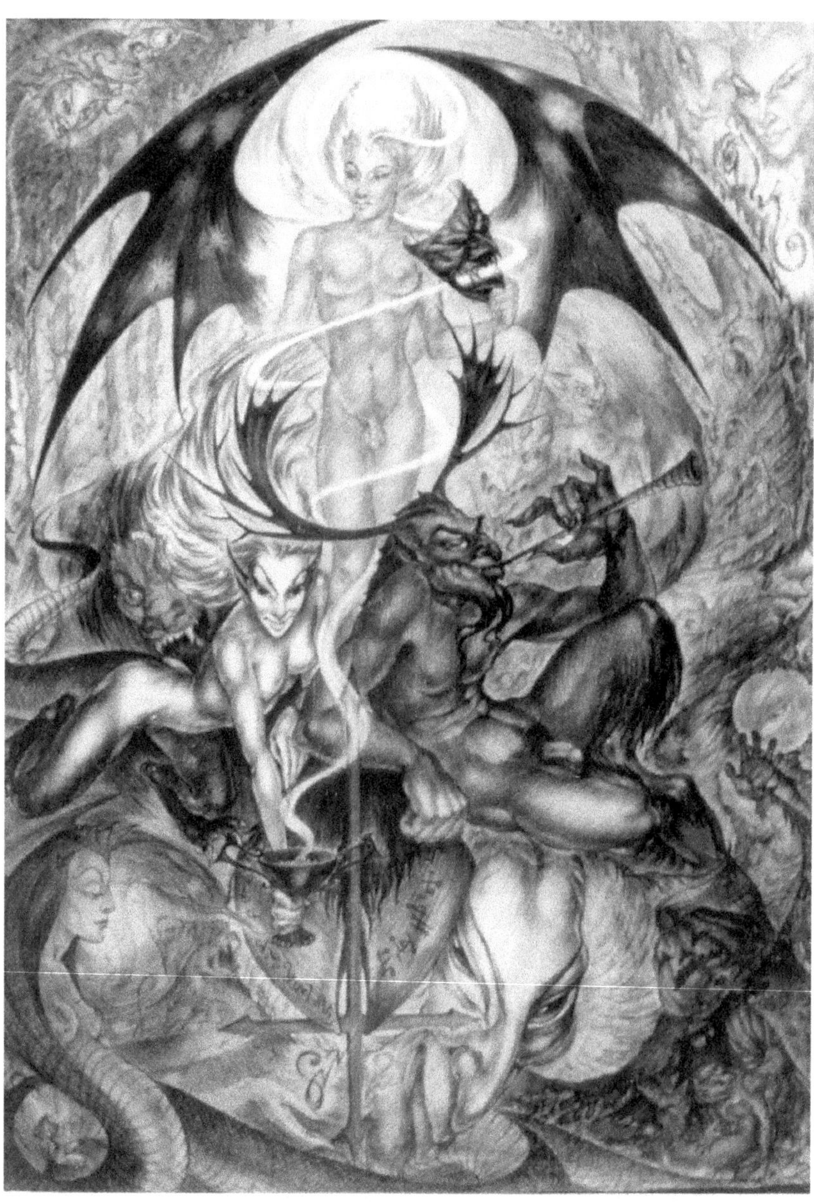

Lucifer – Norton sits in the foreground, beside Pan

culturally appropriate to the consciousness of the beholder. Norton believed that the god-forms themselves provided a mediating link between different levels of reality – the metaphysical and the human – and that human beings could approach the gods by 'rising' through the astral planes towards the manifested god-forms while in a state of trance. Conversely, the gods could 'incarnate' or 'descend' into the astral realms by manifesting in an appropriate form:

> Taking the abstract state of consciousness known as 'Humanity' or Human Consciousness (including all Uni-Planal [sic] variations) as belonging to one Realm of Being – and the next level of consciousness (ie. Deva consciousness, I have used a Sanskrit term, failing any English equivalent) as belonging to another Realm of Being, and as such, completely different from state one, the God-forms comprise a link, or half-way state between the two. Human consciousness, then, can move up into these God-forms during trance, or other exceptional conditions; likewise Deva consciousness can descend into the same form. The inhabiting, or temporary animation of these forms by entities can be likened to an ectoplasmic 'incarnation', during which the entity assumes both the form and the mode of intelligence and perception associated with that form.

From a magical perspective, Rosaleen Norton regarded the astral plane as a type of 'mediating domain' between the gods and goddesses on the one hand, and human consciousness (functioning through the vehicle of the plasmic body) on the other. Norton also formed the view – on the basis of her trance experiences in the plasmic body – that a number of inner-plane 'intelligences' pervaded all aspects of the known universe. These intelligences in turn confirmed the nature of their existence through a range of anthropomorphic images, manifesting as gods and goddesses, demons and archangels – as portrayed in the world's various religions and mythologies.

Norton's cosmology and her conception of magical consciousness lead us in turn to consider some related issues: how did Norton respond to the various gods and goddesses within her personal magical pantheon and how did her response impact in turn on her creative process?

RELATING TO THE GODS AND GODDESSES

Norton's exploration of trance states provided access to a dimension of conscious awareness that was completely unfamiliar to most of her contemporaries. As mentioned earlier, her trance journeys were essentially solitary affairs where her privacy was safeguarded by close family members. However a key discovery made by Norton herself and which distinguishes her from many other occultists operating within the Western esoteric tradition – especially those espousing the philosophy that magic is based, essentially, on directing the will – was that Norton did not believe she was fully in control of the magical energies she was encountering. When I interviewed Norton in 1977 it was evident that she believed that the archetypal gods and cosmic beings she had contacted in trance existed *in their own right.* In their own particular magical realms they held the upper hand – *not she.* To this extent Norton differed from thinkers like Carl Jung, who regarded the sacred archetypes as universal forces deep within the collective human psyche, and not as entities with their own separate existence beyond the mind. While Norton admitted to being influenced by Jung and refers to Jungian archetypes in the L.J. Murphy transcripts, for Jung, the archetypes – the ancient gods and goddesses of religion and mythology – were ultimately sacred personifications of the self.[17]

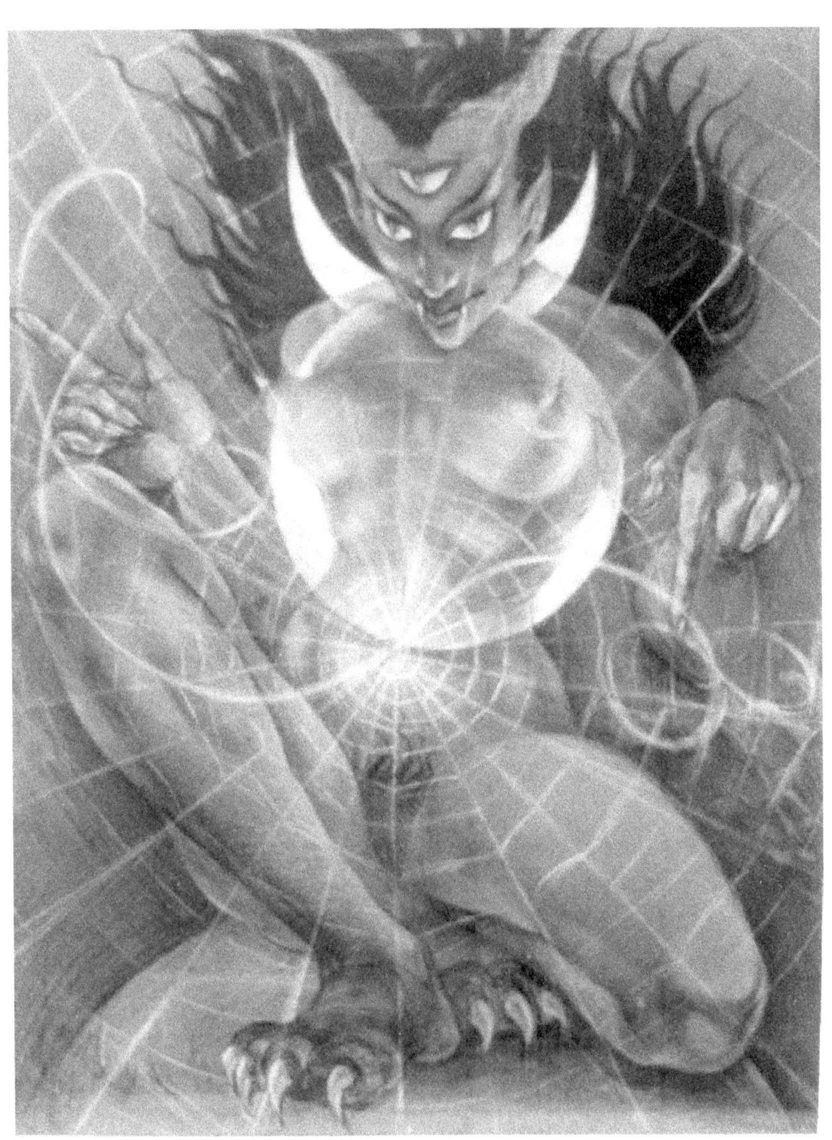

THE SPINNER

On the basis of what she experienced during her trance explorations, Norton did not share this view. For her, magical deities such as Pan, Hecate, Lilith, and Lucifer, as well as other magical entities like Eloi, Fohat and the Werplon were not projections or extensions of her own spiritual consciousness, but powerful – and sometimes terrifying – entities who would grace her with their presence *only if it pleased them,* and not as a consequence of her own personal will or intent. Norton believed she could only depict in her paintings and drawings those qualities and attributes that the god or goddess in question *chose to reveal*, and that those energies would then filter through her 'like a funnel'. Norton maintained that she did nothing other than transmit the magical current. If the gods and goddesses were alive *in her* and *through her*, their presence would manifest in her art and through her ceremonial magical practice.

1 In addition to *Astral Scene* and *The Sphinx*, other artworks which depict Norton in a state of comatose trance include *Nightmare*, a work from the mid-1940s, and *The Initiate*, reproduced in *The Art of Rosaleen Norton* (1952: plate XXII). A coloured rendition of the latter work, slightly different in composition but also showing Norton's head and shoulders, had been included in the Rowden-White Gallery exhibition in Melbourne in 1949.

2 O.M. Broughton 'The art of Rosaleen Norton', *Arna*, Sydney 1948: 18

3 In his article 'The art of Rosaleen Norton', loc.cit.1948, Broughton refers specifically to 'the Yoni (in which the figure of the artist is reclining)...' and says that here the Yoni 'means Receptivity to Forces from other planes and Dimensions of Being'. In *Ecstasy Through Tantra* [988:96], Dr Jonn Mumford writes that 'in Yoga and Tantra...[the Yoni refers to] the female vulva or external genitalia [and is] likened to a lotus bud, soft and sweet smelling. Hindu Tantric sculpture is unique among the ancient civilizations as always clearly

depicting the soft curves and slit of the vulva on female nudes...[the] naked Goddess arched backwards, knees apart, displaying her Yoni for Puja, worshipful veneration.'

4 N. Drury, *Inner Visions: Explorations in Magical Consciousness*, Routledge & Kegan Paul, London 1979: 106.

5 The 'assumption of the god form' in modern ceremonial magic is a practice whereby the magician imitates the posture, regalia and perceived qualities of a mythological deity with the intention of seeking to embody the essence of that deity through an act of ritual and symbolic identification.

6 N. Drury, *Inner Visions: Explorations in Magical Consciousness*, loc.cit. 1979: 106.

7 R. Norton, 'Witches Want No Recruits', *Australasian Post*, Sydney, 10 January 1957.

8 In Mahayana Buddhism the term *Sunyata* refers to the Void, or Supreme Reality, beyond manifested form. For Norton to truly enter Sunyata, she would necessarily have to surrender all vestiges of ego in an act of transcendental Union with the Absolute – hence the term 'trance of annihilation'.

9 Mrs Raphael-Oeser, who sent the present transcript to Walter Glover in 1982, added an annotation of her own, namely that she presumed that Norton had been asked by L.J. Murphy to provide her own personal account of her beliefs and cosmology and also that one preceding page at least, appears to be missing from Norton's account.

10 The whereabouts of this document on automatic writing is unknown – it was not forwarded to Glover in 1982.

11 Norton was married to Beresford Conroy at this time.

12 Presumably Norton means 'faun' and not 'fawn'. She refers to the 'faun shape' later in her account.

13 See P. Van Lommel, 'About the Continuity of our Consciousness', in C. Machado and D.A. Shewmon (ed.), *Brain Death and Disorders of Consciousness*, Kluwer Academic/ Plenum, New York 2004: 115-132.

14 Scientists specializing in the study of altered states of consciousness occasionally work with gifted subjects in an effort to test the validity

of perceptions experienced during willed out-of-the-body experiences (see C. Tart, ed., *Altered States of Consciousness*, Wiley, New York 1969; D. Goleman and R.J. Davidson, ed., *Consciousness: Brain, States of Awareness and Mysticism*, Harper & Row, New York 1979). Paranormal researcher Robert A. Monroe (1915-1995), author of three books on out-of-the-body consciousness (*Journeys Out of the Body*, Doubleday, New York 1971: *Far Journeys*, Doubleday, New York 1985 and *Ultimate Journey*, Doubleday, New York 1984), maintained that religious imagery would be experienced by devout believers as an experiential reality in the after-death state but he also claimed that it was possible to transcend the limitations of religious belief in this state of post-mortem awareness. See N. Drury, *The New Age: the History of a Movement*, Thames & Hudson, New York 2004: 196-200.

15 P. Van Lommel, 'About the Continuity of our Consciousness', loc cit.

16 Ibid.

17 See C.G. Jung, *Psychology of the Unconscious*, Kegan Paul, Trench, Trubner, London 1919; *The Archetypes of the Collective Unconscious*, Routledge & Kegan Paul, London 1959; *Symbols of Transformation*, Bollingen Foundation / Princeton University Press, New Jersey 1956, and *Man and his Symbols*, Dell, New York 1968.

4

Figleaf Morality

Rosaleen's art would soon to come to the notice of a broader audience, and would attract considerable attention through the media. Until now she had only had one real exhibition, at the off-beat and bohemian Pakie's Club in Sydney. Around twenty paintings had been shown there, but few had sold, and she was still very much a figure of the artistic underground.

Some time in early August 1949 she and Gavin Greenlees, together with their pet cat Geoffrey, hitchhiked from Sydney to Melbourne specifically to find a new venue for an exhibition. Both Roie and Gavin were flat broke. Roie had a dim memory of someone called Ian, a student from the University of Melbourne, who had contacted her a few years earlier. It was only a vague recollection, not a detailed memory, and it hardly represented a tangible prospect.

'You don't mean Ian Stapleton, do you?' asked Gavin, having heard his name mentioned by another friend. Although it was a coincidence, it soon seemed after they discussed it, that this was the same person. And Ian Stapleton did prove to be a most enthusiastic ally. Dazzled by the few works that Roie had brought with her, he soon became a type of publicity agent for her. Not only did he book the gallery at the Rowden-White Library at the University of Melbourne, so they could hold the exhibition there, but he also put up some money for out-of-pocket expenses.[1] Not that everything went smoothly, however. Ian had booked Gavin and Roie into the university student hostel in Brunswick Street, Fitzroy. The only trouble was, it was exclusively for men!

Gavin and Roie managed to stay there for about a week, until they received an eviction notice from the warden. It was a silly little scandal, but it refused to go away. It would even result in a court hearing – in March 1951, almost two years later – and Roie would have to explain in Melbourne City Court that she slept in her bedroom only with her cat, Geoffrey, and not with Gavin Greenlees. For the moment, however, despite their eviction their main concern was to hitchhike back to Sydney and get enough paintings together to mount the exhibition.

Getting back to Sydney proved to be troublesome. There were floods along the lower New South Wales coast and, further north, the Camden Vale bridge had been under water for a week. Luckily, just as they arrived, the flooded waters at Camden subsided for twenty-four hours, allowing the traffic, and the two hitchhikers from Melbourne, safe passage across the bridge. Soon the rain and floods would return – this time for a fortnight. However, it didn't matter; Roie and Gavin returned to Melbourne by train.

The works Roie brought back with her included some of her best drawings: *Timeless Worlds*, *Lucifer*, *Triumph*, *The Adversary*, *The Initiate*, an early version of *Individuation*, *Merlin* and *Loosing of the Whirlwind.* All in all, the Rowden-White Library would soon be host to some forty-six works, and Professor A.R. Chisholm would give the welcoming address. The exhibition was scheduled to run from 1-23 August, with the gallery opening from 10 am to 9 pm.

By all accounts the exhibition should have been a relatively peaceful affair, attended mainly by students and a few curious academics. However, two days after it opened, police descended on the gallery, seizing four of the exhibited pictures. Charges would soon be laid under the Police Offences Act of 1928 alleging that these particular works – *Witches' Sabbath*, *Lucifer*, *Triumph* and *Individuation* – were decadent and obscene, and likely to arouse unhealthy sexual appetites in those who saw them.

The raid followed a visit to the exhibition by two policemen, Detective John Olsen and Inspector Tannahill on 3 August. Olsen actually spoke to Rosaleen about the pictures, discussing with her various complaints he had received about the drawings being 'lewd and disgusting'. One person had described the works as 'stark sensuality running riot', while another claimed the exhibition produced 'as gross a shock to the average spectator as a witch's orgy'. Rosaleen was not impressed by these

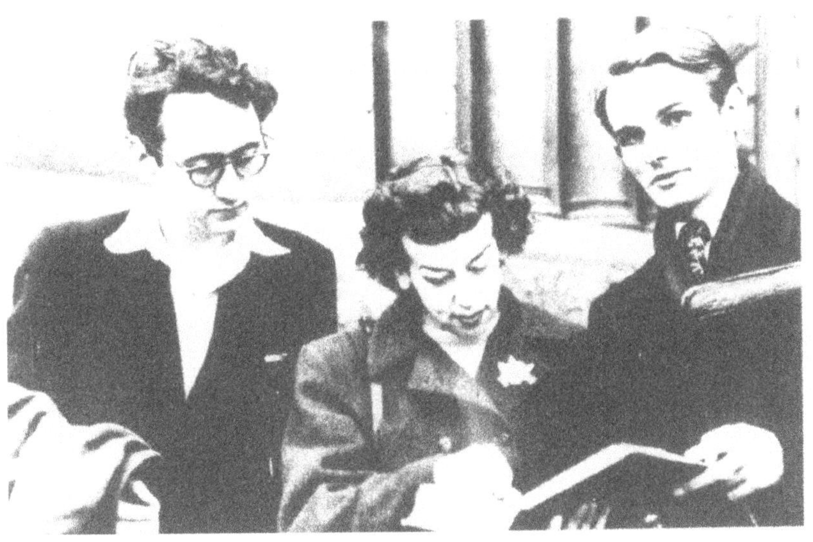

GAVIN AND ROIE WITH IAN STAPLETON, 1949

responses to her work. 'Obscenity,' she countered, 'like beauty, is in the eye of the beholder. This figleaf morality expresses a very unhealthy attitude.'[2]

Olsen persisted, however, asking Rosaleen for an explanation of *Witches' Sabbath*, a controversial work which would later be titled *Black Magic*. She replied that it was a 'symbolistic' drawing: the female figure depicted was a witch, the panther personified the powers of darkness,

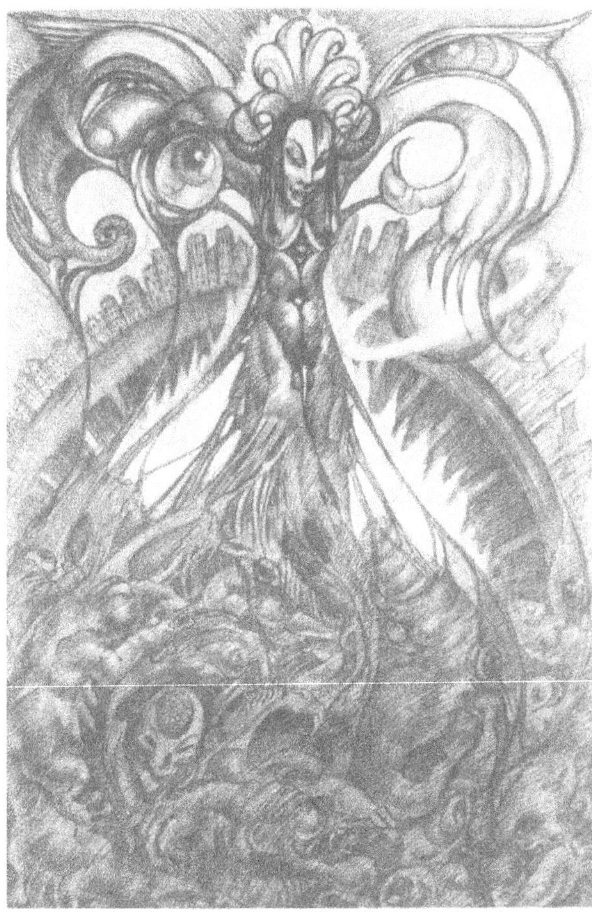

THE EARLY VERSION OF INDIVIDUATION

and their embrace represented the initiation of the witch into the 'infernal mysteries'.

This was all too much for Detective Olsen and his colleague, and in the ensuing court hearing the Crown prosecution would allege that works of this sort could 'deprave and corrupt the morals of those who saw them'. The sessions took place before Stipendiary Magistrate Mr Addison in the Carlton Court while the exhibition was still being shown.

During the hearings, the police detectives put their case quite vigorously, arguing that Rosaleen was displaying works inspired by medieval demonology. However, in Rosaleen's defence, Mr A.L. Abrahams argued that these allegedly obscene pictures were mild compared with illustrations published in *The History of Sexual Magic*, a book which had been cleared by the censors and which was readily available in Australia. 'We have to cater for people with normal reactions to sex,' Abrahams went on to say,

> 'not morons, the subnormal and neurotics.' Driving the point home still further he added: 'The Act under which this prosecution is launched is based on a case heard during Queen Victoria's reign in 1836...' [3]

The Warden of Melbourne University Union, Mr R.R. Barbour, then gave evidence which supported Rosaleen's viewpoint. He was the person who had actually given Rosaleen permission to hold the exhibition, and he did not find her drawings sexually exciting. Keen to reinforce this point, Abrahams then said that for Rosaleen to be declared guilty as charged, her art would have to be found to be of a nature 'likely to corrupt those whose minds were open to immoral influences'.

Fortunately for Roie, the drift of testimonial was beginning to swing her way. Finally Stipendiary Magistrate Addison found in her favour, dismissing the charges against her and awarding £4/4/- costs against the police department. Naturally Rosaleen was delighted with her victory but surprisingly, given the circumstances, the controversy did not help to sell many pictures. Instead, a large flow of penniless students slipped in to see the show and some would ask furtively where they could see the four 'rudies'. And since the viewing audience was largely restricted to students and academics, members of the general public were not able to see the pictures or purchase them. They could only read about them in the newspapers.

Rosaleen finally had to declare that she was still broke – £50 in the red. She had hoped that the university exhibition might lead to further shows in a more central location, such as Flinders Street in the heart of Melbourne. Unfortunately this didn't happen and she then spent several miserable days at the People's Palace and the Salvation Army Hostel wondering what to do next. 'I look like walking back to Sydney and then starving,' she told those who were willing to listen to her sympathetically. 'That's art for you...'

Roie did stay long enough in Melbourne, however, to do a series of psychological tests with L.J. Murphy at the University, in addition to writing her remarkable account of the magical universe referred to in the previous chapter. Murphy recorded several personal details during his interview with her. He was interested to discover that Roie had 'hated' her mother but respected her father, and had a good relationship with her two older sisters. He also recorded several interesting aspects of Roie's sexual history, details of which are fascinating in light of the themes

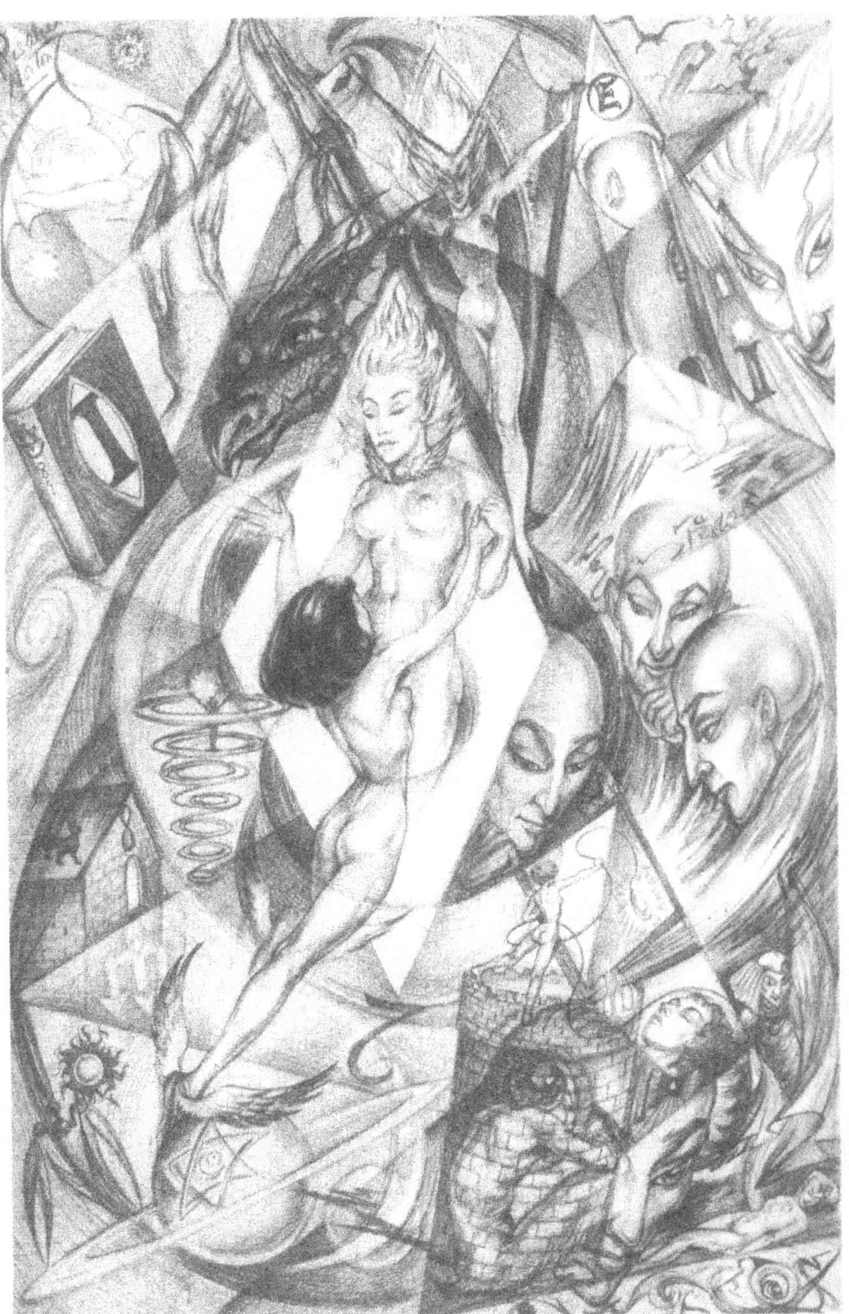

THE INITIATE

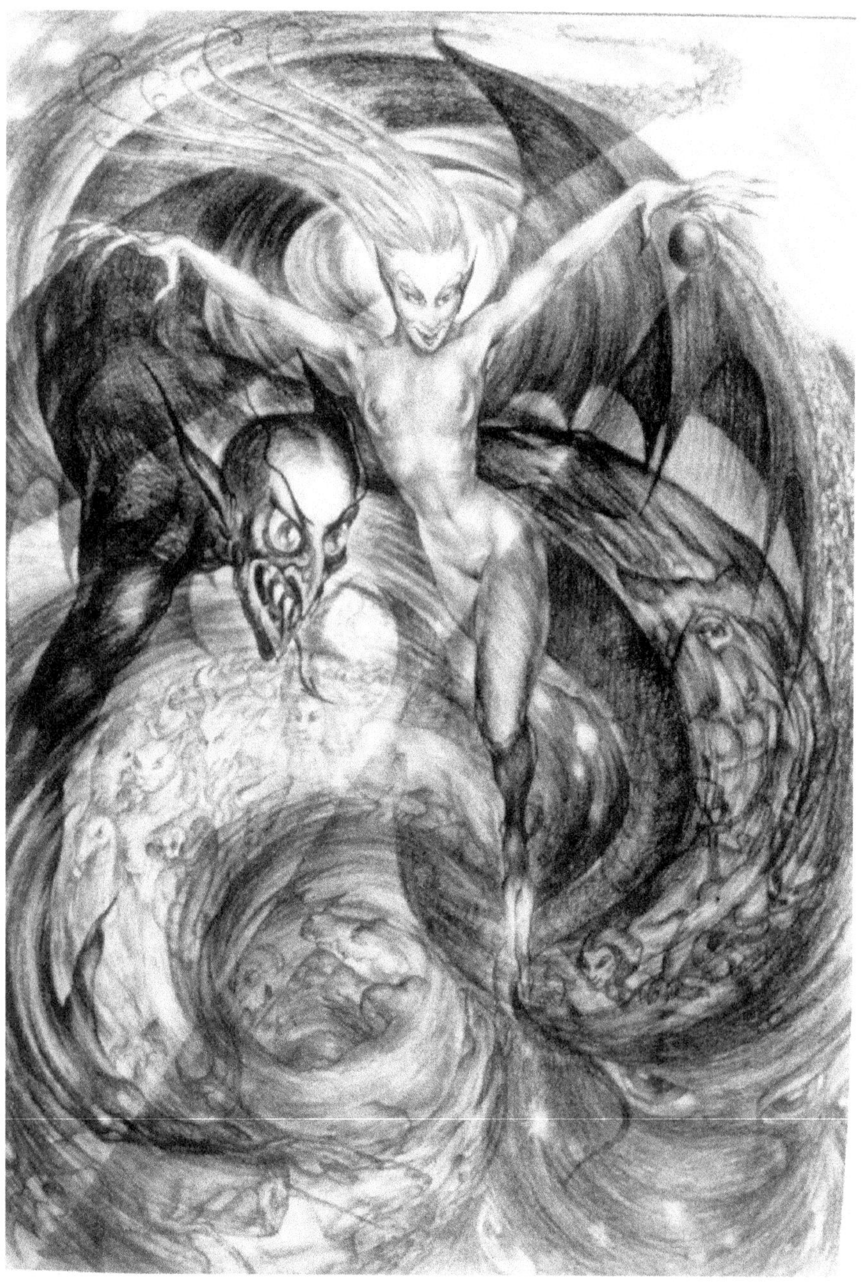

Loosing of the Whirlwind

in her paintings – many of which show naked androgynous figures or phalluses transforming into serpents.

Roie had had her first sexual experience at the age of twelve. It had been 'rather accidental' she told Murphy, 'in that a boy of my own age suggested that we do it. I found it very painful and did not try again...' Roie did not have another sexual encounter until she was seventeen and 'this was a cold-blooded decision on my part: I wanted to find out what it was like.'

During her interview with L.J. Murphy Roie said she had 'no strong sex sensation' at present but continued to have sexual relationships on a continuing basis from time to time. Sex, for her, was something she would often engage in impassively.[4] Perhaps keen to explore different, and more alluring aspects of sexuality – aspects which she had heard about but not yet experienced – she now ventured into areas that would have been considered risqué at the time. Roie claimed to enjoy the company of homosexuals because she could take a more active role with them. She told Murphy: 'Those men are soft and rounded, and they let me do what I like with them. I enjoy most of all their hands softly running up and down my back – sometimes they use pencils and leaves.' She was also fond of manual and oral manipulation with both male and female homosexuals, and had a penchant for sado-masochistic practices. She told Murphy she liked to be tied up and beaten, and to engage in sexual intercourse so powerfully that her partner would hurt her by forcing her back against the pole to which she was tied. During her lesbian encounters, however, she liked to be dominant – kissing and being kissed, stroking and being stroked – but nevertheless remaining the more active partner.

Often, she said, she felt she would like to have a penis of her own, to insert into the woman she was with.

Following a detailed Rorshach-Behn Test, Murphy evaluated Rosaleen as having 'superior' intellectual abilities but felt, surprisingly, that the range of her imagination was not very high. 'The amount of variety and fantasy in the records is clearly not as great as the subject thinks it is... [and] there is a certain stereotyping about them all.' He also found signs of 'emotional rigidity' and a 'high degree of introversiveness', indicative of pronounced 'inner tension and anxiety'. There were signs, too, of a 'schizophrenic type of personality'. However, according to Murphy. 'there is nowhere in the record a lack of intellectual control over the fantasies, which is expected in schizophrenics'.

On the other hand, Murphy wrote, '... there is a straining towards odd and original fantasies which is not completely realised: this suggests that the subject is really malingering in the direction of schizophrenia, that she is trying to be odd and peculiar, and to give way to unconscious fantasies.'[5]

After their brief stay in Melbourne, Gavin and Roie returned to the more welcoming climes of Sydney's Kings Cross, a district which, in line with L.J. Murphy's observations, would surely serve to strengthen their fantasies and enhance their bohemian self-image. Here Gavin and Roie were among friends, for the Cross attracted eccentrics, poets, vagrants and artists as if they were its lifeblood.

Roie and Gavin were now living together and had become lovers although, according to Roie's sister Cecily, that had not been the initial attraction. It is likely that Roie and Gavin first met one another in the last year of the war, when Beresford [Conroy] was still away in New

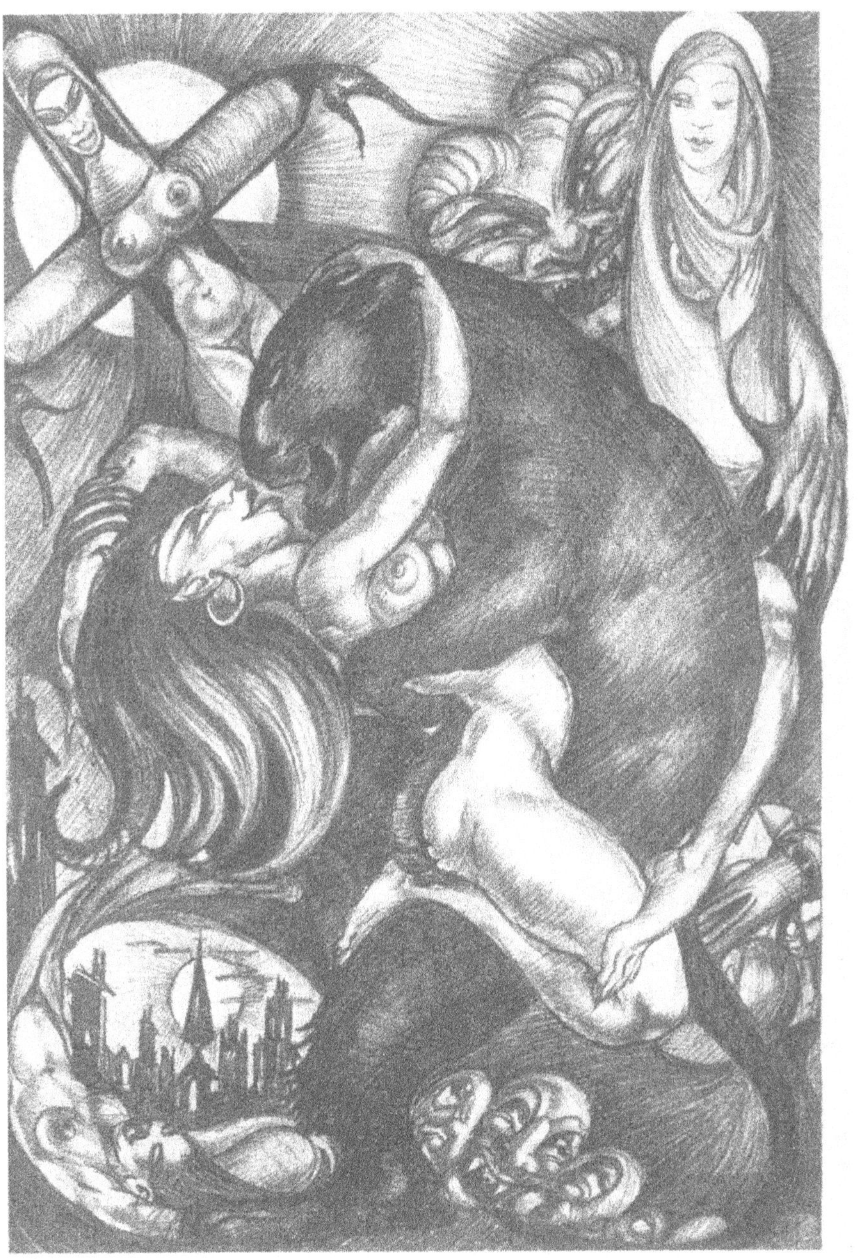

WITCHES' SABBATH

Guinea and Roie was living in the stables in Bayswater Road. Cecily remembered seeing him there, and no doubt their creative contributions to *Pertinent* had drawn them together – she as a visionary artist and he as an aspiring visionary poet.

But if *Pertinent* was the initial common bond, they were also attracted physically to each other, and a sexual relationship soon developed. No doubt, it was a relationship with many different facets. Roie was thirteen years older than Gavin and she was the dominant partner from the start. And while she strongly resisted acting in any way like her mother – she always claimed to have no maternal instincts at all – her relationship with Gavin allowed her to mother him. She became over-protective of him, encouraged his poetry, provided him with warmth and friendship, and gave him a degree of emotional security which he wasn't getting from his own family, especially his journalist father.

While Gavin senior would bully his son, and try to convince him to turn away from fantasy poetry to 'real writing', Roie stimulated Gavin to explore his inner world. Together they investigated mystical symbolism and yarned about surrealist literature. They also enjoyed the same sorts of music – especially Sibelius – and they both explored meditative and hypnotic techniques in order to induce visionary states of consciousness.

Gavin already had a propensity for such altered states since he was an epileptic, although this would not be medically diagnosed until many years later when he fell down one day in the street. For the moment Roie simply accepted Gavin as a person who was sensitive, if highly strung, and prone to what she called 'nerve attacks', when he would rapidly descend into panic and rage.

Generally, however, Gavin was a very mild and gentle youth who wouldn't intentionally harm anybody. Tall and gangly, with spectacles and a mop of unkempt hair, he often seemed balanced on a delicate edge between intellect and madness. He had a dreamy, other-wordly air to him, and this was a powerful attraction for Roie. Most importantly, though, he had a whimsical sense of humour. Both he and Roie loved anything that was ridiculous. Roie would show this side of her personality many years later when she dressed up in a witch's hat for the media. Both Gavin and Roie enjoyed sending themselves up as figures of fun. However, more than anything, Roie simply enjoyed Gavin's company, and in Kings Cross they were truly in their element, for here they could be happily bohemian together. There were also some wild parties – as graphic artist Jim Russell recalls – where Roie's excessive sexual behaviour was on full view for everyone to see:

> … I would see her from time to time at parties with a young man in tow, Gavin Greenlees. A timid sort of bloke with glasses. But it got to the stage where you just dodged her, for she was so outrageous with her Satan and all those things.
>
> One night I was at a party at Chips Rafferty's place. Block of flats up the Cross, third floor. During the party we heard screams from the flat below, and Chips said, 'Aw, Christ. What's this?' And went down. Well Rosie [sic] had this Gavin bloke by the balls. And he was screaming.
>
> Chips said, 'Let 'im go. Let 'im go.' But she wouldn't. So Chips just went BIFF, and knocked her out. And saved him, for the poor fellow was crying, and sobbing. Once he had escaped her, and I use this term advisedly, he told me she was rooting him to death. He pleaded with me to save him from her. She had him locked up in a room. She would be on to him night

and day. And it was just sex, sex, sex, until the poor bloke could hardly raise a fat anymore. [6]

LIFE IN KINGS CROSS

Kings Cross had witnessed a long line of colourful characters as residents, and in its own way it was just as exotic as New York's Greenwich Village or London's Soho district. Originally, the area around Bayswater Road, Darlinghurst Road and Victoria Street had been exclusive, and the province of the well-to-do. Successful merchants had built their mansions there, making it a place of elegant reserve. But then it began to change demographically and in the 1920s, as Frederick C. Folkard observed in *The Rare Sex*, it became 'the hangout of writers and poets, painters and sculptors, musicians and bums'.

During this time the young American 'Wild Bill Kelley', son of a Californian millionaire, threw a series of seemingly never-ending parties in his flat in Royston Square. Through the riotous haze of excitement it seemed that everyone there was simultaneously drinking, singing, carousing, arguing, making love or engaging in fist-fights. These parties continued non-stop until one summer night in 1926, when a girl named Dell Hutton died at one of his wild gatherings from a drug overdose.

Dulcie Deamer, the famous 'Queen of Bohemia', also enjoyed life on the wild side and would often claim in her later years that she had attended over two thousand parties in Kings Cross. Dulcie had worn a dramatic leopard skin costume to the 1924 Artists' Ball and was well known as the lady who used to do the splits on café tables. On one occasion a landlord gave Dulcie notice to quite her residence and she was so upset by this that she procured a quiet old horse and managed to get it upstairs into the living quarters. She then filled the bath-tub with water, put some hay in a corner, and quietly slipped away – leaving the horse in residence.

Dulcie was good fun – a colourful extrovert – but Kings Cross also had its share of crooks and drug pushers. 'Phil the Jew' sold cocaine and sly grog, and was connected to the so-called 'razor gangs' of the 1920s. He became wealthy by operating a chain of sleazy dives which he paraded as night-clubs. They bore such names as the Fifty-Fifty Club and the Four Hundred Club, becoming hangouts for petty criminals. Even the notorious gangster Kate Leigh left her mark on the Cross. Famous in neighbouring Surry Hills as the 'Queen of the Underworld' – a tough and lawless woman who ruled an army of prostitutes, pimps, thieves, thugs and standover men – she also operated a sly grog establishment in Liverpool Street, right in the heart of the Cross.

So Kings Cross could certainly boast a pantheon of exotic characters, some of them charming and some of them dangerous. Roie knew Dulcie Deamer well, and contributed a fantasy drawing to Dulcie's book of poems, *The Silver Branch*, which also had a jacket illustration by Norman Lindsay. Dulcie and Roie shared a love of the supernatural and the mysterious.

Roie and Gavin's flat was in Brougham Street, just off William Street, a short walk from such familiar landmarks as the Mansions Hotel in Bayswater Road and the Arabian café in Darlinghurst Road. At the Arabian, where some of Roie's paintings hung on the walls, you could sit upstairs on a balcony illuminated by coloured lights, or have a more private conversation downstairs in a dimly lit corner. There was also Dickie McGowan's California Coffee Shop, where rough and tumble

Americans hung out, and the sleazy glamour of the night-clubs and strip-joints that had begun to appear since the war.[7]

It was like a river of life, on all levels. Tides of people would pour through the Cross late into the night, aroused by reawakened passion. It was alive, it was exciting, and you could lose yourself in it, for the Cross seemed to go on forever. It was a place where you could come and go as you pleased, where people didn't ask too many questions, and where everyone was both a stranger and a friend. And this was how Roie liked it – for here she could paint her visions, explore the recesses of her soul, and still feel the protective earthiness of humanity all around her. Out there, through the tinsel haze, the old gods were alive and stirring once again.

1 In 'Hitchhiking Witch' Rosaleen refers to Ian Stapleton as 'John Bolton', acknowledging that this was not his real name. In fact, Ian Stapleton was co-editor of the Melbourne University newspaper *Farrago*, and a picture of Stapleton, Gavin Greenlees and Roie was published in the Melbourne *Truth* on 27 August 1949: 21.

2 Quoted in the *Daily Telegraph*, Sydney, 4 August 1949.

3 *Sydney Morning Herald*, 20 August 1949.

4 In the context of comments made by L.J.Murphy in his report, it appears that Roie was rather indifferent to her early sexual experiences. At this stage her marriage to Beresford Conroy was over, although they were still officially married, and her relationship with Gavin Greenlees, while sexually intimate, had other, more important aspects.

5 Interview record between L.J.Murphy and Rosaleen Norton, dated 27 August 1949. These transcipts were supplied by Mrs Y.Raphael-Oeser, widow of the former Professor of Psychology at the University of Melbourne at the time of Rosaleen's exhibition.

6 McCann, N., Interview with Jim Russell, 'And Dangerous to

Know' published on http://nedmccann.blogspot.com.au/2005/09/blog-post_112659887360827086.html, 13 September 2005. Chips Rafferty (1909–1971) was a well-known Australian actor.

7 For further details and photographs see Elizabeth Butel and Tom Thompson, *Kings Cross Album*, Atrand, Sydney 1984

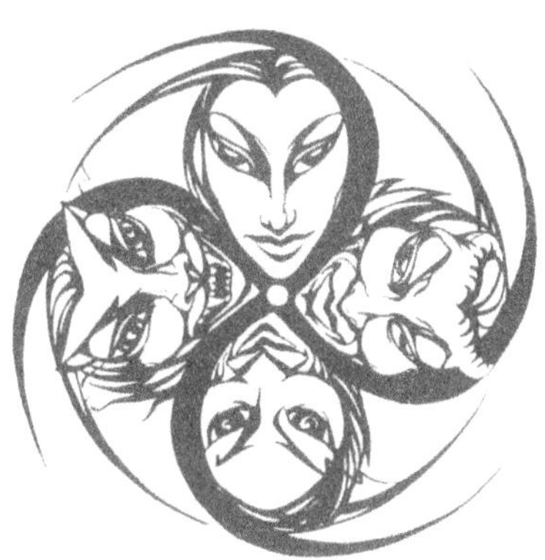

5
Further Controversy

It was 1951 and Roie was becoming well known as one of the 'colourful characters' of Kings Cross. Visitors who had heard of her trance art, or who had seen her paintings on the walls of the Kashmir coffee shop, were anxious to meet her. Here was a woman who seemed to live beyond the confines of respectable society, who reputedly had contact with dark and mysterious forces, and who was irresistibly exotic and intriguing. She was now much in demand socially, even though she and Gavin were living in a squalid tenement where a prominent barrister had recently committed suicide.

179 Brougham Street, Darlinghurst, was a three-storey cream terrace house that had seen better days. The building had originally been edged with ornamental motifs, and the large window beside the front door had two decorative panels, its frames picked out in a contrasting brown. But now the titles were chipped, the paint was flaking badly, the slate roof was in a state of disrepair, and the house was occupied by a mixture of vagrants and bohemians.

Although they later shared the attic, in the beginning Roie, Gavin and several pet cats lived in the basement – in a dingy room which was really a converted laundry, while upstairs in the attic lived a one-handed man named Mick who hoarded piles of newspapers and who would emerge every now and then to pontificate on current affairs. Roie's and

Gavin's room was full of clutter – animal skulls, bones, shells and stones lay strewn around amidst discarded cigarette cartons and forgotten coffee cups.

The main furnishings were an old armchair, a large mirror draped with colourful beads, and an orange crepe paper lampshade which hung down from the ceiling on a long lead. Broken battens in the ceiling had caused sections of the plaster to flake and crumble, and cobwebs now adorned the dimmer recesses of the room. But even in these circumstances Roie was able to ham it up a little, reinforcing her growing

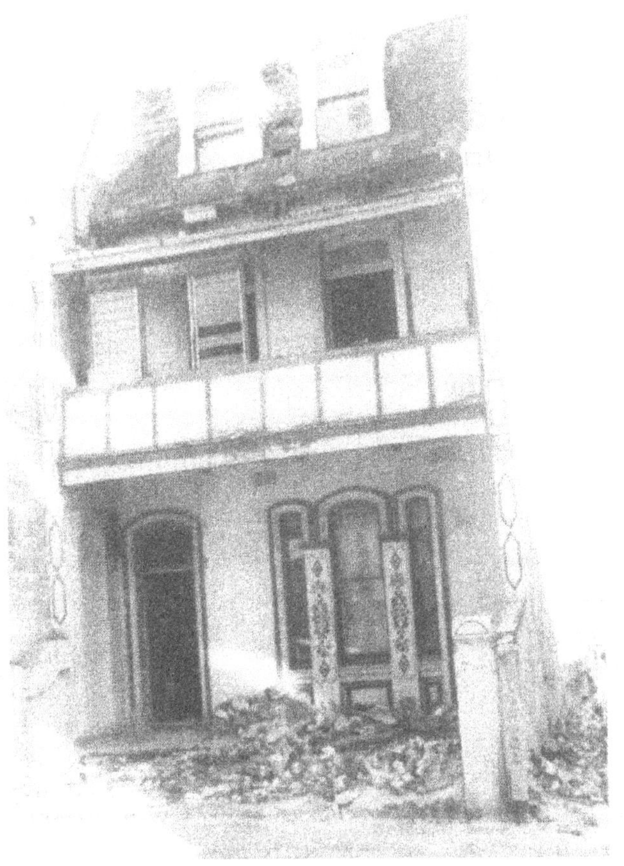

The old terrace house at 179 Brougham Street, Darlinghurst

reputation as an eccentric. A sign in the corridor outside their flat read 'The Female Vagrant' and a placard on the door offered this announcement: 'Welcome to the house of ghosts, goblins, werewolves, vampires, witches, wizards and poltergeists.'

Increasingly, 179 Brougham Street became a mecca for the curious. Visitors to this dilapidated dwelling could always count on meeting someone interesting on the stairs, for all sorts of people passed through the house at one time or another, and no questions were asked. Even members of the local police force would drop in now and then for a cup of tea to break the tedium of their daily rounds. But this happy relationship, unfortunately, did not last long. Some time in September 1951 word reached Sergeant Francis Farrell – popularly known as 'Bumper' – that number 179 was a den of iniquity, and Roie and Gavin were responsible. Members of the Vice Squad were quickly despatched to investigate, and Roie and Gavin were arrested on a charge of vagrancy. They were later remanded at Central Court and given two weeks to find gainful employment.

It was at this point that they made contact with a man who was to play a major role in their future – Wally Glover. Glover himself had had something of a mixed career. Born in 1911, he had left school at thirteen and worked for various trade journals like *Decoration and Glass*, *Package Parade* and *Signs and Showcards*. Then, with the advent of World War II, he had served in New Guinea as a sergeant in the Australian Army, rising eventually to the rank of captain in the Army Education division. After the War he had become a freelance publisher and worked part-time as editor of *The Pastrycook's Review*. As Wally later recalled, ' I conceived the idea of approaching Central Police Station, offering a chance of employment to two people, unknown to me, who had been remanded on a vagrancy charge.' Later, Wally arranged for them to visit him at his office:

> They arrived at my office late in the afternoon, both freshly groomed and sparkling, as if they were straight out of a tub – but they were dressed like hippies two decades ahead of their time. Gavin displayed a propensity for copper. His spectacles

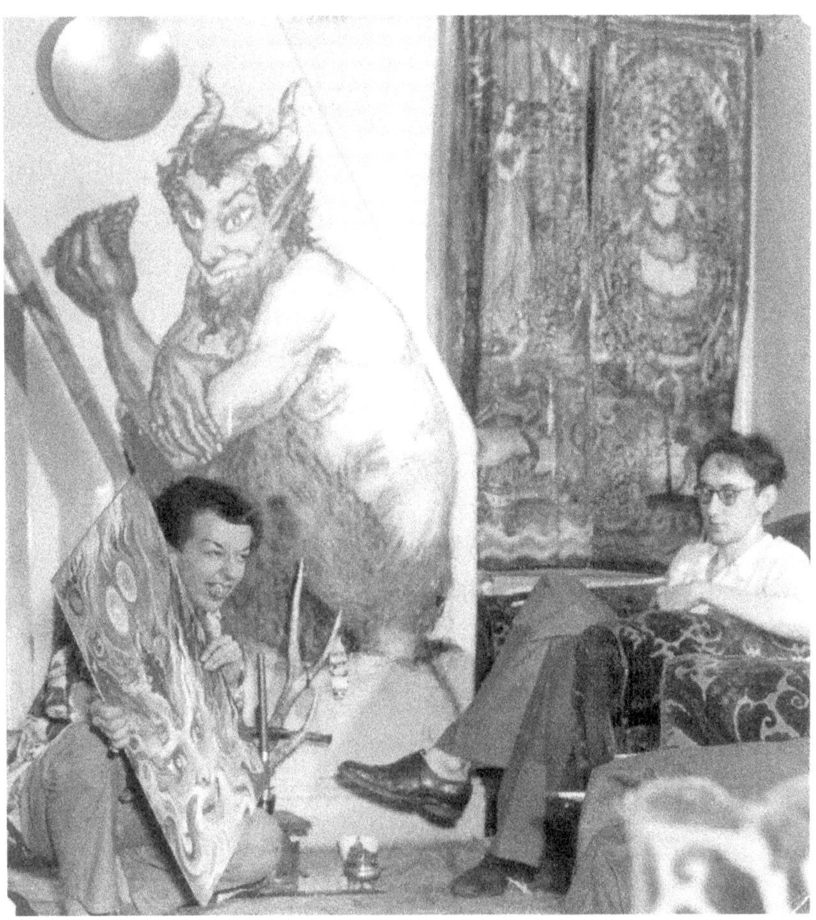

ROIE AND GAVIN AT HOME IN BROUGHAM STREET

> resting on the end of his nose were held together with copper wire, as were his well-worn footwear. Rosaleen was more concerned with demons although at that stage she had not cultivated the acute features that characterised her later appearance.
>
> They showed me their extraordinary work. It had not been prepared specifically for the occasion, hence it was a genuine cross-section of their capabilities. It was so different to anything I had seen, that I was impressed with its obvious potential. [1]

To begin with, Wally Glover did not understand the symbolic content of the work, and at that stage there was no thought of publishing a book. Wally was simply looking for assistants to help him with his freelance advertising and journalism. Gradually, however, it occurred to him that there *could* be a worthwhile publication in all of this, if things were taken in stages. His original idea was to print Roie's illustrations on sheets using an office litho machine, and to tie the sheets together with pink ribbon. He therefore arranged for his solicitor, Bob Benjafield, to formalise a contract with Roie and Gavin which provided them with royalties as an advance against future sums due from the book. Officially Wally was to pay Roie and Gavin £8 a week each, rising to a maximum of £200, against a 15 per cent royalty. In fact, because the book was a year in production, the actual sum paid was much greater than this. However, it was not all one-way. Wally obtained a contract naming him as copyright holder of all Roie's artistic works – present, past, and future.

Wally [Glover] later recalled that, having taken the decision to publish the book, there was then a sudden change in his fortunes:

> Money appeared, as if by magic. Jobs providing funds came in

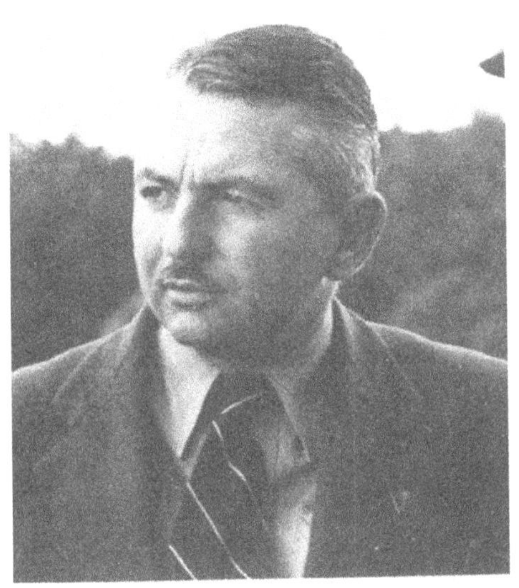

WALLY GLOVER

from most unexpected sources. I was evicted from the tiny one-pound-a-week office I had occupied in a rabbit warren office complex in the city, but learning of my plight, the caretaker of the building offered me an alternative area which turned out to be an entire floor ! In return for a handsome three hundred pounds, the caretaker handed over the keys to an advertising agent who, in turn, presented me with his former office space as a gesture of appreciation.

The office was bare, but on that day I met a pre-War acquaintance who had been in real estate. He told me he would be going to jail the following week and I would be able to select my choice of furniture from a well known repository, where it had been expected to remain for five years.

Rosaleen celebrated our acquisition by painting a giant mural of Baphomet, mythical God of Energy, on the wall... [2]

The next few months saw Roie and Gavin vigorously engaged in selecting works for the book. Gavin's occult and metaphysical poems would accompany the best of Rosaleen's fantastic and evocative illustrations. It was a time of intense discussion, numerous re-writes and textural alterations and, as Roie put it, recurrent bouts of 'Gav's nerve attacks'. The drawings, meanwhile, reflected every dimension of Roie's fertile imagination.

Among the images selected were renditions of Lilith, Queen of Air and Darkness, and a personification of the forces of the Night; a horned devil named Fohat, with a snake for a phallus; and a leonine deity, Eloi, who resembled an ancient Persian monarch. Also included were *Rites of Baron Samedi*, a personal impression of a ritual invocation, and *Black Magic*, which according to Roie represented a mystical experience – 'union with the night'. Here the 'unknown' was personified as a black panther.

Not all the images were sinister or demonic, however. One of the works, *Entombment of Count Orgaz*, was a parody of a celebrated painting by El Greco. *A Room at Castle Issusselduss* showed clocks, vases and chairs coming magically to life as if in a fairytale; *Mosque of Eidolons* and *Fishers of Men* were simply mischievous caricatures of figures in the Church, and *Edith Sitwell* was a tribute to a writer whose work Roie had recently been reading.

Gavin, meanwhile, was engaged in compiling some of his most evocative poetry. The following poem accompanied *The Angel of Twizzavi*, a work intended to depict the dream world as an aspect of the 'astral plane'.[3]

He is the castle of echoes
And the walking mill, sideshow attraction behind sleep
We created those dissolving, mobile corridors
From the dream logged, archaic flesh
Of giants no longer valid.
Units of gravity begotten on science by vertigo
He is the living dictionary of those fashions
Wherein those elegant suites, panelled in fur and fine
mirrors
In fruit and gems, ambassadors tread gathering their reasons,
Like hunters, sly silhouettes, throughout the long night
watches
And strangely fashioned diplomats, in silence,
Stake their claims for the lands, unknown to them, that in
daylight

Will approve or condemn their work.
'Night, night' ... Here are those scenes we all rehearse
When the profile of fixed and obvious purpose fades.
Here rule those iron necessities that in the patter of passing
shapes
Their children, begotten in turning mirrors of the world
You seem to elude, more truly hidden
When daylight's popular music obscure the visible lamps
Although among them, another one, made of our restless
Other, lives
A worker in dark-rooms of space
Moving along a bridge of royal hearts
That, turned to inward dances,
Take all that love and turmoil to their own.
Here are our favourite playful ghosts –
The seance of hands, the travelogue of medieval cities
Wherein a great scholar laboured once
Disturbed by the centuries who mutter dryly their
crepuscular lore
Behind a curtain, amid the more curious exhibits –
Figures born from the changing labyrinth
But spanned by the rainbow of his triumphant art.

While some poems were simply imaginative works, others – like *Esoteric Study* – had seemingly been influenced by Roie herself:

Out of herself the Earth created her own guardian faces
And, using the rule they gave her, out of herself
She made creatures to serve her – animals, poems,
Forgotten beings, men, women... Out of herself

She made the grandeur and its faith, healthy or faded.
Out of that faith all have believed in various moulds
And sometimes, being more like her, a few have lived
Whom guardians taught to know the brooding tarns and
arches
Where cling the flat invisible houses of the shadows.
And all the world's alive with those creators
Who creep, gaunt with their mission, through the hush of
awe.
The old names were shop-soiled. Therefore out of itself
Speech produced Gargos, Anubine, and Fom.
Gargos is monarch of shells and of consistency in decay,
Let us learn and admire the museum
Of his imposing terraces
For gypsies who sport in the forests of infinite Neptune
Are intrepid scavengers of the world's many returns.
Anubine is memory that preserves
As a light of unity
When your face is reflected on the inner stream
His quiet 'face' defies the mocker who cries 'Mirror'
With Law, that is serenity of each limitless actor.
Form, on whose brow sits the diamond of ultimate daylight
Is mouth of such words to which even the earth's gay round
Is brief amanuensis.

One of the poems, a highly evocative work accompanying *Black Magic*, was actually written and initialled by Rosaleen. Not surprisingly, it is one of the most insightful and revealing of all: a personal account of Roie's magical encounter with the forces of the night:

Light's Black Majesty: Midnight Sun: Lord of the wild and
living stars:
Soul of Magic and master of Death;
Panther of Night... enfold me.
Take me, dark Shining One; mingle my being with you,
Prowl in my spirit with deep purring joy
Live in me. giver of terror and ecstasy
Touch me with tongues of black fire.
Fed with the fire at the Black Opal's centre,
I drink living silver in moon-quickened streets,
And star-voices ringing:
All Strangeness is with me
Towering, invisible, changing the Earth.
Hatred and heaven are blending within me: They beat in the
pulse of the stars,
For a god in my heart cries with primitive splendour
'Child of the Shadow, I hate all Humanity!'
Night, freakish Night, sets me free...
Poor fools, sleep on in your deathbeds of life! My home is the
house of the winds,
With great songs of Space ringing wild in my ears
Whose shouting heart leaps to their tune.
I mock at the shapes, plodding thickly, through lamplight:
stupid and cruel – or kind –
They are alien, Other. I'm touched with uneasiness...
Fear of these humans... and glide away sidelong:
Yet knowing in fear, in my stealthy aloofness,,
To know they are They and I'm I.
Towers of old cities are spiralling over me, Night-conjured,

rising from Time
And I hear, through the seething of luminous silence –
Secretive, vibrant, the sound of the Solitude –
Calling of others like me.
Quietly they come, flitting softly as secrets; light-footed,
velvety, swift...
With eyes gleaming green, lambent flame of the Opal.
Kindred... we signal our quick recognition.
I am I... but I know we are we
Panther of silence; god of Night; Lord of the wild inhuman
stars;
You are my own; teeming soul of solitude.
Here is no loneliness, secret Master –
You, Dark Spirit, are with me.

R.N.

While Roie and Gavin were busy with the poems and illustrations, Wally Glover was actively engaged in the logistics of printing and publishing the book. Fine quality deckle-edged Glastonbury Antique paper was ordered from B.J. Ball, Tonecraft of Marrickville were appointed as printers, and a retired flight captain, Alan Cross – whose previous career had been with New Guinea Airways – was selected as bookbinder. Cross was not altogether an incongruous choice. Since his retirement he had made a living restoring family bibles, and Wally contacted him through an advertisement in the *Sydney Morning Herald.* They agreed that five hundred copies of *The Art of Rosaleen Norton* would be bound in leather for the sum of £1 per copy. Prior to this, there had been talk of actually binding some of the copies in tanned bat-skin, since there had been a

The art of Rosaleen Norton

with poems by

Gavin Greenlees

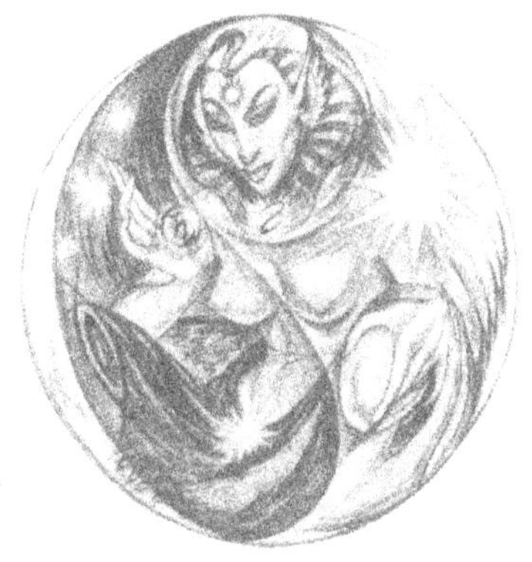

Published by Walter Glover
Sydney Australia

TITLE PAGE OF THE ART OF ROSALEEN NORTON, *1952*

plague of flying foxes in Sydney that year! However, Wally and Alan Cross agreed that standard leather binding was a more practical solution.

Despite his negotiations with Alan Cross and the printers, Wally kept it to himself that he had no great reserves of capital in the bank to cover all the production costs incurred. Whether his suppliers got paid or not would depend substantially on how the book fared in the marketplace.

When *The Art of Rosaleen Norton* finally did emerge in mid-August 1952, it was clear that no pains had been spared to make it a handsome edition. Bound in red leather with gold blocking, it had a Tibetan-blue jacket featuring an impressive Norton line drawing. The price of the book was set at eight guineas a copy – a substantial sum in those days – but trauma would soon follow its publication.

On the very day advance copies were expected from Alan Cross, both Walter Glover's and Rosaleen Norton's fathers died, plunging the release of the book into chaos. Walter Glover would later recall the events of the day:

> I hurried out to my parents' suburban home to assist with arrangements for the funeral. I left at midday, met Alan Cross, collected the books and rushed a copy to each newspaper. Copies of the book were sent off to New York, London and my representative in Paris. Then everything crashed. We had no books and no distribution ... The publicity created demand but nobody knew where to buy the books... [4]

Matters then became complicated when the Post Master General threatened prosecution over registration of what was claimed to be an indecent publication. Certain female figures had been noted in the

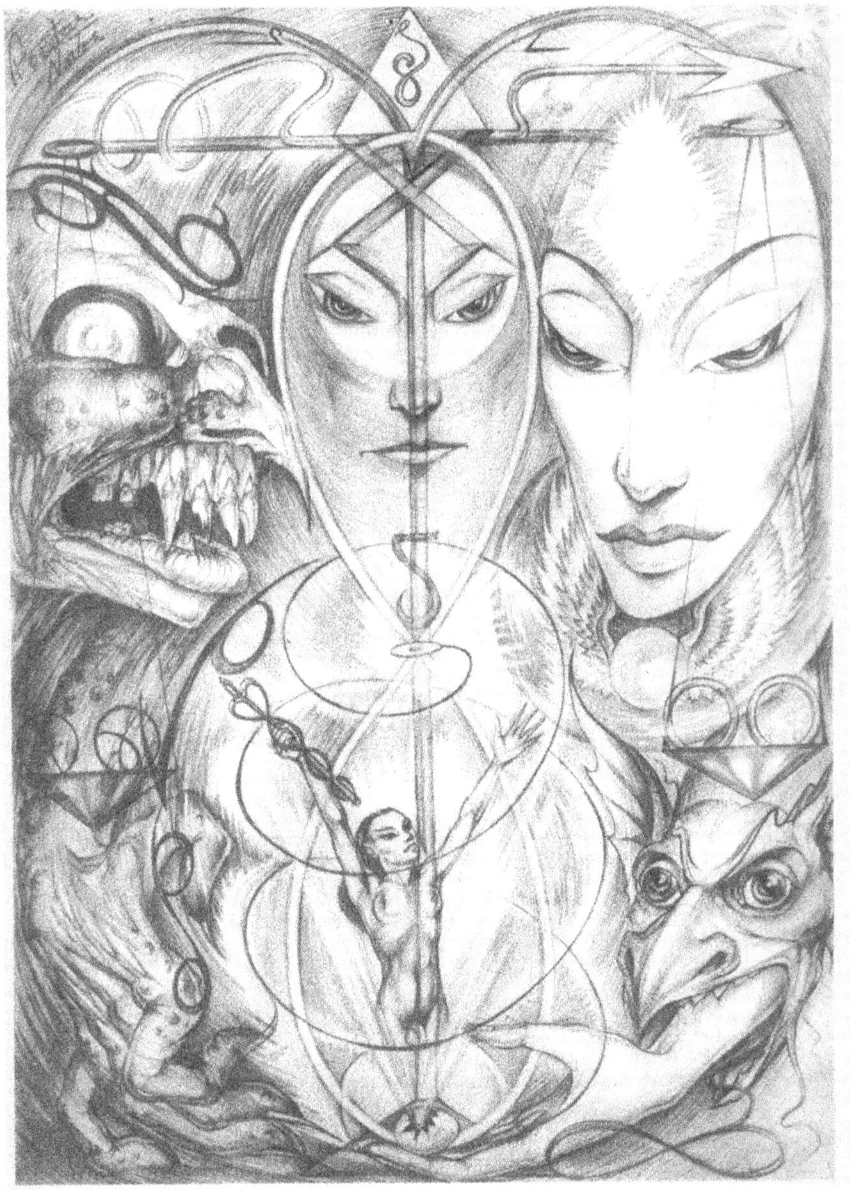

ESOTERIC STUDY

illustrations, complete with pubic hair... Meanwhile, newspapers around the country announced the release of the 'most blatant example of obscenity yet published in Australia'. The Sydney Millions Club, which was including a Norton oil painting in a forthcoming charity auction, hastily removed the piece from view, and the sponsor of the proposed book launch similarly withdrew all support.

However, events then took a strange twist. A big party had been organised at the Sky Ballroom in Elizabeth Street as a tribute to a Masonic Grand Master. Quite unexpectedly, but nevertheless with remarkably propitious timing, the guest of honour suddenly died – and the food, drink and splendid venue then became available. With this opportunity presenting itself, the launch function for *The Art of Rosaleen Norton* was able to proceed. According to one account the function went off 'with devilish abandon' and received a full-page report in a national weekly magazine.

The book obviously had an impact because the American Consul requested a copy bound in bat-skin and the Pakistani Consulate invited both the artist and publisher to produce an erotic art book based on the mythic imagery of certain temples in Pakistan. The threat of Australian government prosecution, however, loomed even larger and refused to subside.

The crunch finally came on 27 August when Wally Glover was officially charged with producing an obscene publication. His first appearance at Central Court was on 25 November 1952, and he registered a plea of 'not guilty'. Representing the Crown was Mr D.J. Vine-Hall, and assisting Wally Glover in defence was Mr Jack W. Shand, QC.

Newspaper magnate Frank Packer, who had taken a personal interest in the case, agreed to pay Glover's legal expenses.

Opening the prosecution before Magistrate Solling, the Crown solicitor maintained that the book itself provided all the evidence required to support a charge of obscenity. But clearly the case would not be as straightforward as that. Debate over the contents proved to be a protracted affair, extending through to February the following year, and

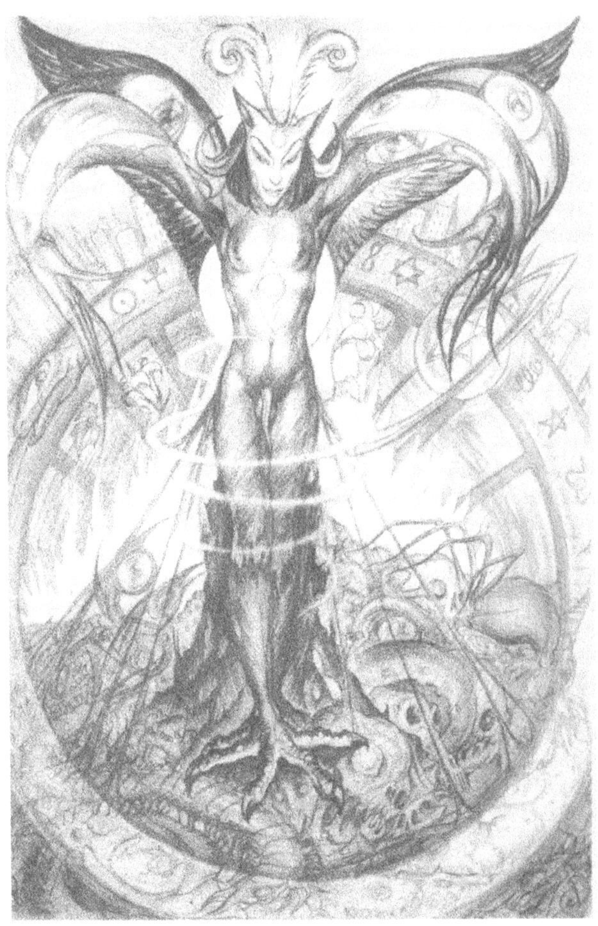

THE NAKED WINGED ANDROGYNE DEPICTED IN INDIVIDUATION *WAS DEEMED ONE OF THE MOST CONFRONTING IMAGES IN* THE ART OF ROSALEEN NORTON

in due course Rosaleen herself would be asked to explain her drawings to the Court.

Mr Vine-Hall drew special attention to the illustrations featuring the black panther (*Black Magic*), a winged androgyne (*Individuation*) and a naked woman rising from an egg (*Esoteric Study*). Rosaleen put up a spirited response in which she talked of the psychology of Jung and Freud and explained that many of her works referred to the 'fusion of the conscious and subconscious mind'. Describing *Black Magic*, one of the works which had been successfully defended in the Melbourne obscenity trial, she said simply that the black panther represented the secret forces of the night, while *Esoteric Study* 'concealed a hidden side of religion which only a select few could recognise'.

Magistrate Solling brought the case to a close by fining Glover £5 plus costs, and ruling that two of Rosaleen's works, *The Adversary* and *Fohat*, were 'obscene and an offence to chastity and delicacy'. Existing copies of the book would need to have these pages blacked out.[5] Meanwhile, Rosaleen wrote an epitaph to sum up how she felt about the magistrate's decision:

Odium Psychopathologicum

Behold, my friends the empty space
That doth this volume thus disgrace.
The drawing that should fill its place
Hath vanished :
          Banned
                    And
                              Banished!
O Puritanic Harpies, rage!

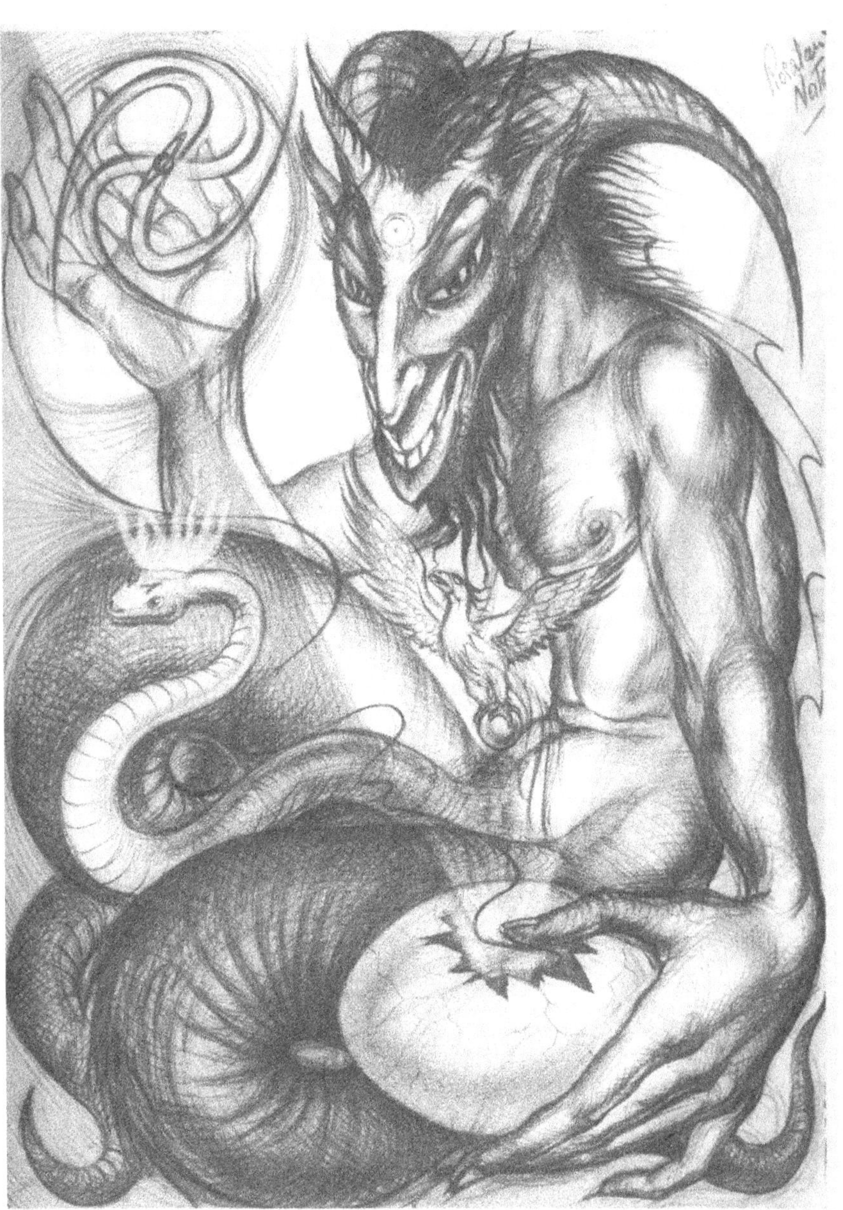

FOHAT

Thy breed alone doth this disgrace,
That mirrored saw its own foul face;
With mind as empty as yon space,
Whose culture (O enlightened Age!)
Is even as a missing page.
Enraged Caliban
(Whose knowledge is, to thy perdition,
Limited as this edition);
Snipping art, in art's expression,
Secrets of thine own repression,
Howl thy malice! Ban –
Yet know, O Ape of little sense
'Honi soit qui mal y pense!' [6]

The book was now attracting widespread publicity and Rosaleen herself was doing well with artistic commissions. But there were still problems with the law – this time overseas. Copies of the book sent to New York were confiscated and burnt by U.S. Customs and this meant that automatically it became a prohibited import to Australia. Nobody taking a copy out of the country could legally bring it back in.

Walter Glover also began to find that his book was too difficult to advertise, and all aspects of distribution then plunged into disarray. By 1957 he was officially bankrupt, publication of the book having contributed significantly to his insolvency. Copyrights to the artworks in the book, which had been assigned to him through his contract with Rosaleen Norton and Gavin Greenlees, were now passed to the Official Receiver in Bankruptcy. They would not be returned to him until May, 1981.

There was, however, an intriguing corollary to the obscenity trial. Bookbinder Alan Cross had, of course, missed out on his money and Wally encouraged him to bind and sell as many copies of the sheets as he could, to help recover his costs. In a consoling gesture, Wally also said that Cross and his wife should select one of Roie's original drawings by way of compensation. Alan Cross had a serpent tattooed around his body, so his wife selected *Fohat* – the erotic and allegedly obscene illustration banned by the magistrate. Fohat's serpentine phallus, she said, was just like her husband's tattoo!

1 Personal communication from Wally Glover. Wally Glover has since died.
2 Ibid.
3 *The Art of Rosaleen Norton*: 56.
4 Personal communication from Wally Glover.
5 For details of this trial see the *Daily Telegraph*, Sydney, 5 February 1953 and *The Sun*, Sydney,
5 February 1953.
6 This epitaph was published in the second edition of *The Art of Rosaleen Norton*, 1982: 9.

6 The Witch of Kings Cross

Over the next three years Roie became notorious in Kings Cross although she laughed at the rumours that circulated about her and seemed impervious to controversy. Certain coffee shops, like the Apollyon and the Kashmir, were said to be the haunt of her 'Devil's cult' and would be crowded out by curious passers-by, in the hope of meeting her. On some occasions visitors would even come into the coffee lounges and cheekily ask for a cup of bat's blood! And the proprietor of one particular coffee shop – a Mrs Pixie Robinson – complained that because she often wore black slacks and a matching sweater, she was always being asked if she was 'the Witch of Kings Cross'. 'No,' Mrs Robinson would tell them, despairingly, 'It's Roie you want...'

The Apollyon was a particularly colourful venue, and something of an institution in the Cross. The top level was simply a place for a cup of coffee, but downstairs was rather like Pakie's – a club for bohemians to gather and chat long into the night. Roie had a permanent exhibition of her paintings in a large room out the back, and for a time the cafe became synonymous with her supernatural art.

So the tourists would come there, hoping to bump into 'the Witch of Kings Cross' in the crowd, and they would always be amazed by the dazzling array of paintings which adorned the walls. Some tourists, though, would take the adulation too far, wandering down William Street to Roie's flat in nearby Brougham Street - specifically to pilfer souvenirs. Some passers-by prised occult symbols from her front door and on one occasion her door number disappeared. This type of activity angered Roie greatly, for despite the flood of exotic newspaper stories about her she was at heart a very private person. A bit of spooky image-building was one thing – it was harmless and a lot of fun – but it got tiresome when the crowds got too close.

As rumours of Roie's strange occult practices continued to circulate, becoming ever more fanciful and embellished by the popular imagination, it was perhaps inevitable that sooner or later someone would report that Black Masses were being conducted in Roie's flat. The revelation finally came on 14 September 1955, straight from the lips of one Anna Karina Hoffmann.

Hoffmann, a migrant from New Zealand, had drifted to Kings Cross after coming to Australia 'to start a new life'. At this stage she had just £75 in an Auckland bank and only £1 to her name in her Kings Cross savings account. She was scraping a meagre living as a part-time waitress, and drifting aimlessly day to day, often sleeping at night on the beach at Bondi or in the Domain.

Late one night Constable Ikin from the Darlinghurst Police Station noticed Anna Hoffmann in Darlinghurst Road, accompanied by a girl who was a reputed criminal. Hoffmann swore at Ikin as he approached her, but then said pleadingly to him, 'I can't stand this life any more. I haven't eaten for days. Please "vag" me while I'm still sane...'

Becoming increasingly hysterical, Hoffmann then went on to claim

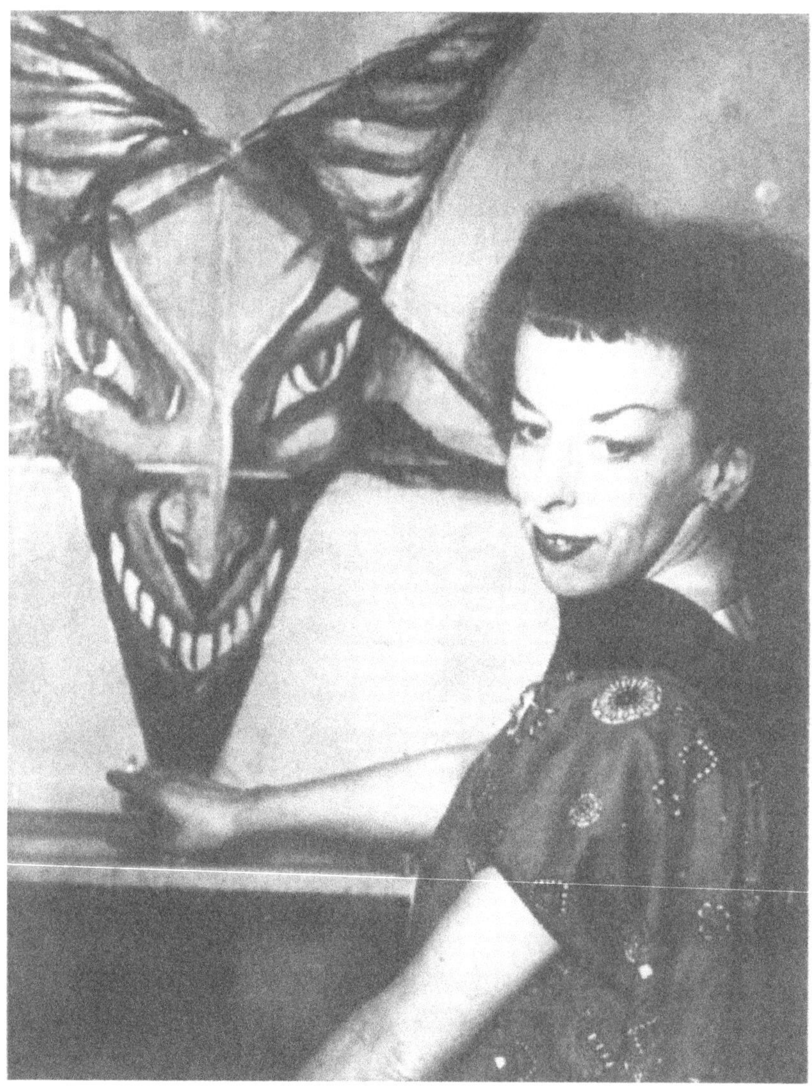

AT HOME

that the main cause of her downfall was that she had attended a Black Mass 'with Roie – the Witch of the Cross'. Ikin arrested Hoffmann on a charge of vagrancy, and she was remanded to appear in Central Court. Appearing a week later before Stipendiary Magistrate Blackmore, Hoffmann at first refused to take the oath, stating that she was not a Christian. She later told the Court that she was a Buddhist, and that 'the evil eye of Buddha would follow Constable Ikin around for the rest of his days'.

Although this fanciful threat should have provided a clear indication of Hoffmann's mental state at the time, further 'evidence' was taken that she had attended rites of Devil worship with Rosaleen Norton, and that all the participants wore black – the Devil's colour. Furthermore, said Hoffmann, they had performed the Black Mass. Asked what this involved, she replied: 'Sex orgies and parties.' Anna Hoffmann would later deny actually taking part in a Black Mass and also confessed that the alleged 'connection' with Rosaleen Norton was based purely on hearsay. Hoffmann was sentenced to two months in jail and later described by Judge Holden in an appeals session as 'a menace'. However, as a result of the widespread press coverage of the Hoffmann allegations, considerable damage was done to Roie's already shaky reputation. She would later have to go to great lengths to explain that the horned god Pan was in no way connected with Lucifer, the god of the Satanists, and that she had never participated in a Black Mass.

Soon afterwards two Sydney newspaper reporters published a detailed eye-witness account of how they had visited a Black Mass in Kings Cross and observed a gowned witch and wizard performing a mock imitation of the Christian Mass during which a rooster was sacrificed. This specific incident made Roie very angry indeed – she would never condone any activity which harmed animals. It later came to light that the incident had been totally fabricated: the participants in the 'Black Mass' were university students who had donned ceremonial robes and used specimen bones from the Anatomy Department to create a bizarre, satanic atmosphere of 'sacrifice'.

Unfortunately, such episodes only served to increase public interest in Roie, and newspaper coverage of alleged 'witchcraft and black magic'

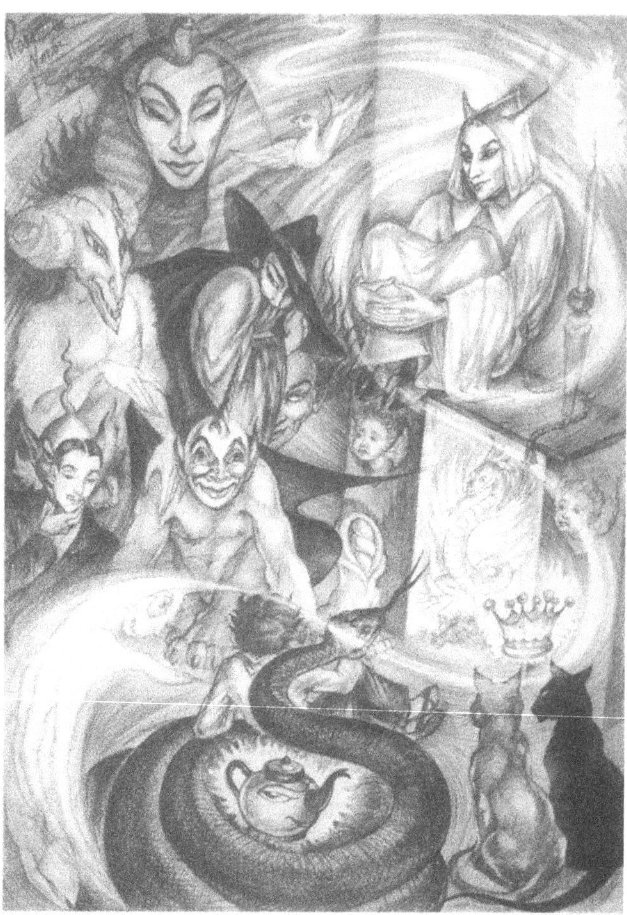

THE WITCH OF KINGS CROSS

activities in Kings Cross continued to appear. Then, as if rising from the ashes, the old charge of obscenity raised its ugly head again. Detective Sergeant Roy McDonald – obviously arriving later on the scene than the tourists – described in court how on 9 September 1955 he had visited the Kashmir Cafe in Macleay Street, Potts Point, and had found several of Rosaleen's paintings on the wall. The owner of the cafe, David Goodman, was subsequently charged under the Obscene Publications Act with having twenty-nine of her works displayed on his premises.

One could be forgiven for having a sense of *déjà vu*. In the Special Court, Mr Dash, SM described the paintings – which included such works as *Black Magic* (again), *Beezlebub* and *Belphagor* – as being 'lewd, lustful and erotic' and fined Goodman £5 plus costs for displaying paintings which could attract the curious and avid.[1] The court hearings dragged on for almost two years. Finally, in Central Court, Roie and Gavin were convicted and fined £25 each. The main charge against them did not involve the paintings themselves, but working with an 'unknown photographer' to produce the 'obscene' photographs taken at the party.

For Gavin and Roie it must have seemed as if their day-to-day lives were becoming surreal. Although Gavin had been teetering on the edge of a mental crisis for some time, Roie found it difficult to take the endless string of charges too seriously. But more controversy was lurking in the shadows – and it would soon unfold with tragic and unforeseen consequences.

Some time earlier Roie and Gavin had struck up an unlikely friendship with Eugene Goossens, the English-born musician who had come to Australia in 1947 and who had been installed as the first permanent conductor of the Sydney Symphony Orchestra. He would also be credited

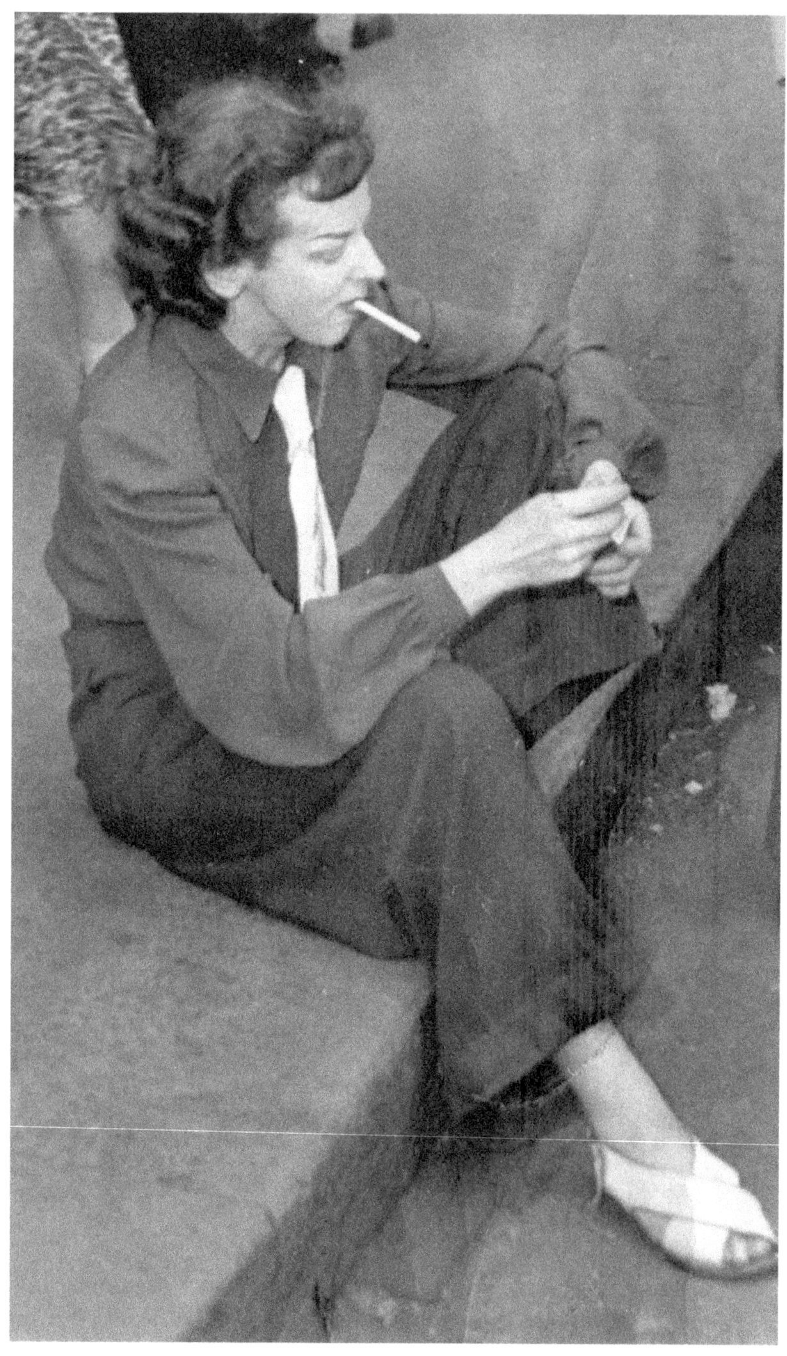

ROIE SITTING ON THE CURB IN DARLINGHURST ROAD

with having the original idea for the Sydney Opera House and was knighted by the Queen in 1955 for services to music.

Eugene Goossens had come to Australia with his American-born wife, Marjorie Fetter-Foulkrod, and they established themselves in a stylish home in Wahroonga, on Sydney's upper North Shore. Mrs Goossens, who was nineteen years younger than her husband and strikingly attractive, soon began to make an impact on the Sydney social scene and her views on fashion were eagerly sought by the women's magazines. Meanwhile after several years of working with musicians at the Conservatorium Eugene Goossens had become increasingly autocratic and had developed a habit of failing many of his most talented students in their exams. It seems that despite his success in lifting the artistic standards of the Sydney Symphony Orchestra he was becoming bored by his work at the Conservatorium. In late 1952 or early 1953 he came across a copy of *The Art of Rosaleen Norton* in a city bookshop – and it immediately rekindled his earlier interest in paganism and magic. Goossens wrote to Roie, expressing admiration for both the book and her artistic work, and she subsequently invited him around to Brougham Street, for an introductory chat over a cup of tea.

Goossens was fascinated by Roie and her seemingly authentic approach to paganism, and soon a friendship began to develop. Eugene had been working regularly in rehearsal rooms at the Australian Broadcasting Commission, just a few minutes' walk away from Brougham Street, so it was easy for him to maintain close contact. Not surprisingly, Goossens soon became a frequent visitor to Roie's flat and a member of the small magical group which would meet periodically to discuss magical ideas and perform rituals sacred to Pan. In addition to their shared interest in the pagan traditions, Eugene, Roie and Gavin also shared a love of classical music, and soon there was talk of all three working together on a musical rendition of Edgar Allan Poe's *The Fall of the House of Usher*. Gavin would write the libretto, Roie would paint the backdrops, and Eugene would compose the music. This project, unfortunately, did not proceed.

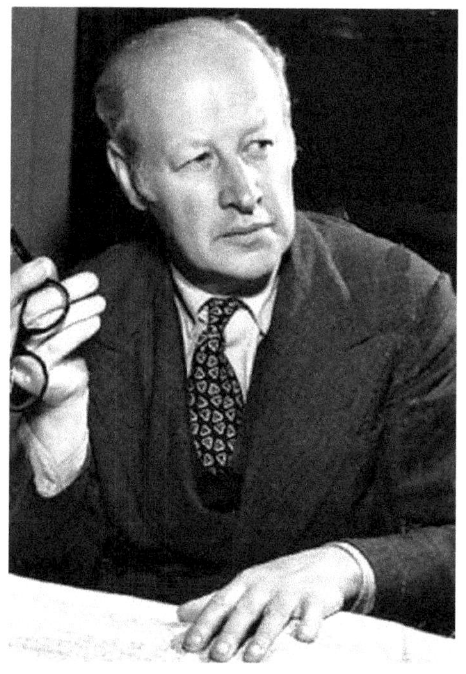

EUGENE GOOSSENS, LATER KNIGHTED BY THE QUEEN FOR HIS SERVICES TO MUSIC

According to journalist David Salter,[2] Goossens' relationship with Roie quickly developed a 'sexual intensity' – he seemed to want some sort of intimate magical relationship with her: 'I need your physical presence very much, for many reasons,' he wrote in one of his letters to her, 'We have many rituals and indulgences to undertake.' It is also clear that he was interested in sexually explicit material, for he closed his letter by adding '...and I want to take more photos.'[3] Roie's remarkable magical explorations with Eugene Goossens are discussed later in this book.

However Goossens did not anticipate that his passionate and erotic interests would plunge him into a career-shattering crisis on 9 March 1956, when he returned to Sydney's Mascot Airport on a flight from London. He was now officially Sir Eugene Goossens, having received his knighthood a few months earlier, and was apparently unaware that a group of detectives and Customs officers had already gathered at the Airport to apprehend him. Alerted by Vice Squad detective A.H. 'Bert' Trevenar, the Customs officials at the airport anticipated that Goossens would be carrying with him a large amount of allegedly pornographic material, and when they searched his luggage they discovered over 800 erotic photographs, a spool of film, and also some ritual masks and incense sticks.[4] Goossens was subsequently officially charged under

Section 233 of the Customs Act, which prohibited the possession or importation of 'blasphemous, indecent or obscene works or articles'

Goossens' case was brought before Mr J.M.McCauley, SM in the Martin Place Court of Petty Sessions, and Goossens was fined the maximum penalty of £100.[5] Four days after issuing his guilty plea Goossens submitted formal letters of resignation to the ABC and the NSW State Conservatorium, his professional career as an internationally

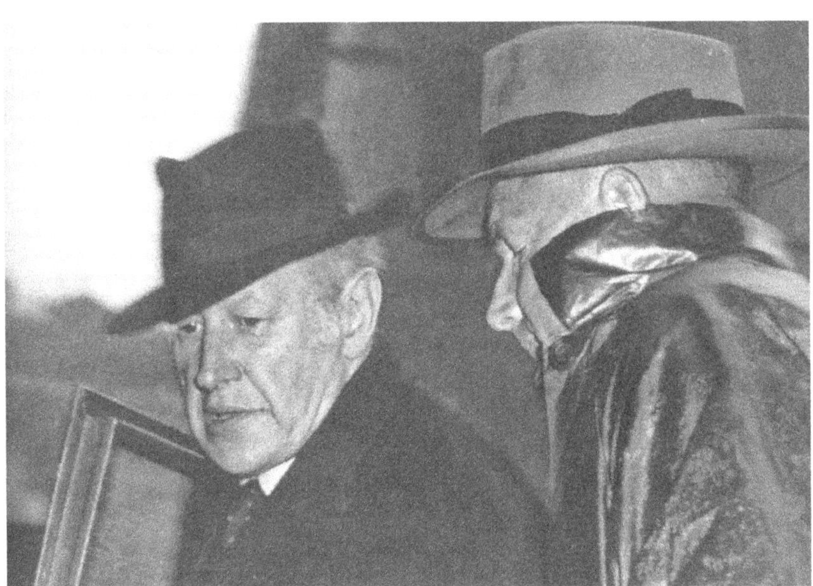

Sir Eugene Goossens arrested at Sydney Aiport in 1956

renowned conductor effectively over. On 26 May 1956 Goossens boarded a flight to Rome, travelling incognito as Mr E. Gray, never to return to Australia again.[6] Soon afterwards Goossens separated from his wife and then tried to reinstate his professional life as a musician by working occasionally for the BBC in London. However as journalist David Salter has commented, 'Goossens was now in decline. News of his antipodean disgrace had undermined the maestro's standing in the British music world. He lived in a succession of London flats and hotel rooms and struggled against failing health...'[7] Goossens died in England from a ruptured ulcer in June 1962, at the age of 69, shortly after returning from a trip to Switzerland where he had visited one of his daughters by an earlier marriage.

Sir Eugene, however, was not the only casualty of this turbulent period. Gavin Greenlees had also entered a period of decline and had been admitted to Callan Park Hospital on 7 October 1955. Details of his condition were released to Judge Clegg during sessions at Darlinghurst Court relating to the earlier incident of the 'pagan photographs'. According to a statement prepared by Dr S.G. Sands, acting medical superintendent of Callan Park, in conjunction with a Macquarie Street psychiatrist, Dr R.J. Kiely, Gavin had been medically assessed as a schizophrenic, suffering from a 'split personality'. Certifiably insane, he was now hallucinating voices which would perpetually torment and ridicule him. His conversation was 'stilted and studded with pseudo-scientific jargon' and he had entered Callan Park in an extremely emaciated state, weighing little over eight stone – considerably underweight for a man of six foot, two inches. According to Dr Sands, Gavin was also 'obsessed with sex' and 'wanted to escape from the real world'. He would take books on occultism into the corner of his room and 'could only be aroused to any action by constant prodding'.[8]

Despite Gavin's decline, however, it was not the end of his relationship with Roie, for she would continue to support him, emotionally

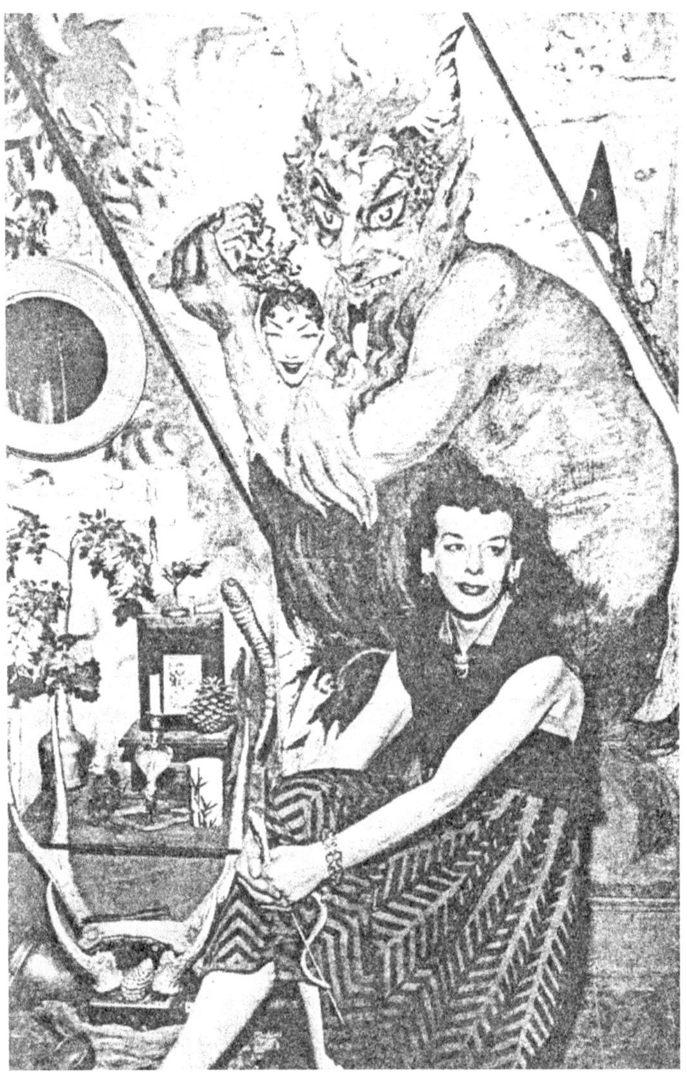

ROIE IN FRONT OF HER RITUAL ALTAR

and maternally, in the way she had from the start. On his allotted visiting days he would come to see her at the Cross and she would visit him regularly at Callan Park, taking him books to read and showing him new drawings and sketches she had completed. She would remain his most valued contact with the outside world, and they would continue to see each other at regular intervals throughout his long period of medical supervision. It would not be until 1983, several years after Roie's death, that Gavin would be fully discharged from the Alma Mater Nursing Home, where he went some years after his admission to Callan Park.

Rosaleen, meanwhile, managed to rise above all her troubles with a sense of style and bravado. Sensational feature stories would soon appear in popular magazines like *Australasian Post*, and the image of Roie as 'the Witch of Kings Cross', with her dark mischievous eyes, plucked eyebrows and devilish grin, would quickly etch itself into popular memory. The public was now openly calling her a witch, so she started to behave like one. It was not a term she had previously used to describe her trance magic, but since she worshipped Pan, and Pan was also a god of Nature, the term seemed to fit – more or less.

Several articles appeared in *Australasian Post* confirming this image. The first, published on 20 December 1956, led with the headline 'I am a Witch! – The chilling admission of Rosaleen Norton, Sydney's worshipper of elder, darker powers'. Roie was pictured sitting beside her altar in front of a mural of Pan. Various adornments were also visible – a mounted set of antlers, a ritual dagger or *athame*, assorted candles, and an especially phallic snake's head. Further on in the article was a photograph of Rosaleen in a particularly dubious looking witch's hat – it looked more like a prop from a Walt Disney movie – and there were also shots of her with her pet cats. 'Familiar spirits are said to take the form of cats,' she was quoted as saying, '...everyone knows that!'

During her interview with journalist Dave Barnes, Roie maintained that she had been *born* a witch – 'Nobody has to teach you' – and that in her case occult powers were a natural part of life. However, true to her real interests, she also sprinkled her references with allusions to the psychoanalytic concepts of Carl Jung and made the revealing statement, which no witch would ever make, that she believed in *all* religions. 'Anything can happen in Infinity,' she remarked casually, her ornamental cigarette holder poised in her hand. 'I believe in lots of Gods, Buddha, and even the Christian God.'

Australasian Post followed the Barnes interview with a three-part 'exclusive': Roie's own account of her life and magical practices. These articles were illustrated, yet again, with provocative photographs and details from several of her more demonic paintings. In the articles Roie recounted details of the University of Melbourne exhibition, her unhappy childhood in Lindfield, and her deep interest in self-hypnosis. She also explained that since her early adolescence she had become aware of the influence of Pan in her life, as he began increasingly to pervade her very being:

> If the Kingdom of Pan had always been with me, it had been mostly in the background, overlaid by what was called reality. Now it had begun to emerge...
>
> [My] awareness grew stronger and stronger that the tedious world of childhood didn't really matter, because this held the essence of all that called to my inmost being: Night and wild things and mystery; storms; being by myself, free of other people. The sense of some deep hidden knowledge stirring at the back of consciousness, and all about me the feeling of

> secret sentient life, that was in alliance with me, but that others were unaware, or afraid of, *because it was inhuman.*
>
> So my first act of ceremonial magic was in honour of the horned god, whose pipes are a symbol of magic and mystery, and whose horns and hooves stand for natural energies and fleet-footed freedom: And this rite was also my oath of allegiance and my confirmation as a witch. [9]

Roie was enjoying the forum offered to her to explain her magical beliefs. She seemed to revel in the fact that she was often being referred to in the popular press as an eccentric, decadent and exhibitionist. 'I am all those things – and glad of it,' she told Dave Barnes, and she was making no apologies for the central role Pan now played in her life. 'If Pan is the Devil, she wrote at the end of one her articles, 'then I am indeed a Devil worshipper.'[10]

1 *Truth*, Sydney, 4 December 1955.

2 See David Salter, 'The strange case of Sir Eugene and the witch' , *Good Weekend*, 3 July 1999.

3 As we will see in Chapter Eight, some form of sex magic was included in these 'rituals and indulgences'. Eugene Goossens confirmed in a police report that he performed acts of oral sex on Rosaleen Norton and that he had been involved in group sex rituals with Roie and Gavin 'four or five times'. It also seems likely that the 'unknown photographer' connected with the Honer and Ager obscenity charges may have been Eugene Goossens.

4 Gavin Greenlees confirmed to Wally Glover in 1982 that the ceremonial masks were for use in their magical rituals at Brougham Street. Personal communication from Glover to the author *circa* 1986.

5 For further details of this case see the newsclippings held by the

Australian Archives, Department of the Navy, SP551, Log Books of HMC, HMS, HMA ships, 1855-1957.

6 D. Salter, 'The strange case of Sir Eugene and the witch', loc.cit.:21.

7 Ibid.

8 *Truth*, Sydney, 18 November 1956.

9 Rosaleen Norton, 'Witches Want No Recruits', *Australasian Post*, 10 January 1957: 35.

10 Ibid.

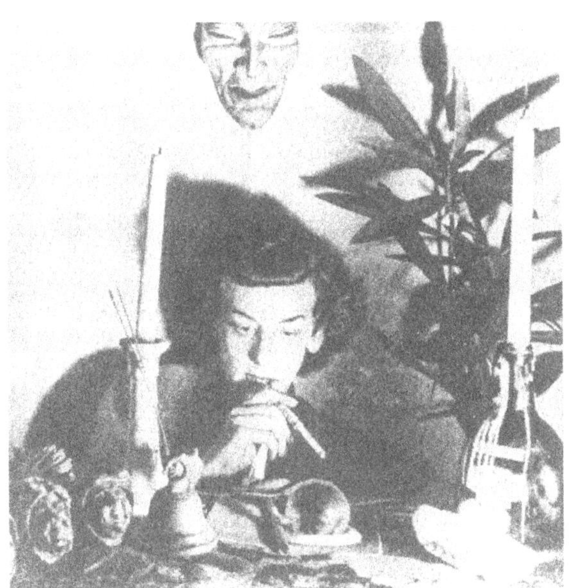

ANOTHER PICTURE OF ROIE ENGAGED IN RITUAL

7

Rosaleen Norton's Magical Cosmology

Throughout her life Rosaleen Norton consistently maintained that she had been born a witch and was essentially self-taught. In a series of informative autobiographical articles published in the mid-1950s[1] she described how this had come about: 'If you are a witch nobody has to teach you. In my case, it came naturally, and nobody had to teach me.' Later, when she was asked by an interviewer whether she had a 'Devil's mark' on her body – 'proof' that she was an authentic witch – Norton confirmed that she had some unusual physical attributes that she associated with her witch-identity: 'My bodily peculiarities include a pair of freak muscles (extending from armpit to pelvic bone on either side) not normally found in the human body' [and] 'a rare, atavistic formation of the upper ears known as "Darwin's Peak"'. She also alluded to 'two small blue dots on my left knee, which are one of the traditional witch marks' and to her 'quasi-feline vision – sharper and clearer in subdued light than in bright light'. In one of her articles, 'I was born a Witch', Norton mentions that the two distinctive blue marks appeared suddenly on her body when she was a child:

> At seven years old two small blue marks very close together appeared on my left knee, and they are there still. I have since learned that two (or sometimes three) blue or red dots together on the skin are among the traditional witch marks. Although,

of course, I didn't know this at the time, I remember noticing them the year we arrived in Australia and wondering what they were; they seemed important in some way that I couldn't define.[2]

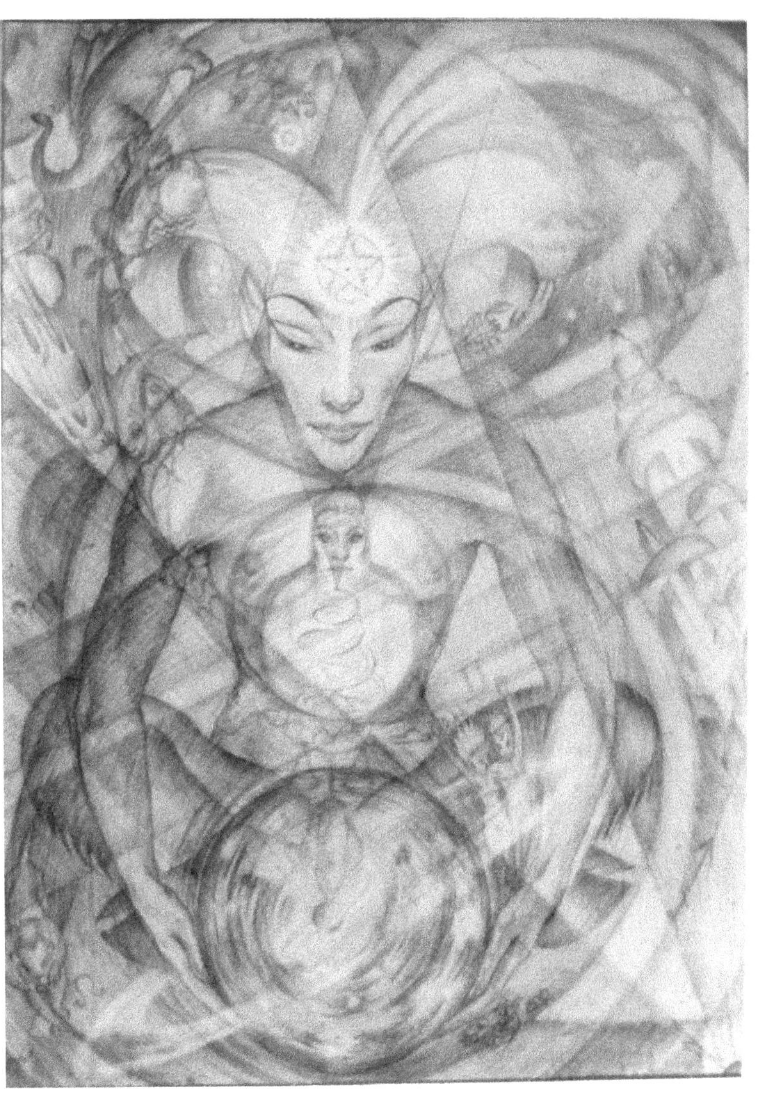

THE BLUEPRINT –
AN EARLY DEPICTION OF PAN

Witchy and supernatural themes came naturally to young Rosaleen. In fourth grade at school she developed a fondness for Dracula and played the title role in an improvised play about the famous vampire. Draped in blackboard cloths with two open umbrellas serving as wings, Norton gave several spirited performances that were eventually terminated by an irate headmistress who claimed that her cries of 'Give me blood to drink' were putting the school boarders off their food! But for young Rosaleen the figure of Dracula was both dramatic and confronting – exactly what was needed to stir up her fellow pupils at the exclusive Church of England girls' school. Her fondness for vampires, and Dracula in particular, reflected her rapidly developing fascination with all things pagan, and soon a further step along this path would be taken. Exploring ancient Greek mythology, Rosaleen soon came across the ancient deity Pan – god of the wild, untamed forces of Nature. On a personal level, discovering Pan was enormously significant. Rosaleen's view of the outside world – a view rapidly reaching beyond the confines of her exclusive Anglican upbringing – would never be quite the same again.

In classical ancient Greek mythology Pan was variously considered to be the son of Hermes and the nymph Dryope, or the offspring of Zeus and Callisto. Pan was part man, part goat, and was represented with the horns, tail, hind legs and hoofs of a goat and also with a flat snub nose and beard. Sometimes he was depicted with the ears of an ass, a symbol of acute perception. Fond of music and dancing, Pan was associated with shepherds and the woods and also possessed prophetic powers. Because the woods were considered a place of fear at night, and because Pan often frightened unwary travellers in the countryside, Pan's name gave rise to the idea of 'panic' or alarm, and Pan himself was considered unpredictable, lascivious and lecherous. Pan's distinctive shepherd pipes or pan-pipes, his own invention, were fashioned from seven reeds and were referred to as a syrinx. Pan's name literally means 'all', and the philosophical and religious concept of pantheism (which derives from a combination of the Greek *pan* = all, and *theos* = God) conveys the idea that the universe as a whole is divine and that there is no divinity other than the universe and Nature.[3]

According to an article published in *Squire* magazine in April 1965, Norton's deeply felt attraction to the ancient Greek god Pan coincided with her rejection of her family's Christian beliefs and specifically with her parents' wish that she should be 'confirmed' into the Anglican faith at the age of twelve. Norton's interest in the mythic figure of Pan led in turn to improvised magical rituals:

> She started to take more than a passing interest in Pan, the horned...half-man, half-goat Greek deity who spent most of his time rolling young nymphs in the Arcadian meadows. This interest, generated by the confusion which accompanies adolescence and fired by Ro's inherent rebellion, became a fetish. She devised worship rituals, using robes, Chinese joss sticks and wine she pinched from a stock hidden by her parents. At this stage she hadn't discovered the true meaning of the bright blue dots which had appeared mysteriously on her knee a few years before. She rejected Christianity entirely and embraced Pantheism...the identification of God with all that exists...Ro believes that everything is equally a manifestation of her God – rather Gods – because she has divided her divinity into several gods. These are Satanic spirits which manifest themselves to her in the classical satyric image. 'I often see them,' she told *Squire*.[4]

Norton had also provided an account of her belief in Pan in an autobiographical article published in *Australasian Post* in January 1957:

> Some occult theories hold the stars and planets to be the bodies of great beings and so do I. I think the God Pan is the spirit whose body – or such of it as can be seen in these four dimensions (the fourth being time) – is the planet Earth, and who, therefore, in a very real sense, is the ruler and god of this world. Perhaps that is why he was given the name 'Pan', which in Greek means 'All', for he is the totality of lives, elements and forms of being – organic, 'inorganic' and otherwise, comprising the planet as a whole: much as an animal body is a totality of myriads of cells, bacteria etc, in which ordered whole these live and function, having their own forms of "intelligence" and perception, according to type. *Such a body would be the "world" to any of its micro-organisms*, and the integrated consciousness of the body's owner would exist in another "world", and on a different plane from theirs.'[5]

In this particular article Norton also speculated about the nature of this metaphysical being who, in her view, ruled the world:

> If a man could communicate with any of his body cells on its own plane, it would perceive its 'god' in terms fitted to its understanding. To see him as he is to himself, ie. as a man, the cell consciousness would have to unite with and 'become' that of the man, in a world outside anything conceivable in its entire experience. Of course, this is only a parallel, and shouldn't be regarded as exact: a god, for one thing, is a very different form of life, involving other laws and dimensions, and could (as far as I know) manifest si-

> multaneously in any number of places and shapes, to those who form part of him, or others, without disturbing any plane of his multiple consciousness and activities elsewhere.'[6]

Norton's cosmology is based on an understanding that Nature and the Cosmos are innately sacred. Divinity is 'divided' into a number of gods and goddesses and these ruling deities – headed by Pan – are able to exist and function in more than one dimension of reality. Norton's concept of a hierarchy of spirits headed by Pan – 'whose body is the earth' – is reminiscent of the ancient Gnostic *archons* who were thought to rule different regions of the heavens while also maintaining governance of the earth.[7] Archons were celestial rulers – 'gate-keepers' guarding entry to the higher spheres – and their powers transcended and encompassed all aspects of human activity. In Norton's conception, Pan equated with the totality of human experience and existence – although she expanded his reach to embrace the totality, or 'ground', of all being. In a sense Pan, for her, embodied and represented the furthest reaches of the sacred universe – extending to infinity in all directions. It is all the more remarkable that Norton began to develop this concept of Pan while she was still an adolescent:

> The onset of adolescence often awakens the religious as well as the sexual urge, and this was so for me. For some time previously I had been constantly aware of a world wherein moved vast and mysterious powers, the sense of gay daemonic [sic] presences and hauntingly familiar atmospheres, elusive yet powerful and compelling, when everything round me seemed to change focus like patterns in a kaleidoscope. [8]

For Norton this led to the development of an instinctual ritual desire, an emotive and worshipful response to the mysterious powers that seemed to surround her and which demanded that she should forsake her childish frivolities in favour of serious and respectful pagan worship:

> If the Kingdom of Pan had always been with me, it had been mostly in the background, overlaid by what was called reality: *Now it had begun to emerge and pervade the latter.* Awareness grew stronger and stronger that the tedious world of childhood didn't really matter, because this held the essence of all that called to my inmost being: Night and wild things and mystery; storms; being by myself, free of other people. The sense of some deep hidden knowledge stirring at the back of consciousness; and all about me the feeling of secret sentient life, that was in alliance with me, but that others were unaware, or afraid of, because it was unhuman.
>
> So my first act of ceremonial magic was in honour of the horned god, whose pipes are symbol of magic and mystery, and whose horns and hooves stand for natural energies and fleet-footed freedom: And this rite was also my oath of allegiance and my confirmation as a witch. I remember my feelings on that occasion well, and they are valid today: If Pan is the 'Devil' (and the joyous goat-god probably is from the orthodox viewpoint) then I am indeed a 'Devil' worshipper.'[9]

Norton shows here that, even as an adolescent, she is willing to trust her intuitive sensibilities, opening her spirit to the wild forces of Nature. Perhaps anticipating her emerging allegiance to the heretical powers of magic she already senses she is stepping forth on a path that will take her into a realm of 'deep hidden knowledge'. Ahead she faces some sort of initiation into secrets and mysteries. And yet Norton knows

– even as a teenager – that she is venturing well beyond the confines of conventional religion. She is ready to embrace Pan, who may very likely

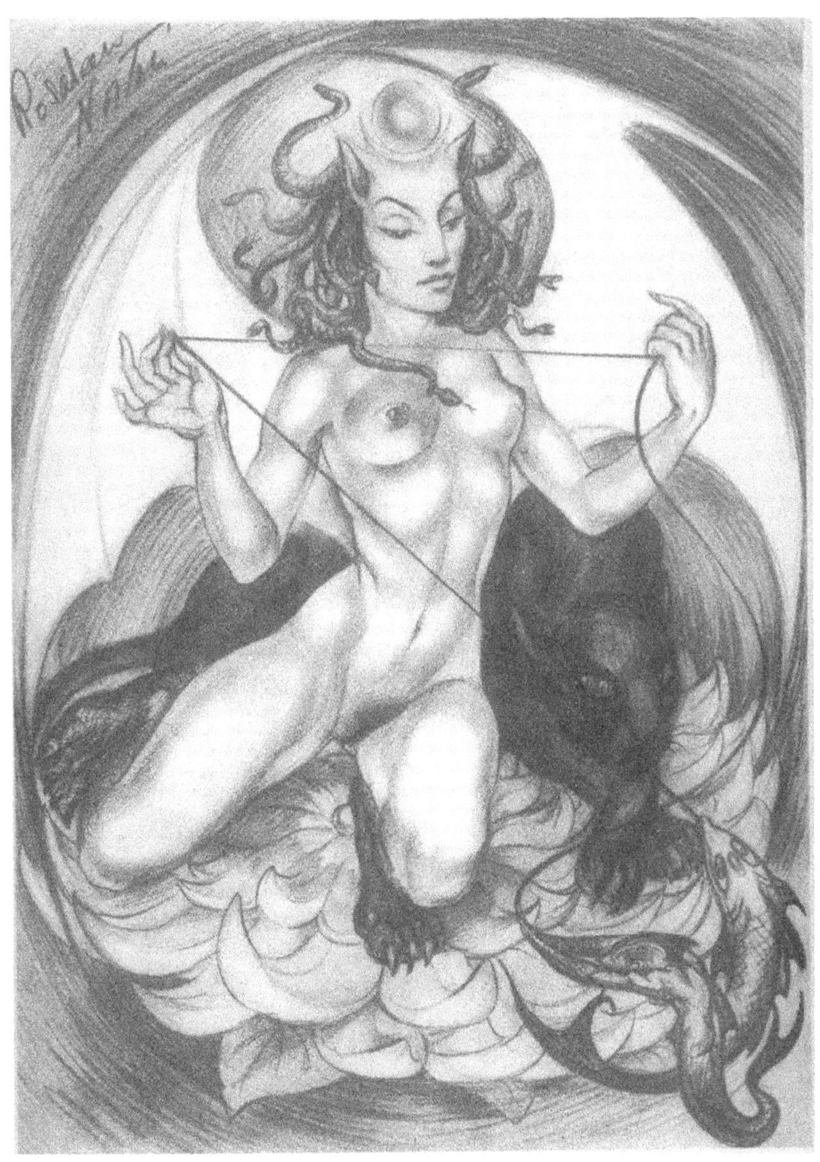

Lilith, Queen of the Night

be seen by others – among them the more 'orthodox' Christian members of her family and community – as the Devil incarnate.

HECATE, LILITH AND LUCIFER

Pan quickly became the supreme deity in Norton's magical pantheon – she acknowledged very early on her allegiance to the 'Kingdom of Pan' and would later refer to herself as the 'High Priestess at the Altar of Pan'. However other ancient deities and supernatural entities also provided inspiration and guidance. Prominent among them were Hecate, Lilith and Lucifer, the latter in his role as 'the Adversary'.

Hecate In classical Greek mythology, Hecate, or Hekate, was usually considered to be the daughter of the Titans Perses and Asteria, although in other accounts she is the daughter of Zeus and Asteria. Hecate was goddess of the night and darkness, and ruler of the hidden aspects of Nature. As a goddess of transitions, Hecate was associated with birth and death, and from the fifth century BCE onwards, she is also specifically associated with ghosts; Hecate could also cause nightmares. Accompanied by barking dogs and hordes of spirits of the 'restless dead' – those people unable to find their way to Hades – Hecate was sometimes called *kleidophoros* ('key-bearer') and as a gate-keeper of Hades she was able to let spirits in and out of the Underworld. A triple goddess, Hecate revealed three different personae and from the Roman period onwards she was linked to the moon: as a moon goddess she was associated with Selene (Roman counterpart: Luna) and Artemis (Roman counterpart: Diana), and as a goddess of the Underworld she was also linked to Persephone (Roman counterpart: Proserpine). Hecate was only worshipped at night; dogs and black lambs were offered to her as sacrifices.[10] Often shown entwined in coils of snakes, which in ancient Greece were associated with the dead, Hecate was a goddess also associated with the crossroads, especially three-way intersections – such crossroads being in turn considered supernatural places and associated with magic and spirits.[11]

In an interview I conducted with Norton in Sydney in 1977, two years before her death, she told me that she regarded Hecate as a more imposing deity than Pan because Hecate was known to be a dealer in death and a purveyor of curses. Norton felt Hecate was often very frightening because she was a shadowy goddess flanked by cohorts of ghouls and night-forms. However Norton maintained that Hecate could also be a protector. If ever Norton was required to curse people with her 'witch current' in order to redress what she believed to be an unfair 'balance of events', Norton called on Hecate's hexing powers and believed this was a legitimate use of the magical art.

Lilith Although Norton tended to link Hecate and Lilith in her pantheon of ancient female magical deities, Lilith's mythic origins are quite different to Hecate's. Lilith is an exotic she-devil who first appears in Sumerian mythology in the middle of the 3rd millennium BCE before entering the Jewish tradition during the Talmudic period (2nd-5th centuries CE) and then finally emerging as a queenly consort at God's side during the Kabbalistic era.[12] In the Sumerian tradition Lilith was acknowledged as a 'beautiful maiden' but she was also regarded as a harlot and vampire who would never willingly let her lover depart. During the Talmudic period Lilith was known as Adam's first wife but their relationship was deeply troubled and when Lilith came to believe that Adam intended to overpower her, she uttered the magical name of God, rose into the air, and flew off to the Red Sea, a place believed to be full of lascivious demons. There she indulged herself in unbridled promiscuity giving rise to more than a hundred demonic offspring each day.

Norton discovered references to Lilith in Carl Jung's *Psychology of the Unconscious* and quoted from Jung's text in the unpublished notes which accompanied her illustrations in *The Art of Rosaleen Norton*:

> ...Adam, before Eve, already possessed a demon wife, by name Lilith, with whom he quarrelled for mastership. But Lilith raised herself into the air through the magic of the name of God and hid herself in the sea. Adam forced her back with the help of three angels. Lilith became a nightmare, a Lamia, who threatened those with child and who kidnapped the modern child...[13]

For Norton, Lilith was 'Queen of Air and Darkness – symbol of Night'.[14] Gavin Greenlees, whose poem on Lilith accompanied Norton's drawing in *The Art of Rosaleen Norton* referred to Lilith as 'the Queen of Night and Sympathy' and described Lilith as an 'image of the Unconscious with its power to align images and draw together those spirits who have the true affinity – holding man by the soul image.' Lilith was also traditionally depicted as a Lamia who threatened children, and it is interesting to note in passing that Norton herself was totally opposed to ever having children of her own. For Norton the very notion of ever being a mother was repugnant. In 1964 she told an interviewer from the television station Channel Nine, Sydney, that she had no wish to be a mother and in her autobiographical article 'Witches Want No Recruits', published in 1957, she made a similar remark:

> ...nothing would ever induce me to have a baby; the very idea of it was always repugnant, chiefly because, I feel, it would detract from my own completeness...[15]

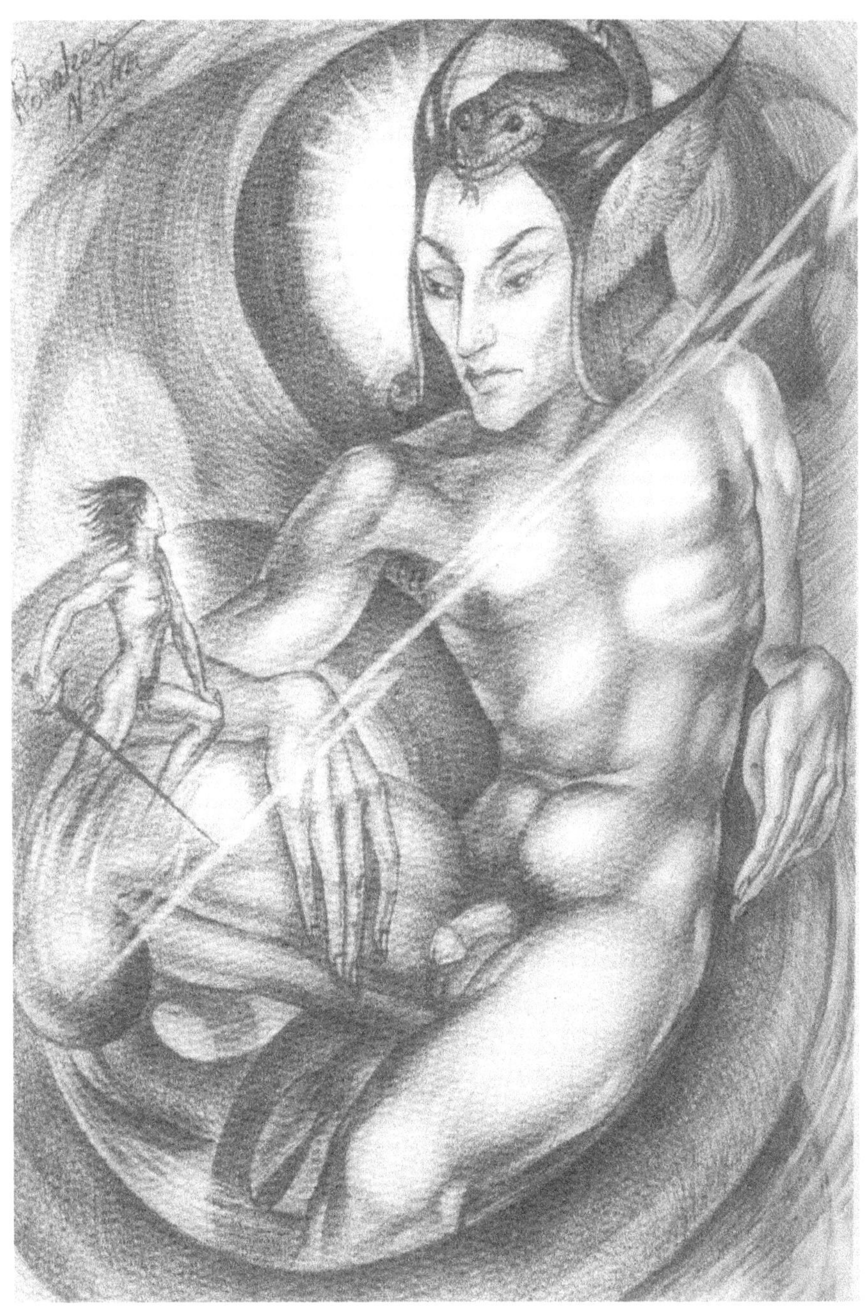

Lucifer in his role as the Adversary

However, for Norton the defining quality of Lilith is that she is a *powerful symbol of the Night.* Lilith is the 'Queen of Air and Darkness' and mirrors Hecate's chthonic role as Goddess of the Underworld and the secret forces of Nature. Norton acknowledges her attraction to the potency of darkness, writing in the introductory essay in *The Art of Rosaleen Norton* that her 'vision… is one of Night'. Norton's fascination with the powers of darkness is also evident in the powerful poem, written by Norton herself, which accompanies her controversial drawing *Black Magic* – a work that shows a naked woman (presumably Norton herself) in a passionate and intimate sexual embrace with a black panther. As we saw earlier, the poem reads like an invocation:

Light's Black Majesty: Midnight Sun: Lord of the wild
and living stars;
Soul of Magic and master of Death;
Panther of Night… enfold me.
Take me, dark Shining One; mingle my being with you,
Prowl in my spirit with deep purring joy,
Live in me, giver of terror and ecstasy,
Touch me with tongues of black fire…'[16]

Norton's ecstatic vision of the night is powerful and deeply felt. She is fully at home enfolded by the 'luminous silence' of the Night, and her poem ends triumphantly: 'You, Dark Spirit, are with me…' As a visionary magician, Norton clearly has her mythic home in the realm of the Midnight Sun: this is the domain where her soul resonates with the primal pulse of the Universe itself.

LUCIFER/THE ADVERSARY

The figure of Lucifer/The Adversary completes the lesser triad in Norton's magical cosmology. For Norton, Lucifer was closely associated with the spirit of rebellion and the quest for secret knowledge. In her illuminating essay, *A Vision* – written in the.1940s – Norton reminds her readers that '…we seek knowledge and truth and… "Lucifer" means "Light Bringer"…our greatest reward is in the eternal adventure of the search itself.'[17]

At least two major art-works relating to Lucifer form part of Norton's *oeuvre*: the painting *Lucifer*, which was exhibited in the 1949 exhibition in Melbourne, and the drawing *The Adversary*, reproduced in *The Art of Rosaleen Norton* in 1952 and shown here . In the Judaeo-Christian tradition Lucifer [Latin: 'light-bearer'] is another name for Satan. In Isaiah 14.12 the reference to Lucifer relates to the King of Babylon but was misunderstood to refer to a fallen angel and subsequently passed into Judaeo-Christian theology as a name for the Devil. Isaiah 14.12 opens with a dramatic pronouncement:

'How art thou fallen from heaven, O Lucifer, son of morning! How are thou cut down to the ground which didst weaken the nations! [from the Authorised Version].' These words, said to predict the impending doom of the King of Babylon, were taken by St Augustine and other Christian theologians like Origen [18] to refer to the fall of a mighty archangel who had rebelled against God in heaven and who had been cast out in punishment. In heaven this archangel had been known as Lucifer but on earth he would be known as Satan [Hebrew: 'the adversary']. In heaven Lucifer had sought to be sufficient unto himself, refusing to admit that he was dependent on God. His sin was therefore that of pride, his ensuing punishment on being cast headlong from heaven absolute and eternal. As a consequence of his fall from grace Lucifer was then filled with hatred for God.

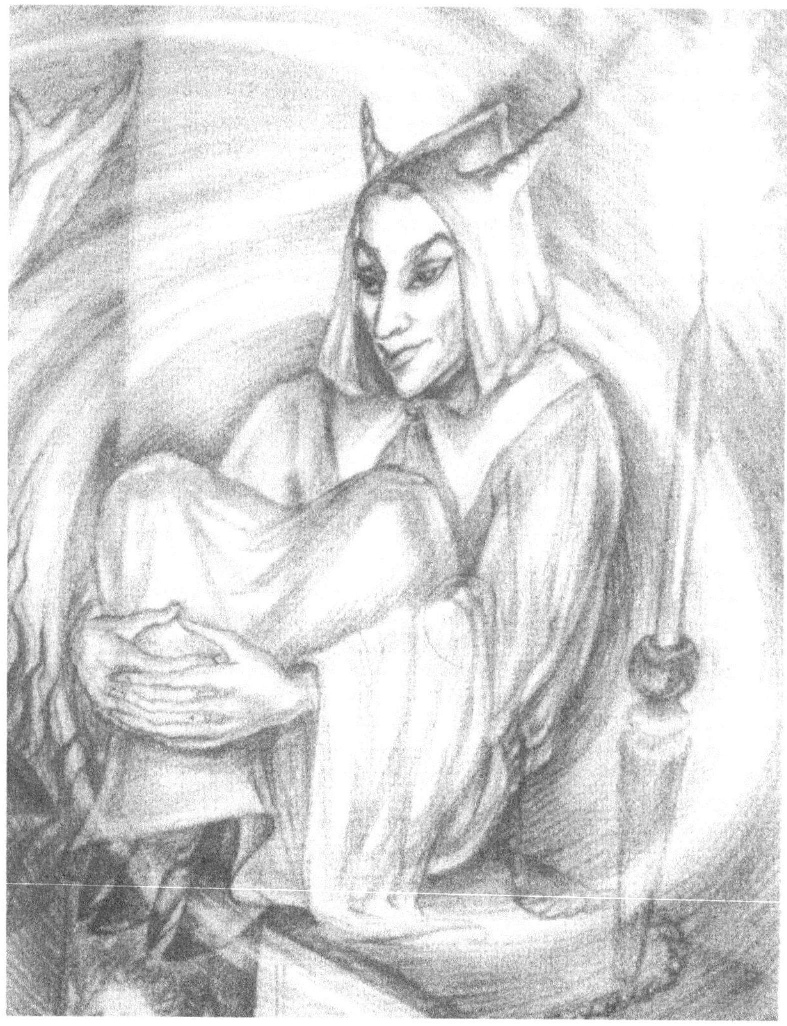

JANICOT – A DETAIL FROM AT HOME

From the time of Origen onwards, when Lucifer and Satan were identified as one and the same, any distinction between fallen angels and demons began to disappear in Christian theology. As historian Richard Cavendish has observed:

> In this tremendous vision most of the main threads of the later Christian conception of the Devil are drawn together – 'the satan' who accused men before God; the war in heaven, with the forces of God led by Michael; the expulsion of Lucifer from heaven; the fallen angels or stars who were his followers; the seven-headed dragon Leviathan; and the belief that the Devil's vengeful fury has been let loose on earth...[19]

Although they depict essentially the same supernatural being, Norton's *Lucifer* and *The Adversary* are nevertheless quite distinctive as artworks. In *Lucifer*, we are shown the figure of the light-bearer, winged and resplendent, standing naked as he presides over his domain. Lucifer's body shines with golden light but by way of contrast his wings are dark and in his left hand he holds a devilish mask that represents the other, demonic, side of his character. At Lucifer's feet sit the horned figure of Pan, playing on a pipe, and a naked feline demon with clawed feet, based on the figure of Norton herself. Other humanoid forms are also depicted at the periphery and in the background of this complex composition, including a mysterious bare-breasted snake-creature and a number of supernatural beings who seem caught up in the vortex of a nightmare. *The Adversary* is a much simpler, though nevertheless powerful, composition and depicts the fearsome encounter between a small and vulnerable, naked human being and a much larger and imposing winged entity – the Adversary, or Satan, also shown naked – whose head-cap is surmounted by a snake. In both of these works the central figure is depicted as arrogant and aloof and clearly commands both authority and respect. In my 1977 interview Norton told me that although she considered Lucifer's role to be that of an adversary, this did not necessarily make him 'evil' As Norton commented at the time:

> He binds and limits man when it appears that he is growing too big for his boots. He tries to trick man, not with malicious intent, so much as exposing the limitations of the ego and man's pride in his own existence.' [20]

In addition to Pan, Hecate, Lilith and Lucifer, who collectively represent the major figures in Norton's pantheon, a range of other magical and mythic entities are referred to her in her writings and in her art. Because Norton claimed an existential reality for several of these entities they should also be considered as significant, contributing to both her artistic oeuvre and also to her personal magical cosmology. In the glossary included in *The Art of Rosaleen Norton* she makes reference to a number of magical beings from different cultural traditions, thus reflecting her own eclectic and idiosyncratic interests. They include Bucentauro, whom Norton describes as a 'type of eidolon' or phantasm; Eloi, the 'phantasy spirit of Jupiter';[21] Makalath, the Laugher, described as 'an archangel who expresses himself cosmically through the power that manifests itself in this world as humour'; Fohat, 'the dynamic energy of cosmic ideation'– an entity referred to in Theosophical literature;[22] Erzulie, a 'voodoo Priestess of Mamaloi'[23] and The Dubouros, whom Norton identifies as 'a being representing Mind ...similar to the Egyptian god Thoth as the detached, enigmatic Recorder'. Norton also lists Val, Kephena, Borzorygmus and Mwystingel as 'imaginary beings of Twizzari', the latter

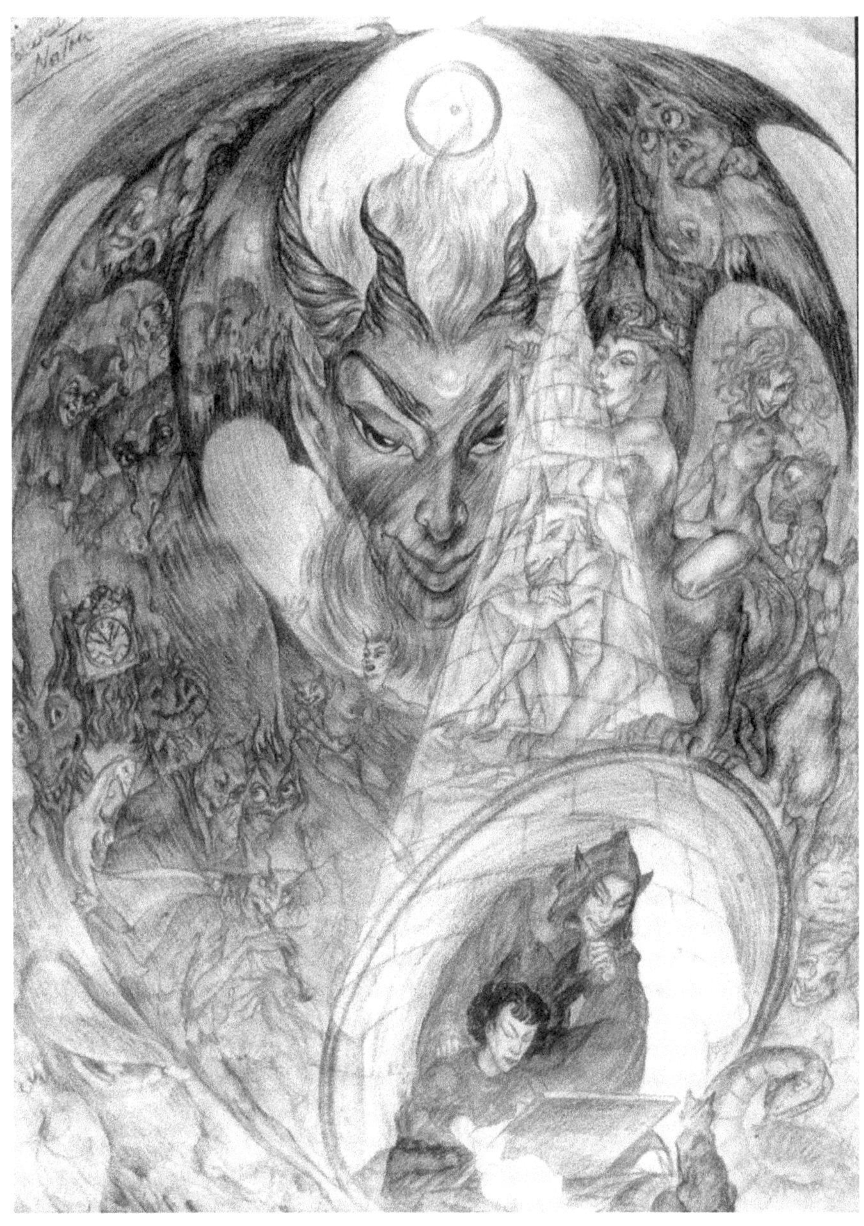

ROSALEEN NORTON WITH JANICOT – AND PAN LOOKING ON

her name for the 'Dreamworld...an aspect of the Astral Plane', and she makes reference also to Trudgepig, whom she describes as 'another imaginary creature ... [a] symbol of hypocritical gravity and gloom'.

In addition to this eclectic assortment of mythical entities, there is also an important magical figure whom Norton refers to as her 'Familiar Spirit-in-Chief'– a being she knew by many different names, including the Monk, Frater Asmodeus and Brother Hilarian. This particular magical servitor, however, was more generally known as Janicot – Norton gives his name as Jannicot – and he in turn has fascinating occult connections, for his origins derive from Basque cosmology and witchcraft.

THE POWERS OF JANICOT

Norton's magical journals indicate that she regarded Janicot as the guardian of all portals leading to magical awareness. In the text accompanying her drawing *At Home* Norton says that Janicot 'manages most of my occult activities, supervises trances, escorts me into other planes of Being, and sometimes assists the Sphynx in selecting visions for me.' In traditional Basque witchcraft Janicot, or Jaincoa, was depicted as the Horned God – *Basa-jaun*, the 'Goat-man'– otherwise known as the Lord of the Woods. Janicot was the Basque god of the oak and also god of doorways and the Wheel of the Year. Janicot was a satyr-like being with a human torso and the legs and feet of a goat. There is an immediate affinity here with the figure of Pan, but the mythic connection is more specifically with Dianus or Janus, the Roman two-headed God of the Oak Tree. Janus has been described as 'the Door God, the God of the Hidden Portals into the Netherworld, and the "portal" or gate between one time and the next', and this would seem to be how Norton regarded him as well.

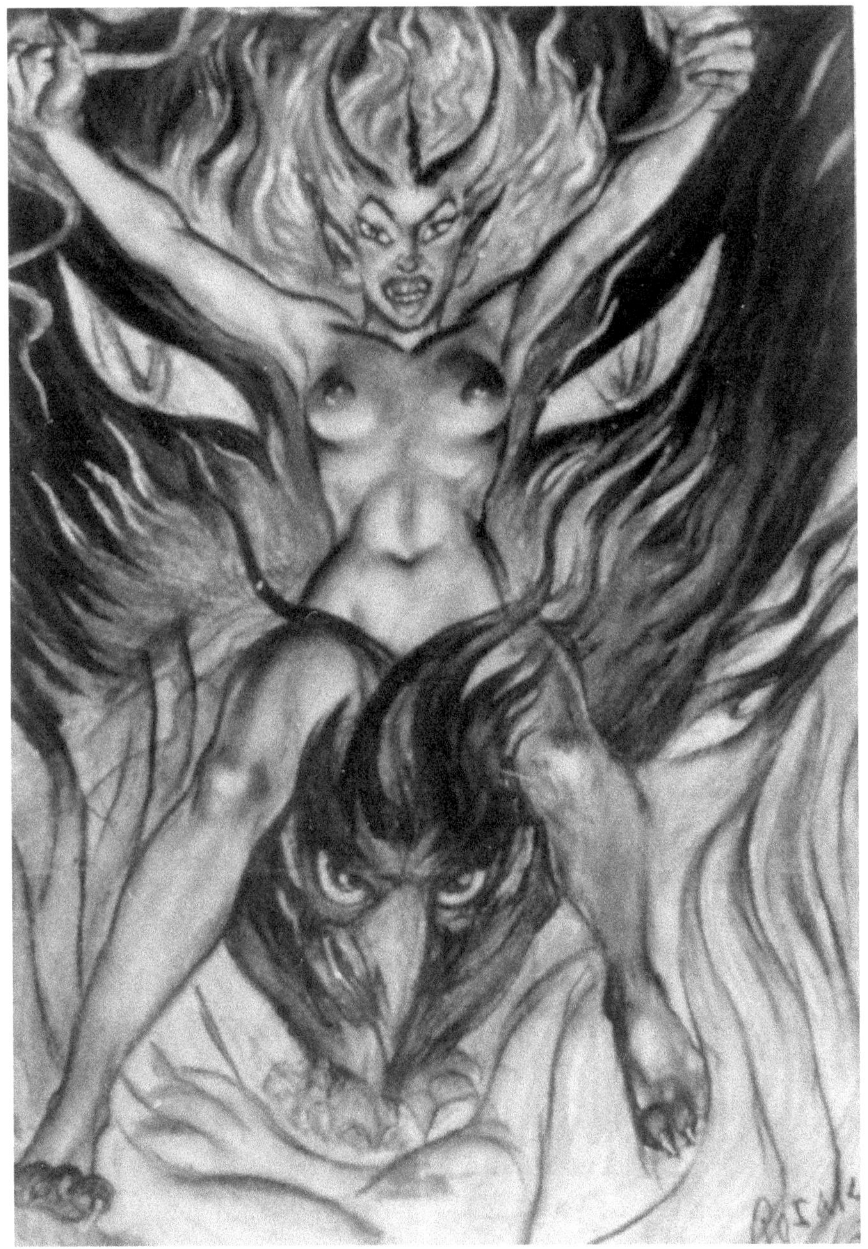

FIREBIRD

The Basque witches of France and Northern Spain traditionally paid homage to Janicot in graveyards or forests, dancing around an altar of rock on which a goat's skull had been placed with a glowing candle positioned between the horns. Norton apparently drew on this ancient Basque tradition, modifying the procedure for her inner-city magical rituals: she depicts her Janicot altar – a horned skull surmounted by a blazing candle – in her drawing *Rites of Baron Samedi,* published as Plate XIV in *The Art of Rosaleen Norton.* Contemporary Wiccan author Timothy Roderick describes Janicot's powers in terms that resonate with the way in which Norton may well have viewed him – as a servitor and guardian of the gateways opening to magical awareness: 'When you tap into the ancient archetypal energies of Janicot,' writes Roderick, 'you evoke your ability to see the big picture, to understand the true nature of things... [Janicot] also evokes your ability to see the true nature of your spirit... to see each moment in time as a doorway.'[24]

THE KABBALISTIC TREE AND THE QLIPHOTH

Both in her writings and in her art, Rosaleen Norton makes frequent reference to the Jewish Kabbalah as one of her principal maps of magical consciousness, and in her glossary listings she reveals her detailed knowledge of the ten spheres of consciousness, or *sephiroth*, associated with the Kabbalistic Tree of Life. Drawing on Dion Fortune's classic text, *The Mystical Qabalah*, a work which heads the list of esoteric publications in her bibliography, Norton refers to Binah, representing the sphere of the 'Supernal Mother', and Geburah, the sphere of 'Rightful Destruction' on the Kabbalistic Tree. It is significant that Norton gives the spelling as Qabalah, rather than Kabbalah, which is the variant used by Fortune in her text. Whether the mystical qualities associated with

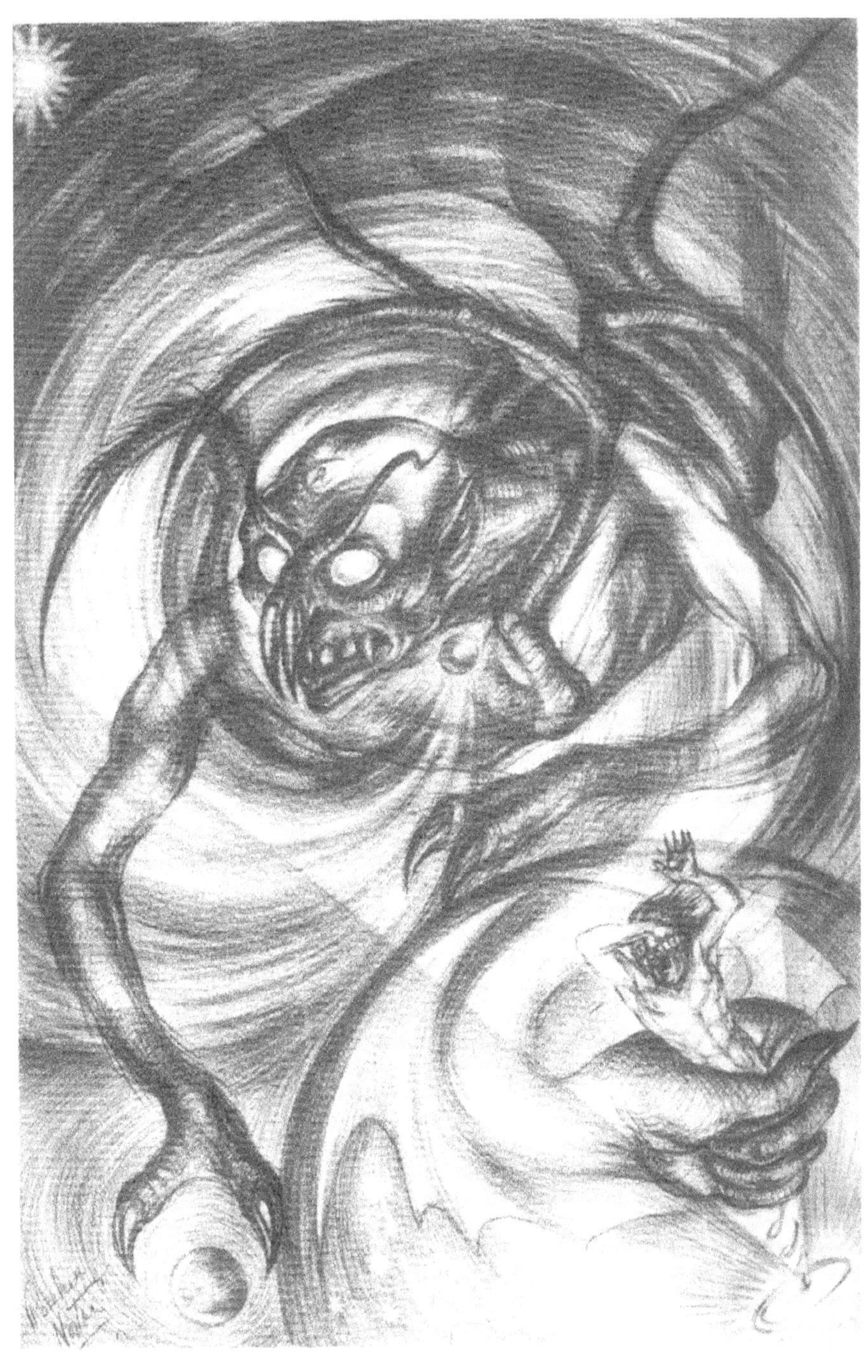

QLIPHA – *THE ARTIST'S DEPICTION OF THE TERRIFYING WERPLON*

Binah or Geburah were theoretical points of reference or experiential realities for Norton is impossible to determine. Norton's personal knowledge of the historical origins of the Jewish Kabbalah, for example, is called into question by her reference to the Qabalah as 'originally the ancient Chaldean secret doctrine which was known in Egypt under the name of the Book of Thoth...' a summation that probably owes more to Madame H.P. Blavatsky's Theosophical theories in *Isis Unveiled* – a book also listed in Norton's bibliography – than to sound Jewish scholarship.[25]

In addition to citing familiar references from the Kabbalistic Tree of Life, Norton also makes frequent allusions to the 'dark' or negative aspects of the Tree known as the *Qliphoth*. Norton seems to have had several experiences involving these dark, negative energies and documents these experiences in her drawings and magical journal.

Thelemic magician Kenneth Grant describes the *Qliphoth* – the plural form of the Hebrew *Qlipha*, meaning 'harlot' or 'strange woman' – as 'shells' and 'shades' of the dead.[26] According to Grant the *Qliphoth* signify 'otherness' and refer to 'the shadowy world of shells or reflections... power zones [that] form the Tree of Death'.[27] It is within the magical domain of the *Qliphoth* that Norton claims to have encountered the threatening magical entity she called the Werplon, a hostile humanoid insect-creature illustrated in *The Art of Rosaleen Norton*. The Werplon is by far the most hostile and confronting creature in Norton's magical cosmology. An entry from her magical journal describes her encounter with this terrifying entity:

> ...I realised that my consciousness was united with that of a totally different Order of Being. Temporarily I was experiencing the sensations of one of those great – and to this world

WAR, *ANOTHER QLIPHOTHIC IMAGE*

terrible – entities called Werplons. ...Sensation was intense; swift vibrant power and precision, and awareness below the surface, of some constant danger... Deep purple predominated with overtones of black, lit by splashes of vari-coloured [sic] light at certain of the power points...Suddenly a shock of apprehension

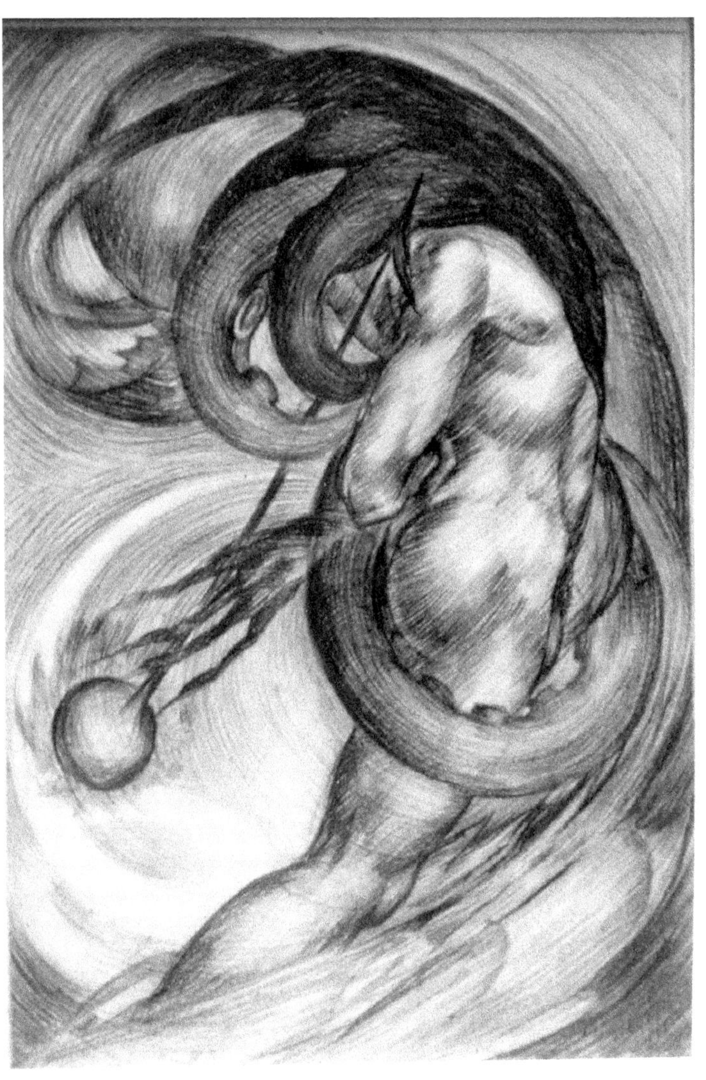

> electrified the Werplon. That needle-keen precision of operation seemed to waver, to become slightly clumsy. A wave of fright and disgust swept me as one of the Werplon's senses registered the loathsome human vibration... I knew terror... Waves of pain invaded my aetheric body. My mind screamed...[28]

Rosaleen Norton was fascinated by the dark polarities of magical consciousness and experienced the potency of these magical forces first-hand. What is especially significant about Norton's magical encounter with the Werplon is that she says it took place while she was utilising her 'aetheric body', a reference to her out-of-the-body exploration of the 'astral planes' accessed through trance and self-hypnosis – as we saw in an earlier chapter.

1 R. Norton, 'I was born a Witch, *Australasian Post*, Sydney, 3 January 1957; 'Witches want no Recruits' *Australasian Post*, Sydney, 10 January 1957 and 'Hitch-hiking Witch', *Australasian Post*, Sydney, 7 February 1957.

2 R. Norton, 'I was born a Witch', loc cit: 4.

3 P. Harrison, *The Elements of Pantheism*, Element, Shaftesbury, Dorset, 1999: 1.

4 'Inside Rosaleen Norton', *Squire*, Sydney, April 1965:42.

5 R. Norton, 'Witch Was No Class At School', *Australasian Post*, Sydney, 24 January 1957:15.

6 Ibid.

7 Gnostic scholar Hans Jonas defines the Archons as planetary rulers and believes that they were originally Babylonian in origin. Jonas notes that in Gnostic cosmology the Archons 'collectively rule over the world, and each individually in his sphere is a warder of the cosmic prison…As guardian of his sphere, each Archon bars the passage of souls that seek to ascend after death, in order to prevent

their escape from the world and their return to God.' See H. Jonas, *The Gnostic Religion*, second edition, Beacon Press, Boston 1963: 43.

8 R. Norton, 'Witches Want No Recruits', *Australasian Post*, Sydney, 10 January 1957: 35

9 Ibid.

10 See 'Hecate', in P. Turner and C.R. Coulter, *A Dictionary of Ancient Deities*, Oxford University Press, 2000: 208. According to Rabinowitz, other offerings to Hecate included bread, eels and mullet. See J. Rabinowitz, The Rotting Goddess: The Origin of the Witch in Classical Antiquity, Autonomedia, New York 1998: 62.

11 See R. Von Rudloff, *Hekate in Ancient Greek Religion*, Horned Owl Publishing, Victoria, Canada 1999:113, 122.

12 R. Patai, *The Hebrew Goddess*, third enlarged edition, Wayne State University Press, Detroit 1990: 221.

13 C.G. Jung, *Psychology of the Unconscious*, Kegan Paul, Trench, Trubner, London 1919: 153-154

14 From unpublished notes accompanying Norton's illustration *Lilith*, reproduced in *The Art of Rosaleen Norton*, Sydney 1952.

15 R. Norton, 'Witches Want No Recruits', *Australasian Post*, Sydney, 10 January 1957:5.

16 R. Norton, *The Art of Rosaleen Norton*, Walter Glover, Sydney 1952:48.

17 R. Norton, 'A Vision', included in the *Supplement to the Art of Rosaleen Norton*, Walter Glover, Sydney 1984.

18 See J.B. Russell, *Satan: the Early Christian Tradition*, Cornell University Press, Ithaca 1981:130.

19 R. Cavendish, *The Magical Arts*, Arkana, London 1984: 289.

20 See N. Drury, *Inner Visions: Explorations in Magical Consciousness*, Routledge & Kegan Paul, London 1979:106.

21 Despite its resemblance to a Jewish god-name, Eloi is not strictly Kabbalistic. The god-name of Chesed, the fourth sphere upon the Tree of Life associated with Jupiter in Dion Fortune's *Mystical Qabalah* [1935: 161], is given as El and not Eloi. It is likely that Norton derived the reference to Eloi from Madame H.P. Blavatsky who refers to the Eloi of Jupiter in *The Secret Doctrine* [1897] 1962,

Theosophical Publishing House, Adyar, Madras, India: ii :301 and iv: 108. Blavatsky ascribes this reference to the planetary spirit of Jupiter to the early Christian theologican Origen, who in turn is said to have ascribed it to the Gnostics.

22 See H.P. Blavatsky, *The Secret Doctrine* [1897] 1962, Theosophical Publishing House, Adyar, Madras, India:. Blavatsky refers specifically to Fohat as the 'dynamic energy of Cosmic Ideation' and 'the guiding power of all manifestation' (I:81) and later describes him as 'the personified electric vital power, the transcendental binding unity of all cosmic energies, on the unseen as on the manifested planes, the action of which resembles – on an immense scale – that of a living Force created by Will...Fohat is not only the living Symbol and Container of that Force, but is looked upon by the Occultists as an Entity; the forces he acts upon being cosmic, human and terrestrial, and exercising their influence on all these planes respectively.' (I:170-171. Capital letters in Blavatsky's text).

23 In Haiti Erzulie is revered as the Voodoo goddess of love, beauty, flowers and jewellery. She also enjoys dancing and fine clothes. See Maya Deren, *Divine Horsemen: the Voodoo Gods of Haiti*, Thames and Hudson, London 1953; 62 (second edition 1970). During her lifetime Norton could have had access to this well-known book, a classic study of voodoo, although it was first published a year after *The Art of Rosaleen Norton.* It is likely that Norton drew at least part of her enthusiasm for voodoo from William B. Seabrook's *Magic Island* (New York, 1929) which she lists in the bibliography in *The Art of Rosaleen Norton* (1952:79) as a reference under the heading 'witchcraft and demonology'. Norton lists its title incorrectly as *The Magic Isle* in her bibliography.

24 T. Roderick, *Wicca: 366 Days of Spiritual Practice in the Craft of the Wise*, Llewellyn, St Paul, Minnesota 2005:284.

25 Traditionally the Kabbalah is regarded as a mystical commentary on the Pentateuch – the written Torah, or 'five books of Moses'. The Hebrew word 'Kabbalah' itself means 'that which has been received' and refers to an oral mystical tradition. Evcen though the

Kabbalah did not exist in written form until the Middle Ages, it is thought that the *Sefer Yetzirah*, or *Book of Creation*, was composed in Palestine between the third and sixth centuries CE. Another early Kabbalistic text, *Sefer ha-Bahir*, emerged in Provence, where there was a Jewish community between 1150 and 1200 CE. Around 1280 a Spanish Jewish mystic named Moses de León (1238-1305) began circulating booklets among his fellow Kabbalists. These texts were written in Aramaic and de León claimed that he had transcribed them from an ancient book of wisdom composed in the circle of Rabbi Shim'on bar Yohai, a famous disciple of Rabbi Akiba, who lived and taught in Israel in the second century CE. These booklets gradually formed the text known as Ha-Zohar ha-Qadosh, usually referred to as the *Zohar (The Book of Splendour)*. Although Moses de León may have drawn on early material received through the secret oral tradition, it is now thought that he himself was probably the author of the Zohar. Norton's assertion in *The Art of Rosaleen Norton* (1952:78) that the Kabbalah is an 'ancient Chaldean secret doctrine which was known in Egypt under the name of the Book of Thoth' is completely fanciful. For the origins of the Kabbalah see G. Scholem, *Origins of the Kabbalah*, Princeton University Press, New Jersey 1990, and M. Idel, *Kabbalah: New Perspectives*, Yale University Press, New Haven 1988.

26 K. Grant, *Outside the Circles of Time*, Muller, London 1980: 287.

27 K. Grant, *Nightside of Eden*, Muller, London 1977; 275-276.

28 R. Norton, *The Art of Rosaleen Norton*, 1952:44

8

Magic in the Coven

For most of her adult life Rosaleen Norton lived in squalid, dimly lit apartments and frequently her rituals were performed within a relatively confined space, in what otherwise served as her living quarters. As mentioned earlier, 179 Brougham Street was in a very run-down condition when Norton and Gavin Greenlees lived there in the 1950s. When they first moved in, having returned to Sydney after the Rowden White Gallery exhibition in Melbourne, the paint on the terrace house was flaking badly, the slate roof was in a state of disrepair, and the house was occupied by an assortment of vagrants and bohemians. At the beginning of their tenancy, Norton, Greenlees and a number of pet cats shared the basement flat, which was actually a converted laundry. At this time the attic was occupied by a one-handed man named Mick who emerged periodically amidst piles of assorted newspapers. Later Greenlees and Norton shared the attic as a living space. They also constructed their ritual altars in this room. At one end of the attic a huge painted mural of Pan served as a backdrop to one of the altars; a second, smaller, altar was located in the opposite corner of the room.[1] The attic also contained what journalist Dave Barnes described as a 'long low couch' as well as other items of domestic furniture.

Several journalists who visited Norton during the 1950s and 1960s in order to interview her have provided detailed descriptions of the Brougham Street flat and its embellishments. In *Sydney Observed* (1968) Gavin Souter describes the ambience of Kings Cross during the 1950s and goes on to provide fascinating details of his personal visit to the Norton apartment in Brougham Street:

> From...the top of William Street, King's Cross has projected its identity up Victoria Street as far as the Slamat Makan Indonesian restaurant, and down as far as the Swiss Inn; up Darlinghurst Road as far as the Tabou near Elizabeth Bay Road; down Macleay Street to the Chevron-Hilton; down Bayswater Road to the All Nations Club; and down William Street to Brougham Street, where Rosaleen Norton used to burn her incense to Pan and Hecate. Perhaps she still does. It is a few years now since I visited Miss Norton's terrace house, but I recall the occasion clearly; it was about 11 a.m. and although bright sunlight was slanting through the leaves of the plane-trees downstairs, the Norton living-room was kept dark with heavy drapes. Against one wall stood an altar decorated with a painting of Pan, a set of stag's antlers, a red cactus flower in a brass urn, a cobra's head candlestick holder, and a few blobs of candlegrease from the last ritual. The name *Uriel* had been chalked in several places on the wall. 'I must take those off,' said Miss Norton apologetically. 'They were put up for a particular operation – an invocation.'
>
> Before I left, Miss Norton jokingly put on a rubber lizard's head mask. 'A friend of mine wore this to the Kashmir one night,' she said. 'It had all the *tapuls* quite worried. A tapul, in case you are not familiar with the word, is a dummy mask

> made for occult purposes by a Tibetan sorcerer.... Miss Norton, her eyebrows pencilled upwards in mephistophelean curves and a talisman around her neck, may sometimes be observed sitting among the tapuls at the Kashmir coffee-lounge – an object of timid curiosity, like a lovebird among sparrows.[2]

A visit to the same Norton apartment in 1962 is described by Bob Walker and Richard Neville in 'Deliver us to E-ville', an article written for the University of New South Wales student newspaper, *Tharunka*:

> Timorously, 'Tharunka' entered the King's Cross coffee shop which exhibits those of her paintings not condemned by the Vice Squad, and were given a variety of directions to follow. Finally they found themselves outside a dingy tenement house in a locale of dubious reputation. The windows were boarded up, paint had long since peeled from its walls. The time, midnight, when Cinderellas go to bed and witches rise.
>
> They knocked at the door, and waited. They knocked again. Finally, as one went to ring a bell suddenly noticed high up on the door, it creaked open and a dark figure said 'Yes?'
>
> In the flickering light of a brass lamp they caught glimpses of a narrow face, prominent nose and teeth, with eyebrows angled sharply upwards. In fact, somewhat like the mask-like paintings in the coffee-shop.
>
> They were led into a cramped basement room. The low ceiling was of bare boards, cobwebs hanging like stalactites. A red covered bed was along one wall; opposite there was an altar draped with blue cloth, on top of which were gilded antlers, porcelains of entwined snakes, panthers and a vari-

> ety of lamps and candles. Masks grinned form the walls; four mirrors glinted in the half-light, and shelves of grey-old books were variously placed in what space remained.
>
> Rowie [sic] was dressed in black tights and a red sweater. The room was heated by a makeshift gas ring [on] the floor, illuminated by a red lamp whose shade was decorated with daemonic faces. There was no source of ventilation.[3]

The lack of ventilation in Norton's apartment was something that Dave Barnes had also noticed in 1956 when he interviewed her for a second time, accompanied by a staff photographer. At this stage Norton and Greenlees had moved upstairs from the basement to the attic. 'For the first time the room seemed oppressive,' Barnes wrote. 'We noticed that the black curtains seemed to keep out nearly all the sunlight. And air. The attic seemed suddenly nearly as dark and damp as that four-years-ago basement.' [4]

The confined ritual working space in the Brougham Street attic suggests that the number of magical practitioners working closely with Norton was very restricted. When journalist D.L. Thompson visited Brougham Street in 1955 to interview Norton and also to meet other coven practitioners he was told that Norton's immediate magical group consisted of seven members. And yet Norton herself later gave widely varying responses to different interviewers who asked the same question about her coven membership. When Bob Walker and Richard Neville asked Norton in 1962 how many people belonged to her cult she gave the figure as 'roughly 300' and in the Channel Nine television documentary on Kings Cross, *The Glittering Mile* (1964), in which Norton was interviewed, Norton at first claimed 'thousands' of followers and then admitted to exaggerating before revising the figure down to 'hundreds'. In 1972, when Norton was asked the same question by *Sunday Telegraph* journalist Kerry McGlynn, she claimed she had 'at least 200 followers in Sydney and hundreds more throughout the country'.[5] However the wildly varying figures may conceal a different issue. If Norton had begun to think of herself at this time as the titular head of all the witchcraft covens in Australia, a situation suggested in a by-line in Dave Barnes' 1967 article 'Confessions of a Witch', the larger numbers may be approximately correct. However, in this case the estimates of coven membership numbers would not be referring specifically to Norton's inner group of close magical associates, which would have been very small – around seven, as the Thompson article suggests. It is interesting to note, in this context, that Norton's sister and confidante Cecily denied that Norton's Brougham Street coven actually existed, in terms of the usual meaning of the expression 'witches' coven'– which generally means a group of up to thirteen initiated members.[6] My handwritten notes from my first interview with Cecily (c.1982) say that according to her, 'Roie didn't have a coven as such – Roie had a group of "occult friends".' This is probably understating the situation, however. Roie used the magical rune name *Thorn* in her magical meetings,[7] which suggests that each of her occult colleagues had initiatory names. Two close magical associates of Norton's were also included in D.L. Thompson's interview at the Brougham Street flat in 1955. They were not identified by their real names but were referred to in the article according to the ritual masks they were wearing. One of the coven members – described as 'plump, dark, and middle-aged, with a face like a successful dentist'– was initially introduced to Thompson as 'Mr Abrahams' but later conceded that this was not his real name. He did claim, however, to be an electrical engineer, which provides us with a clue to his possible identity.[8] Mr Abrahams later donned a green Toad mask and is subsequently referred to in the article as the Toad. Norton changed into her ritual clothing, emerging in a loosely hung 'witch's apron' and a black shawl. She was also wearing a Cat mask that had an opening allowing her to continue smoking a cigarette through her long cigarette-holder. Thompson refers to her as the Cat. The other group member present at the interview was the Rat, whom Thompson describes as a 'taciturn, squarely built type'. The interview took place in the Brougham Street attic through a haze of incense smoke, in front of the large painting of Pan, a figure Thompson mistook for the Devil:

> To the left, in the shadow was an old settee; above it a nude and rather shy-making [sic] picture painted by Miss Norton. Further left was what was clearly the coven's place of worship – an altar, with a man-sized picture (painted by Miss

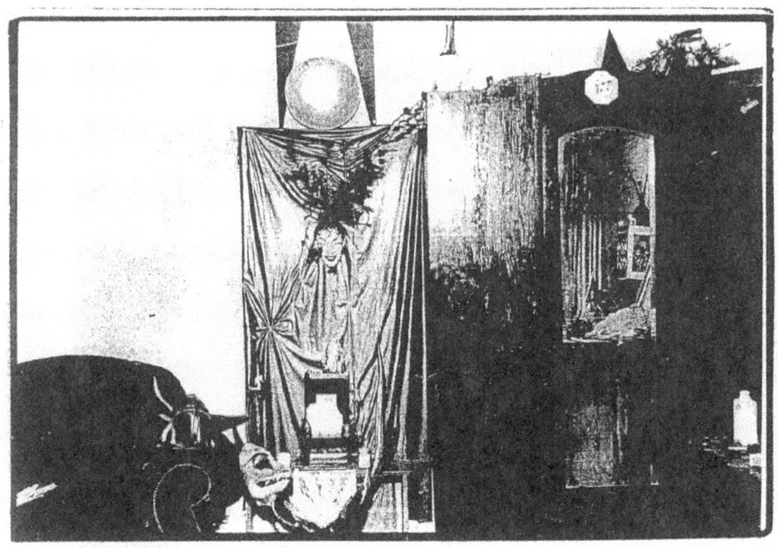

ROIE'S HECATE ALTAR

> Norton) of a particularly toothy devil. To the left and right of Lucifer two candles burned, while in front a spirit lamp added its quota of smoke to the generally murky atmosphere. Odd horns, devil's potions, and other black magic bric-a-brac stood around... Behind us, almost lost in gloom, was a deep easy chair, and beside it a smaller altar with a sea-shell full of bat's blood or something of the sort...'[9]

Thompson began his interview by asking how many members were in the coven and the Cat's response was: 'Seven.' Thompson now asked

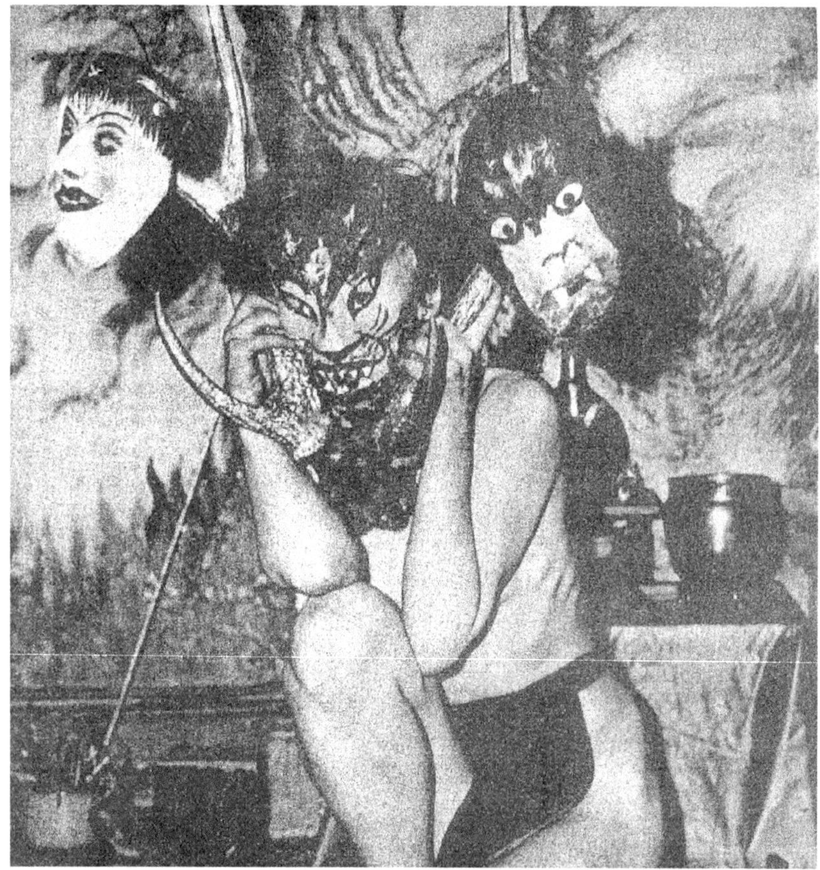

Rosaleen Norton in her ritual mask – and very little else

whether this was the only coven in Sydney, to which the Toad replied: 'No, this is only one of half a dozen.... As you see, we are quite well equipped, although perhaps a little restricted for space. There is one coven which I visit which is much better equipped. However, this serves our purpose admirably, and we are all indebted to Miss Norton for accommodating and decorating it.' Thompson now asked whether the coven practised 'certain cruelties' as part of its rites, to which the Toad responded: 'That is completely false. Cruelties have been only too common in all the so-called religions since history began, but the followers of Lucifer practise no cruelty to man or animal.'

Thompson turned again to Norton who was now sitting topless in her skimpy witch's apron, having discarded her shawl, and asked her somewhat ingenuously: 'But what do you get out of witchcraft? If you don't do it for the dressing up or for the ritualistic posing, which we have just photographed, why on earth do you do it all? Thompson records her response:

'What do I get out of it?' said Miss Norton. She pushed the cat mask to the back of her head and lit another cigarette. The cool air from the window chilled her bare body and she reached for her shawl again. 'I get a life that holds infinite possibilities and is entirely satisfying to me in all planes of consciousness.' [10]

The Thompson article is a significant document because in addition to providing details from the interviews it also contains details of the group's magical activities written by Norton herself, details acknowledged as such in the text. Norton confirms that she was 'self-initiated' and that she took the Oath of Allegiance to the Horned God when she was 13. She also writes:

'I had not been taught any ceremonial magic, nor had I read anything technical on the subject – it just "came through" instinctively.' Norton then goes on to provide important information relating to the group's structure and ritual practice:

> Sorcerers or witches (the term applies to either sex, although males are generally known as warlocks, and the more advanced as wizards) are not confined to any age, class, professional or social sphere. The youngest I have encountered (apart from myself) was a male of 17, the oldest a witch of 65.
>
> As I said, this coven has seven members. The oldest is 51 and the youngest 25. There are also several associate or honorary members of both sexes, and our last meeting was held in my own studio temple here. Other meeting places have included two North Shore suburbs and an eastern suburb. In summer we meet anywhere out of doors that is suitable.
>
> Initiation rites differ somewhat according to the coven, but are broadly, the same. The neophyte, after a period of probation, is asked certain questions. After that he or she assumes a ceremonial posture (one hand on the crown of the head, the other under the sole of one foot) to take the oath of allegiance to the presiding deities of the covens, male and female, sometimes called Pan and Hecate. A ritual to the four Elemental Powers, either before or during the initiation, is also necessary.
>
> After initiation comes a form of baptism, when a new name is given to the initiate. It is usual for him to be presented with a magnetised talisman and a piece of cord known as

> the Witches' Garter. Ceremonial attire ranges from nakedness to full regalia – robes, hood, sandals, and accessories. Different types of incense are used, according to the nature of the rites in progress, and special herbs are sometimes infused and drunk.[11]

Norton concluded her interview with the journalist by commenting that she was 'proud of being a witch, sorceress, or what you will' and that she had provided this information to counteract the tone of a number of articles published previously by *Australasian Post*, which may have conveyed a quite different impression of the 'Witch Cult'.

DOREEN VALIENTE'S ACCOUNT OF THE NORTON COVEN

Information about Norton's coven is also included in a book titled *The Rebirth of Witchcraft* by the noted British witch Doreen Valiente, who was at one time High Priestess in Gerald Gardner's coven and who helped develop key ritual procedures in the modern witchcraft revival. Valiente had gained this information about Norton and her ritual activities from a British journalist named Leslie Roberts who also worked as a waiter on the ocean-liner S.S. *Orcades* which covered the sea-route between Britain and Australia in the late 1950s. Valiente had earlier told Roberts about Norton and he in turn became interested in the possibility of meeting her. Norton had sent Gerald Gardner a copy of *The Art of Rosaleen Norton*, and this is how Valiente herself had first heard of the Australian witch and artist.[12] According to Valiente, Roberts located Norton shortly after the *Orcades* docked in Sydney in 1959, and they got on well together. Valiente writes about Roberts:

> It was not long before he was initiated into her coven. I have his scribbled notes of the events, autographed by Rosaleen Norton herself. He also recorded a good deal of personal information about Rosaleen.[13]

According to Roberts' notes, Norton's tradition of witchcraft was known as 'The Goat Fold' and this branch of the Old Religion had been brought to Australia by some of the people who were deported from Britain as convicts during the colonial era.[14] Valiente says there was a Welsh flavour to some of the names associated with Norton's coven and this may have arisen because 'Rosaleen's family was of Welsh extraction':

> The first degree of initiation is called 'Consurier', which is a form of an old Welsh word meaning 'wise woman' or 'cunning man'. A phrase from the ritual says: 'Walking on the heath, I met some friends. I have been in the cauldron and out again. They told me I am one of the green shoots of Pryderie.' This word is evidently a version of the name Pryderi, one of the heroes of the old Welsh romance called the *Mabinogion*, which is full of magic and mystery. Its heroes and heroines are probably the ancient gods under a medieval guise, as they were sung about by the Welsh bards after Wales became Christianized. Pryderie seems to have been the miraculous child of Queen Rhiannon, who is the version of the mother goddess herself.
>
> It was perhaps because of his Welsh connection that Rosaleen accepted Leslie so readily as a member of her coven. His full name was Leslie Tudor Roberts, and he believed himself to be descended from a Welshman called Tudor Roberts who was a chamberlain at the court of Henry VIII.[15]

With regard to magical tools and ritual nudity, according to the notes Valiente received from Roberts the following ritual practices were a feature of Norton's coven:

> Some of Rosaleen's rituals were conducted in a state of ritual nudity, but often she preferred to dress in robes and she and her coven made much use of ritual masks in the form of heads of animals and birds....
>
> The Sabbats were the same as those observed by European witches, though of course in Australia midsummer and mid-winter would be at the opposite times of the year from those in Europe, so the witches' year had to be adjusted accordingly...
>
> Like Gardnerian witches, Rosaleen and her coven used 'working tools', though not so many as are enumerated in Gardner's rituals. They had only five, namely the athame (air), the cup (water), the censer (fire), the pentacle (earth) and the cord (spirit). They made much use of consecrated cords in their workings. They also had a ritual meal of wine and cakes, the latter being specially made of wholemeal flour, olive oil and honey. The wine was drunk from a horn, which was passed round the circle deosil (clockwise).[16]

Valiente also provides details of a text address from the initiation ritual which Roberts says he received from Norton. This was called *The First Knowledge* and, according to Valiente, Leslie 'let her copy this down'. The text reads as follows:

> The Craft is only part of the Way and must not be mistaken for all of it. But in itself it is important, for it can be used to lighten burdens and to help in the Great Work. It is not for

> the weak. Had you been such, you would not be here. Therefore, know this: some have the power, most have it not. If you have it, it springs from within you, from the will, the mind and the spirit; and it can be joined to external symbols. It must grow through practice, as you gain knowledge and skill. The implements, words, symbols and spells are your working tools. You must be guided by the Gods who dwell in the mind and body. The Officers of the coven will tell you of the Gods, for this knowledge is too secret to be written. Always remember that you must be stronger than the powers you evoke. Knowing how this is done is one of the signs of mastery. Therefore to the Work, and to the knowledge that is joy and strength and light and life everlasting.[17]

Valiente admits to slightly amending the grammar of the original and writes: 'I think it gives a good idea of Rosaleen's attitude to witchcraft.' However it is highly doubtful that Norton would have written this text herself. Norton was never one to lapse into a pontificating, formal style of writing and the contrived seriousness of such phrases as 'Therefore, know this: some have the power, most have it not' and the almost Christian tone of 'Therefore to the Work, and to the knowledge that is joy and strength and light and life everlasting' are most unlikely to have come from Norton's lips or pen. She was, after all, a creature of the night and had said so on numerous occasions in the past. Norton does not refer to her magical procedures as 'the Work' in any of her earlier articles or interviews so we must infer that, if it is authentic, *The First Knowledge* was a document that Norton had acquired from another source. It was most likely of British origin, where ritual formality was more valued in occult circles. It is possible that around the time Roberts met her in Sydney, Norton may have incorporated *The First Knowledge* into the activities of her local magical group although it is not referred to in the 1955 Thompson interview referred to earlier, which includes ritual details provided by Norton herself.

It is possible that by 1959 – three years after the departure of Sir Eugene Goossens – the act of asserting a sense of 'occult lineage' may have become important to Norton, or one of her close magical associates,[18] as had also been the cases with witches in Britain who were keen to demonstrate that they were restoring the forgotten lineage of the Old Religion. The allegedly Welsh orientation of Norton's personal witchcraft lineage is also very much open to question. Her father was English and her mother a New Zealander of Jewish extraction.[19] Even more significantly, from the beginning, Norton had made it clear – and this is supported by her autobiographical articles in the *Australasian Post* in 1956 and 1957 as well as by references in the 1955 Thompson interview – her central deity was Pan and not one of the Welsh Celtic deities, and the other central deities in both her art and her personal magical cosmology were Hecate, Lilith and The Adversary (Lucifer). Other elements of Norton's ritual practice – as is clear both from textual evidence that links some of her thinking and ritual practice to the writings of Aleister Crowley and photographs, already referred to – that show she invoked Jewish archangels like Uriel – indicate that she was more influenced by the magic of the Hermetic Order of the Golden Dawn and *Thelema* than by Celtic tradition.

There is one additional, somewhat surprising statement in Valiente's account. Valiente writes that

> members of Rosaleen Norton's coven had a special handshake which they used between themselves. Leslie was taught this handshake and he always used it from then onwards among his closest friends. I do not know of any other coven which uses a sign like this. Perhaps it may have been derived from Masonic sources. [20]

The founding members of the late 19th century Hermetic Order of the Golden Dawn were all Freemasons, and if this handshake was indeed part of Norton's coven procedure in the late 1950s it too seems to have been a practice introduced for effect to reinforce the notion of a secret occult lineage – an idea that may have been suggested by one of Norton's magical associates but which is unlikely to have come from Norton herself. Nowhere in Norton's own writings or in her lengthy interview with L.J. Murphy at the University of Melbourne, which was very probing, is there any mention of a Masonic component to Norton's magical practice.

However other statements made by Valiente are definitely supported by corroborating data. Valiente writes that 'The deities invoked by Rosaleen and her coven were called Pan and Hecate, though other names were also used.'[21] This assertion is certainly supported by earlier statements from Norton as well as by photographs taken in 1956 by Vice Squad detective Bert Trevenar which confirm D.L. Thompson's observation a year earlier, namely that there were two altars in Norton's Brougham Street flat – one dedicated to Pan and the smaller one to Hecate. Dave Barnes' interview with Norton in 1956 similarly alluded to a ritual altar in both North and South. There is also supporting evidence for Valiente's statement that Norton's coven made much use of ritual masks in the form of heads of animals and birds: photographs of masked coven members, including Norton herself, were published in the *Australasian Post* in October 1955.

Valiente was aware that several aspects of Norton's ritual practice were improvised and spontaneous, a point reinforced recently by magical practitioner Dave Robinson (aka Wayland the Smith) who was a friend of Norton's and a regular visitor to the Brougham Street flat in the early 1960s.[22] And Valiente was aware that Norton had taken a private oath of allegiance to Pan for she writes: '...she had never read of this ritual anywhere. It just "came through" instinctively...', [23] a statement which is clearly at odds with the notion that Norton was continuing a Welsh Celtic witchcraft lineage dating back to convict days. It is therefore apparent that while some details in Valiente's account can be substantiated by reference to other sources, including Norton's own statements, other details supplied by Leslie Roberts remained contradictory and unresolved.

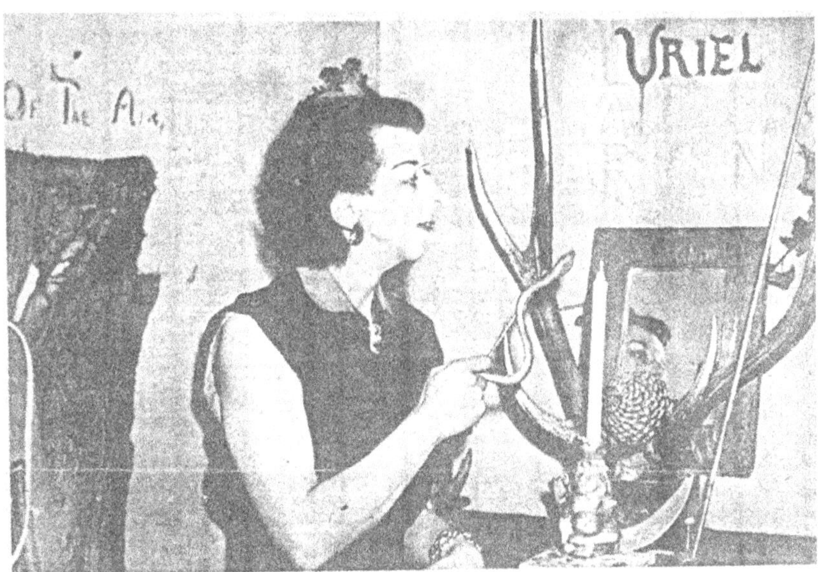

ROIE INVOKING URIEL – WHOSE NAME IS CLEARLY VISIBLE BEHIND HER, WRITTEN ON THE TEMPLE WALL.
PHOTOGRAPH TAKEN IN 1955

Nevertheless, despite the contradictory elements in the Norton coven material that Leslie Roberts shared with Doreen Valiente one point is indisputable: the name of Leslie Roberts is one of the few that can be definitively linked to Norton's magical group in the 1950s – we know this because Valiente was able to witness documents from the Australian coven that bore Norton's own signature.

Who else is known by name as an early member of Norton's magical coven? One of Norton's long-standing 'occult friends', to use Cecily Boothman's somewhat quaint expression, was Bill Turnbull – also known as Druid Alpha – to whom Norton bequeathed her *athame* and other magical equipment in her will.[24] The fact that Turnbull was bequeathed personal ritual equipment that had belonged to Norton herself, including her prized ceremonial dagger, strongly suggests that he was one of her most valued occult associates and perhaps a member of her inner magical circle.[25] Norton's publisher, Wally Glover, claimed to know of three other individuals who were rumoured to be members of Norton's magical group: he named them as Jack Davey, the prominent radio announcer; George Nathan, a wealthy Jewish bookmaker, and Henry Foster, an engineer who specialised in oven maintenance and who worked at a bakery in Bondi Junction.[26] Glover understood that Foster was the 'high priest' in Norton's coven and the circumstantial evidence provided earlier suggests he may have been the coven member who referred to himself first as Mr Abrahams and then as the Toad, in D.L. Thompson's interview.[27] More recently, in June 1999, Sydney-based crime writer Ned McCann was told by Detective Bert Trevenar that there were 'malicious rumours' circulating around the time of Sir Eugene Goossens' departure claiming that Sir Charles Moses, General Manager of the Australian

Broadcasting Commission, and his assistant, A.N. (Huck) Finlay were also members of the coven, but this assertion had not been proven.[28] Aside from these possible connections – several of which are speculative and unsubstantiated – further information on Norton's inner circle of magical associates has not been forthcoming. There is, however, one close associate of Rosaleen Norton whose magical activity in her inner circle *has* been documented in some detail. This figure is Sir Eugene Goossens, and the sorts of practices he and Norton were engaged in included various forms of sex magic based largely on the *Thelemic* teachings and practices of Aleister Crowley.

1 Norton referred to these as the North and South altars respectively. It is not known what specific purpose the Southern altar served. In an interview with Dave Barnes in 1956, Norton said it 'used in certain rituals' but did not provide any details. It may possibly have been a shrine to Hecate. See D.Barnes, 'I am a Witch', *Australasian Post*, Sydney, 20 December 1956:8.

2 G.Souter and G.Molnar, *Sydney Observed,* Angus & Robertson, 1968: 68-71. Molnar provided the illustrations for this book; Souter supplied the text.

3 B. Walker and R.Neville, 'Deliver us to E-ville', *Tharunka*, University of New South Wales, Sydney, 3 July 1962: 8. This interview was apparently conducted in the basement of the Brougham Street house and there is no mention in this article of the Pan mural. This suggests that at this time Norton had acces to both the attic and the basement flat. She seems to have taken her ritual stag antlers with her from one room to another because they appear in different locations in various photographs from the period.

4 D.Barnes, 'I am a Witch' , loc.cit, 1956: 8.

5 K.McGlynn, 'Going to the Devil', *Sunday Telegraph*, Sydney, 16 July 1972.

6 In the British Wiccan tradition when membership of a witches' coven looks like exceeding 13 members, senior members may branch off and form a new coven.

7 Information provided by a former coven member and close associate of Norton's, who does not wish to be identified.

8 Wally Glover advised me in 1981 (my written notes survive) that he had heard a rumour that one of the coven members was Henry Foster, who worked as an engineer in a bakery at Bondi Junction, where he was involved with oven maintenance. Glover had heard that Foster was High Priest of Norton's coven. In the Thompson article the Toad describes himself as '...a warlock...almost a wizard, although I am perhaps not fully qualified for that distinction'. This nevertheless suggests that the Toad and – if he was indeed Foster – was reasonably 'senior' in Norton's group.

9 This, presumably, was Norton's South altar. Thompson notes that to the right of the Pan painting was another wall with a recessed window. D.L. Thompson, 'Devil Worship Here!', loc cit.: 4. This window faced onto Brougham Street. Because the house itself faced east, this allows us to confirm that the Pan altar was the North altar.

10 D.L. Thompson, 'Devil Worship Here', loc cit: 5.

11 R. Norton's text in D.L. Thompson, 'Devil Worship Here!', loc cit.:37

12 In *The Rebirth of Witchcraft* Valiente says the contact between Gardner and Norton was 'limited' (1989:154). She also notes that Norton told Gardner she was working in Sydney as a witch and already had a coven, which indicates that Norton did not derive her coven structure from Gardner, if indeed she ever had her own 'coven' in the literal meaning of the word. According to Valiente, Norton had read about Gardner in the Australian press (1989:155) and then sent him her own book. Two articles featuring large photographs of Gardner appeared in the popular tabloids in the 1950s and it may have been one of these articles that prompted Norton to make contact with him. They were 'Witchmaster!' (subtitled: 'The Devil is on our Doorstep') published in *Australasian Post* 14 July 1955, an anonymous article which also contained pictures of Aleister Crowley

and one of Crowley's lovers, the Australian-born violinist Leila Waddell, and 'Witches in the Nude' by Peter Lucas (subtitled: 'Boss Gardner Won't Allow Unpleasant Spells At All') published in *People*, Sydney 5 March 1958.

13 D. Valiente, *The Rebirth of Magic*, loc.cit: 155

14 Loc.cit: 156

15 Loc cit: 156-157

16 Loc.cit: 157

17 Ibid.

18 There is a hint of mock seriousness and formality in the Toad's responses in the D.L.Thompson interview: when the Toad refers to his interviewer as 'sir' on 'brother' on several occasions. See D.L.Thompson, ' Devil Worship Here !', *Australasian Post*, Sydney, 6 October 1955: 4.

19 Norton's father, Albert Thomas Norton, was a native of London and Norton's mother, Beena Salek née Aschman was born in New Zealand (*Australian Dictionary of Biography*, vol.15.,Australian National University, Canberra 2000).

20 D. Valiente, *The Rebirth of Magic*, loc.cit:159

21 Loc cit: 158.

22 Personal communication to the author from D. Robinson, 10 October 2006.

23 Quoted in D. Valiente, *The Rebirth of Witchcraft*, loc cit: 158.

24 Personal communication to the author from Cecily Boothman, c.1986. Turnbull died in 2004.

25 According to Norton's sister, Cecily Boothman, Norton's will, which was 'written in scratchy handwriting' also specified that certain objects should pass to Cecily herself and to a close friend, Eve Finney. After Norton's death in 1979 Cecily received various books and drawings - one of them from Norton's classic 1940s period. A 'special cat art-work', Norton's last painting, was bequeathed to Eve Finney (notes supplied to the author by Cecily Boothman, c.1985).

26 Notes by the author taken during an interview with Wally Glover, c.1986 during the writing of the first draft of *Pan's Daughter*.

27 D.L. Thompson, 'Devil Worship Here !', loc.cit.

28 N. McCann, interview with Detective Bert Trevenar, 19 June 1999, available on-line at http://nedmccann.blogspot.com

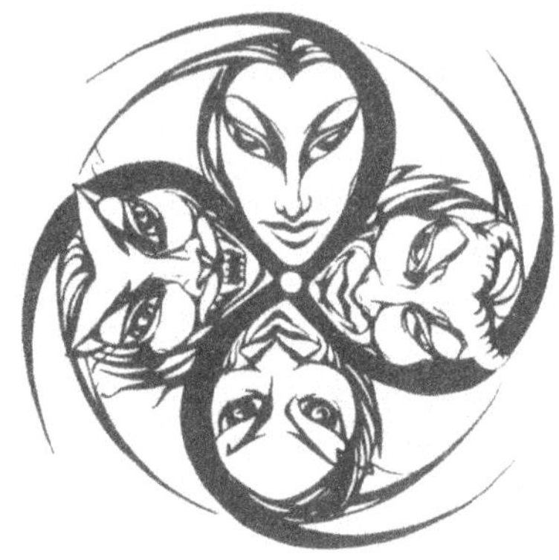

9

Rosaleen Norton and Thelemic sex magick

Modern sex magic (or sex magick) derives substantially from the *Thelemic* philosophy and ritual activities of Aleister Crowley – an account of how it developed as a key component of the Western esoteric tradition is provided in Appendix A. Other notable esoteric practitioners of sex magic include Paschal Beverly Randolph (1825-1875), Theodor Reuss (1855-1923) and Kenneth Grant (1924-2011),[1] but their writings are not acknowledged by Rosaleen Norton in her bibliography and it is unlikely that she was aware of them. Very few of Grant's major writings were available in Norton's lifetime, Reuss was known primarily in Germany and died when Norton was only six, and an accessible English-language version of Paschal Beverly Randolph's 19th century text *Sexual Magic* was published only as recently as 1988, nine years after Norton's death. On the other hand, Crowley's *Magick in Theory and Practice* is listed in Norton's bibliography and there are several references to Crowley in the private correspondence between Norton and Goossens. *Magick in Theory and Practice* [1929] was an extremely rare item during Norton's lifetime – the undated pirated edition released in New York during the 1960s was not available in 1952 when *The Art of Rosaleen Norton* was published so it is somewhat surprising that Norton even knew of its existence. However we now know that Norton collected rare and relatively obscure volumes on magic and erotic verse issued by Crowley. This latter point is demonstrated by the fact that a limited edition volume titled *Konx Om Pax*,[2] which was self-published by Crowley in London in 1907 [restricted to 500 numbered copies and printed on handmade paper], was part of Norton's estate following her death: it was listed for sale in 1996, along with several of Norton's original etchings and drawings.[3]

In addition to drawing on the ceremonial sex magic practices of Aleister Crowley, Norton's sex magic approach also involved the practice of arousing *Kundalini* energy. Norton had alluded to the Kundalini in the symbolism of her controversial drawing *Fohat*, which was reproduced in *The Art of Rosaleen Norton* in 1952: this was one of the two offending images that had to be blacked out from this edition before it could be legally released for sale in Australia.[4] According to Norton the image of *Fohat*, which depicted him as a goat-headed deity with a large serpentine phallus, was intended to convey 'the dynamic energy of cosmic ideation'. As Norton wrote in a personal commentary on *Fohat* which she later passed to Wally Glover, 'The goat is a symbol of energy and creativity: the serpent of elemental force and eternity.' Norton went on to link her drawing to the power of the Kundalini, which is unleashed through Tantric sex practices in order to facilitate the release of cosmic consciousness. The following details are previously unpublished notes relating to the *Kundalini* and the image of Fohat which Norton prepared while she was selecting art-works for inclusion in *The Art of Rosaleen Norton*:

> *Kundalini* – the undifferentiated elemental and potential creative power of the Self (collective unconscious, personal and impersonal or racial), generally symbolised as the serpent and

traditionally associated with the spinal cord. When latent it manifests itself only sporadically and partially in the sex force and sometimes in artistic creativity. Active, it confers supernormal powers in various directions. Kundalini is generally represented as a serpent: the serpent penis of Fohat is the same symbol used here to denote macrocosmic creativity. The phoenix is an emblem of immortality. [5]

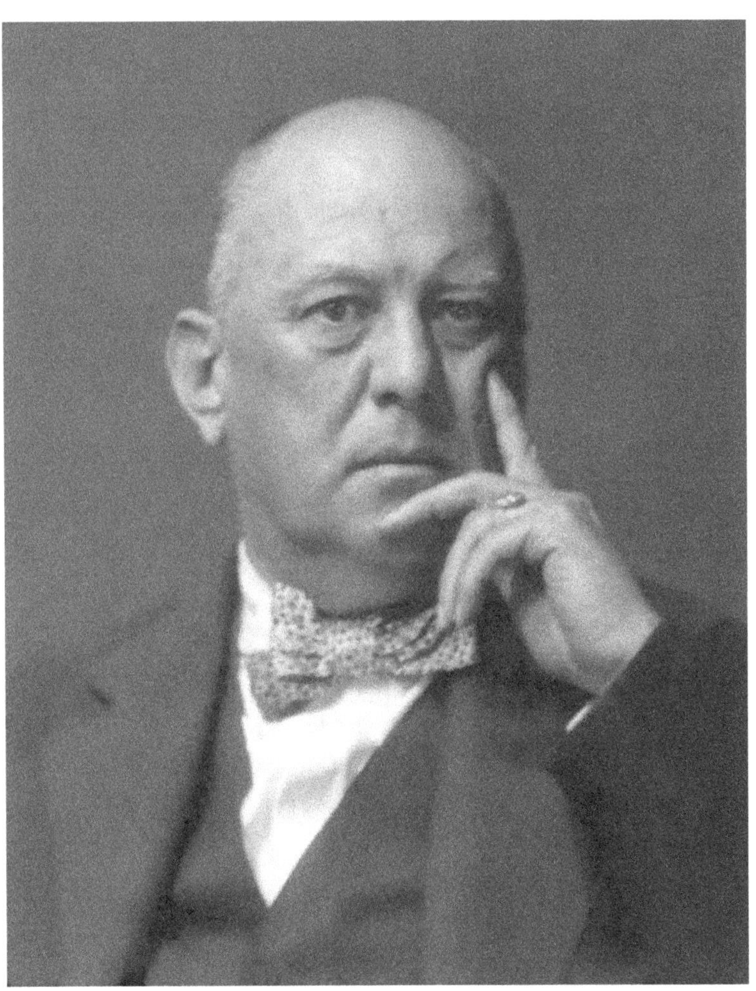

ALEISTER CROWLEY

SEX MAGIC AND HOMAGE TO PAN

Norton's practice of sex magic reflects her own sexual preferences which, as we saw earlier, were recorded in the 1949 sessions with psychologist L.J. Murphy in Melbourne. To recap the main points documented in the Murphy interview: Norton was originally heterosexual but around the age of 23 she became more interested in male homosexuals. She favoured sexual intercourse with male homosexuals because she could take a more active role, although she also stated that after around three months of sexual activities with male homosexuals she also liked to participate in manual and oral manipulation with female homosexuals. The Melbourne transcripts also make reference to the fact that [Norton] 'likes very much to be tied up, beaten, [and] then have S.I. [sexual intercourse] when her partner hurts her by forcing her back against the pole to which she is tied'. This particular aspect of Norton's sexual behaviour is reflected in a controversial and far-reaching incident that occurred in October 1955, when Norton and her lover, Gavin Greenlees, were charged by police with engaging in 'an unnatural sexual act'.

On 3 October 1955 two members of the New South Wales Vice Squad, Detective A.H. 'Bert' Trevenar and Detective N. Hayes, raided Norton's Brougham Street flat and laid charges against Norton and Greenlees. The police raid had taken place because two men, Francis Honer and Raymond Ager, had earlier offered the Sydney-based *Sun* newspaper a series of allegedly obscene film negatives and photographs which purported to show evidence of a Kings Cross witchcraft cult. Honer had stolen the film negatives from Norton's flat and, with Ager as an accomplice, had attempted to sell them to the *Sun* newspaper for £200. Honer and Ager had been apprehended by police and two naked figures had been identified in the photographs: Norton and her lover, Gavin Greenlees. Later, during the court hearings, Norton maintained that she and Greenlees had been engaged in a sexual ritual dedicated to Pan. The offending photographs would not be available for public viewing for many years. A few of the photographs were screened on the ABC television programme *Rewind* on 5 September 2004 and showed Norton naked and tied by her wrists and ankles to a pedestal in a staged act of sex-bondage, while Greenlees performed acts of flagellation on her. Greenlees had also been photographed engaging in cunnilingus and anal sex.

During the first court session Norton adopted a defiant attitude to the charges of alleged obscenity brought against her. Dressed flamboyantly in a red skirt, black top and leopard-skin shoes, she defended her belief in pantheism, which she described as the heathen worship of ancient Greek gods. At the end of the court hearings Honer and Ager were jailed for four months, while Norton and Greenlees were eventually acquitted. As one might expect, the court case against Norton and Greenlees attracted extensive coverage in the popular press.

The Honer/Ager incident suggests that Norton and Greenlees had begun to formulate the rudiments of a sustained practice of sex magic by the mid- 1950s: Norton specifically claimed during the court proceedings that the controversial sex-bondage photographs 'depicted aspects of ceremonial' and that they had been taken 'during a ceremony of worship of the Greek mythological [figure] of Pan and not during a witchcraft ritual'. Detective Trevenar confirmed that Greenlees was 'dressed in ceremonial garb' in several of the photographs. He also confirmed that he had been advised that Greenlees and Norton had lived together in the Brougham Street studio since 1949 and had committed similar sexual acts 'quite often'.[6] However, there was a more specific connection between the Honer/Ager photographs and Norton's practice of sex magic – and it related to the unique sexual relationship between Rosaleen Norton, Gavin Greenlees and the resident chief conductor of the Sydney Symphony Orchestra, Eugene (later, Sir Eugene) Goossens.

Before coming to Australia, Goossens had been friendly with the pianist and composer Cyril Scott, who had Theosophical interests and was the author of *An Outline of Modern Occultism.* Goossens was also friendly with the composer, critic and editor Philip Heseltine, who had a strong interest in black magic and paganism. Heseltine had met Crowley around 1914,[7] was a member of Crowley's O.T.O.,[8] and was known in artistic and musical circles by his *nom de plume*, Peter Warlock. On one occasion Heseltine used magic squares from the *Book of the Sacred Magic of Abramelin the Mage* in order to get his estranged wife to return to him: his ritual method included the act of engraving one of the *Abramelin* magic squares 'neatly on his arm'. In the posthumously published *Magick Without Tears* (1982) Crowley notes: 'I don't know how he proceeded to set to work; but his wife came back all right, and a very short time afterwards he killed himself.'[9] As mentioned earlier, according to Goossens' younger sister, Dame Sidonie Goossens-Millar, it was Heseltine's involvement with magic that first attracted her brother to the occult, and it is also of interest, in this context, that Heseltine was a friend of the poet Victor Neuburg, who had been involved with Aleister Crowley in sex-magic ritual activities in the Algerian desert in 1909. As an O.T.O. member, Heseltine provides the key link between Crowley's sex magic practices on the one hand, and the *Goetic* sex magic techniques that Eugene Goossens offered to teach Rosaleen Norton.

Detective Bert Trevenar already knew about Goossens' close relationship with Rosaleen Norton and Gavin Greenlees prior to the police raid on the Brougham Street apartment on 3 October 1955. Trevenar had in his possession a collection of intimate and personal letters Goossens had sent to Norton: he had obtained them from Joe

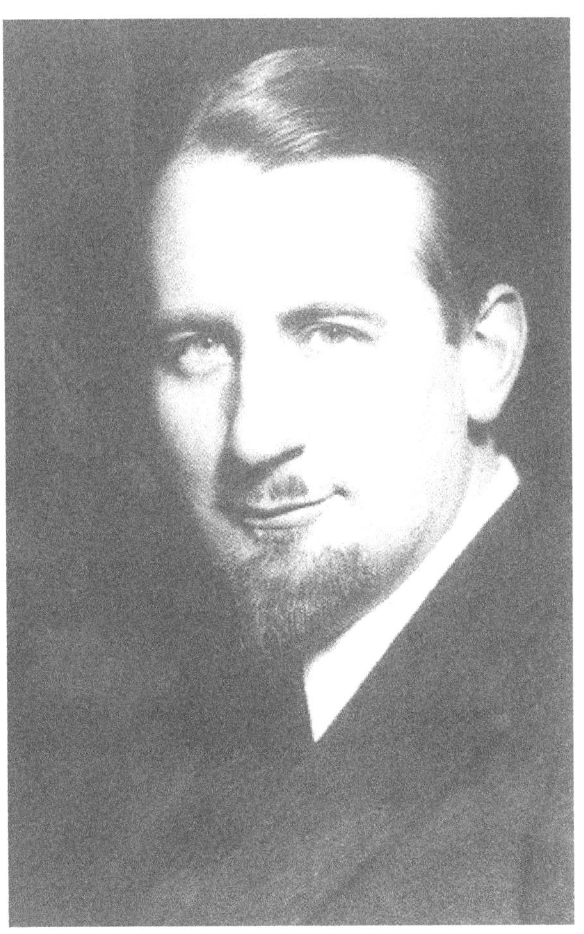

Philip Heseltine, also known as Peter Warlock – the link connecting Crowley, Goossens and Norton in the practice of Thelemic sex magick

Morris, one-time senior crime roundsman for the Sydney *Sun*, who had infiltrated Norton's coven and secretly removed them. When Norton and Greenlees were charged with engaging in 'an unnatural sexual act' following discovery of the Honer/Ager photographs, Goossens feared being caught up in a scandal and hurriedly destroyed his private collection of pornography and black magic paraphernalia. Not to be outdone, Trevenar swiftly obtained approval from Detective Inspector Ron Walden, head of the Vice Squad, to monitor the relationship between Norton, Greenlees, and Goossens – specifically with a view to securing evidence of sex perversion – and this included tracking Goossens during his visits to Europe with assistance from connections provided by the Sydney *Sun* newspaper. In London Goossens was observed making 'unorthodox purchases in grubby newsagencies and bookshops in Soho and around Leicester Square'.[10] It is significant that a leading occult bookshop, Watkins, was located close to Leicester Square in Cecil Court; Goossens could easily have acquired rare works by the Thelemic sex magic practitioner, Aleister Crowley, at this specialist outlet for *esoterica* – Watkins is well known in London as a source of rare magical texts.

Following Goossens' arrest at Sydney's Mascot Airport, Trevenar had a unique opportunity to interrogate him about his sex magic interests. A section of Trevenar's record of interview reads as follows:

> 'I said: "How is that Rite [ie. sex magic] conducted?" '
>
> 'He said: "We undressed and sat on the floor in a circle. Miss Norton conducted the verbal part of the Rite. I then performed the sex stimulation on her." '
>
> 'I said: "How did you do that?" '

> 'He said: "I placed my tongue in her sexual organ and kept moving it until I stimulated her." '[11]

Further allusions to sex magic rituals are also found within Goossens' personal correspondence to Norton, copies of which Trevenar had secured through his informant, Joe Morris.[12] When Trevenar interviewed Goossens he showed the conductor photocopies of the letters taken by Morris from the Brougham Street flat and Goossens in turn confirmed that he had written them. Some were signed *'Djinn'*, which was a magical name used by Goossens when he corresponded with Norton. It also seems likely that Djinn was Goossens' magical name in the Norton coven.[13]

In her research paper 'The Witching Hour: Sex Magic in 1950s Australia', Dr Marguerite Johnson notes that there are eleven extant letters written by Goossens to Norton and Greenlees, one them incomplete and another a set of instructions possibly related to another piece of correspondence, probably lost. Johnson writes:

> Each of the letters extends to two-and-a-half handwritten pages approximately; they had been composed in Australia and overseas; seven open with a greeting to Norton; four either refer to and/or send greetings to Greenlees (one is actually a postcard from Lord Howe Island addressed to Greenlees); three are signed with Goossens' magical name, Djinn; five include references to caution and anonymity; six contain small sketches, two of which are sex magic images. The letters are not dated, although one has an intact envelope stamped 4 June 1953 with a Canberra postmark. Another includes a series of potential meeting times which suggest four possible dates: March 1952 (too early), August

> 1953, May 1954 or January 1955. Each letter deals with magic and sex magic is expressly mentioned in all of them...[14]

There are several references to sex magic in the correspondence and these references are clearly associated with a specific type of ritual practice: the Thelemic sex magic of Aleister Crowley. 'A.C.' is referred to specifically in four of the letters. In one, which begins 'For Roie, to whom secret greetings...' Goossens writes: 'Thanks too for that quite needless assurance regarding the inviolability of my MSS and notes...also for retaining the A.C. writings' – a clear reference to the published works of Crowley. In another, which begins 'Roie – the savoury witch...,' Goossens makes a passing reference to the well known libertarian attributes of Aleister Crowley when he writes: 'And how I agree with you about all that normality "pap"! Let's "piss it out" of existence as A.C. used to say...' However in a third letter, which is of considerable interest from a magical point of view, Goossens provides Norton with travel details of how to get to his cottage near Mount Victoria in the Blue Mountains, so she can come and visit him. In this letter there is also a key reference to Crowley. Goossens writes: 'Obviously a pied-à-terre is necessary, hidden and private...' He then continues: '*Yes, I'll instruct you in the grimoire.* The diagrams are necessarily crude but none the less effective, being all from unimpeachable sources. *You will be my best – and only – pupil*, and I shall appoint you keeper of the seals (You nearly hit the nail on the head in your bit about A.C. and self in June letter!). Unfortunately, I didn't bring the book, but shall bring it to you next week for lesson one.'

It is interesting that Gavin Greenlees was not involved in this secret meeting in the Blue Mountains: Goossens refers to Norton as his 'only' pupil in matters relating to the grimoire. The last two sentences provide us with a useful insight: here Goossens is offering to instruct Norton in an area of the magical arts relatively unfamiliar to her: *namely how to make use of the magical seals, or sigils, contained within a medieval grimoire*. This is an important point because here we see Goossens offering knowledge of specific magical techniques to Norton and not the other way around. This clearly contradicts the statement issued by Goossens' solicitors issued after Goossens' departure for Europe in May 1956 to the effect that the conductor believed he was responding – in a ritual context – to 'persistent menaces…involving others'.[15] Here is a case of Goossens 'luring' Norton into the magical practice of *Goetia* and not the other way around. In addition, there is a clear inference that Norton appreciates the magical connection between Crowley and Goossens, for the letter makes reference to something previously noted in relation to 'A.C. and self' [ie. Crowley and Goossens].

Grimoires are spell-books containing the magical sigils or 'seals' assigned to various demonic spirits, and they were largely unknown in the West until the 13th century.[16] Crowley had himself financed publication of an edition of the *Goetia, or Lesser Key of Solomon the King* in 1904, a 16th century work which contained the magical seals used to evoke 72 'evil spirits'.[17] In the *Goetia* these spirit-entities are described as the '72 Mighty Kings and Princes which King Solomon commanded into a Vessel of Brass, together with their Legions... Of whom Belial, Bileth, Asmoday and Gaap were chief.'[18]

The *Goetia* is very likely to be the book Goossens is referring to above, because A.C. (ie. Aleister Crowley) was not only directly involved with its publication but also supplemented MacGregor Mathers' presentation of the actual grimoire text with an essay titled 'The Initiated

Interpretation of Ceremonial Magic' which was included as a separate chapter in the same volume when it was published in 1904.[19] During the mid-1950s, when Goossens' letter was written, the *Goetia* was probably the most accessible magical grimoire and source of magical seals for occultists seeking this sort of information. A further indicator that the *Goetia* was very probably the text in question is provided by the fact that in the same letter, referred to above, Goossens makes reference to 'Ashtaroth cream' which was intended for Norton alone, 'and no-one else'. This was probably a magical unguent that Norton was to rub into various parts of her body – we know that Goossens had purchased such 'unguents' for Norton in Paris.

In relation to the use of seals from magical grimoires, Astaroth – also known as Ashtaroth – is listed as the 29th spirit in the *Goetia*; the following text describes his specific attributes:

> He is a Mighty, Strong Duke, and appeareth in the form of a hurtful Angel riding on an Infernal Beast like a Dragon, and carrying in his right hand a Viper. Thou must in no wise let him approach too near unto thee, lest he do thee damage by his Noisome Breath. Wherefore the Magician must hold the Magical Ring near his face, and that will defend him. He giveth true answers of things Past, Present and to Come, and can discover all Secrets. He will declare wittingly how the Spirits fell, if desired, and the reason of his own fall. He can make men wonderfully knowing in all Liberal Sciences. He ruleth 40 Legions of Spirits.[20]

After describing the particular attributes of each of the 72 evil spirits, including Astaroth, the text of the *Goetia* includes the following commentary on what happened when the legendary King Solomon 'commanded' these spirits 'into a Vessel of Brass':

> And it is to be noted that Solomon did this because of their pride [ie the pride of the evil spirits], for he never declared other reason why he thus bound them. And when he had thus bound them up and sealed the Vessel, he by Divine Power did chase them all into a deep Lake or Hole in Babylon. And they of Babylon, wondering to see such a thing, they did then go wholly to into the Lake, to break the Vessel open, expecting to find great store of Treasure therein. But when they had broken it open, out flew the Chief Spirits immediately, with their legions following them; and they were all restored to their former places except Belial, who entered into a certain Image, and thence gave answers unto those who did offer Sacrifices unto him, and did worship the Image as their God.[21]

When we consider that the spirits described in the *Goetia* had such a specific connection with King Solomon it is perhaps not surprising that Goossens decided to use *'Djinn'* as his magical name. One can also speculate on how.

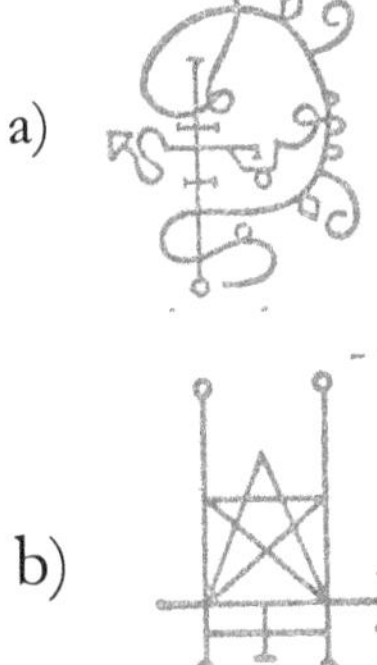

c) 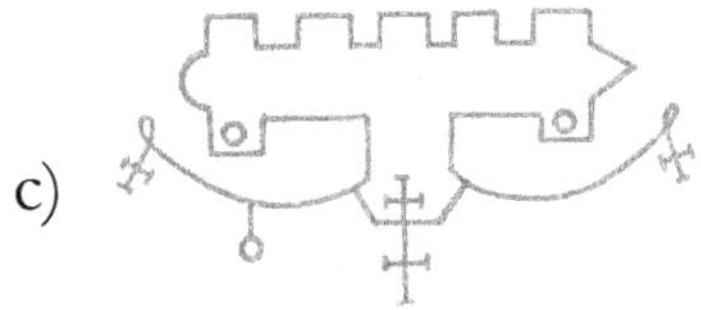

d) 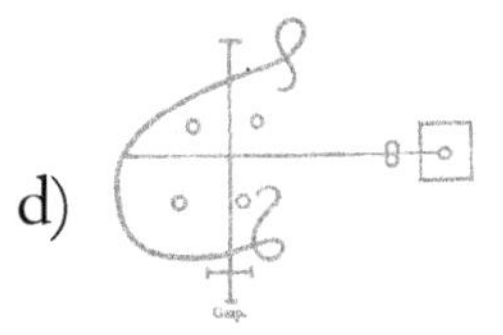

DEMONIC MAGICAL SEALS (SIGILS) FROM THE LESSER KEY OF SOLOMON *(*GOETIA*): A) ASMODAY B) ASTAROTH C) BELIAL D) GAAP*

Goossens himself would have made use of the magical sigils contained in the grimoire. In a fourth letter, headed ' Salaam Roie', Goossens mentions that he has just located a second-hand copy of 'G.B' and is leaving it propped up against Norton's door awaiting her return. In all probability the initials 'G.B' refer to a major biography of Crowley, *The Great Beast*, by John Symonds, published in London in 1951.[22] Goossens goes on to explain that he had 'since read it and [it] confirms all I knew of A.C. though [it] exaggerates certain things overmuch...' In the same letter Goossens also mentions that he has been experimenting with 'cakes of light' and he adds a note of encouragement to Norton: 'I hope you will have better luck with the unguent...' We should note here that the reference to 'cakes of light' is a specifically Crowleyan allusion to sex-magick ritual offerings made from meal, honey, menstrual blood and sexual secretions (See Appendix A). Given Goossens' Thelemic orientation, one can assume that Goossens would have employed magical seals, or sigils, in the same way that Crowley did: by activating them with semen. It is possible that Goossens wanted to be alone with Norton in the Blue Mountains to simulate the Great Beast / Scarlet Woman sex-magic partnership advocated by Crowley and this could explain why Greenlees was not invited on this particular occasion. Also, as mentioned earlier, it was part of Crowley's Thelemic approach to sex magic to masturbate and ejaculate onto magical sigils like those contained in grimoires like the *Goetia*. As O.T.O. historian P-R. Koenig has noted:

> ... masturbating on a sigil of a demon or meditating upon the image of a phallus would bring power or communication with a (or one's own) divine being...In the IXth degree, one identifies oneself with an ejaculating penis. The blood (or excrements) from anal intercourse attract the spirits/demons while the sperm keeps them alive.[23]

ALTARS, RITUAL PARAPHERNALIA, AND VOODOO-INSPIRED PERFORMANCES AT BROUGHAM STREET

Mention has already been made of the fact that Rosaleen Norton's Brougham Street attic apartment was small, and that when she and Gavin Greenlees resided there during the 1950s and early 1960s this space had to double as a living area and a ritual working area. Detective Trevenar took photographs of the attic studio during his police raid and these are of interest because they reveal details of the ritual aspect of the room. It is also useful to compare the Trevenar photographs with details reported in Dave Barnes' profile article on Norton, 'I am a Witch!' published a little over a year later, and also with photographs reproduced in Norton's autobiographical article 'Hitch-hiking Witch', published in February 1957.

According to Barnes, Norton's Pan altar was located 'at the end of the room'.[24] A large figure of Pan had been painted directly onto the wall, and the large, opening photograph in the Barnes article shows Norton sitting next to various ritual implements and assorted bric-a-brac, including stag antlers, a candle-holder, dishes and pine-cones. The word 'Pan' is visible on the wall beneath a circular mirror on the left-hand side. Taking into consideration details from D.L. Thompson's 1955 interview, referred to earlier, it can be established that the altar dedicated to Pan was located at the northern end of the attic, the northern quarter being the traditional position for a witch's altar.[25] However, Detective Trevenar's photographs, taken in October 1955, indicate that there were two altars in the Brougham Street attic. We know from other sources that the second altar was dedicated to Hecate.[26] The Hecate altar, which was located at the southern end of the attic, was squeezed in between an armchair and a wooden wardrobe whereas the Pan altar stood alone and effectively occupied the full width of the room, with heavy curtains draped on both sides.

A photograph taken of Norton in the Brougham Street apartment in 1957[27] shows that the stag antlers had been moved from the Pan altar to a different location and were now part of an improvised altar in the corner of the room.

The mounted stag antlers which in the Barnes article had been photographed on the floor in front of the Pan altar (December 1956) had now been lifted up and placed on top of an item of furniture that is not clearly visible but which is waist-high. In the 1957 photograph Norton stands beside the antlers pointing a curvy snake implement which seems to be some form of magical wand. A solitary candle is also placed centrally on the altar in front of the antlers. Behind the candle and the antlers a medium-size, heavily framed mirror has been mounted so that the mirror-glass is visible between the V-shape of the antlers. Although one could surmise that Norton may have moved some of her ritual paraphernalia around the room to pose for photographs, there are some indications that the altar arrangement in the 7 February 1957 photograph had some degree of permanency. The name Uriel has been painted on the wall. In the Golden Dawn magical tradition Uriel is the archangel of Earth and his 'sphere' is in the North. The words 'Of the Air' are also visible in the photograph and have been painted on the wall behind Norton. This would locate the element Air in the West. In the Golden Dawn tradition the element Air is associated with the archangel Raphael and is traditionally located in the East as part of the well-known Banishing Ritual of the Lesser Pentagram. Golden Dawn magicians used the Banishing Ritual to purify the ritual circle by banishing negative influences and establishing the protection of the four elemental archangels over the sacred space. West is the symbolic domain of Gabriel, the archangel of Water, but the photograph indicates that Norton has located Air in the West. This suggests that Norton did not follow the Golden Dawn system exactly although the very presence of a reference to the archangel Uriel behind her ritual altar suggests that part of her magical practice was based on familiar Golden Dawn procedures. Since Uriel is traditionally associated with the North and is a symbol of Earth it was appropriate that her main ritual altar, dedicated to Pan in his role as the ancient Greek God of Nature, was located symbolically in the North.

Norton's Hecate altar, however, appears to have been at least partially improvised. In the photograph introducing Barnes' article 'I am a Witch!' (December 1956), in which Norton posed in front of the mural of Pan, a small female mask has been mounted on the wall; here it has become part of the altar backdrop, nestling between Pan's outstretched hand and his chin. In Detective Trevenar's photographs of the Pan altar, taken approximately a year earlier, the female mask is missing. However this same female mask occupies a central position in Trevenar's photograph of the second altar, which Norton confirmed to D.L.Thompson was dedicated to Hecate. Barnes remarked in his 1956 article that this particular female mask had a surprising resemblance to Norton herself, and she may have used it to reinforce her sense of symbolic and personal connection with both Pan and Hecate, on different ceremonial occasions.

Norton confirms in the Thompson article that the ritual initiations which took place at Brougham Street were dedicated to 'the presiding deities' of the coven, Pan and Hecate, and that neophytes were required to take an oath of allegiance to these deities.[28] Norton also confirmed in an interview with *Sun* journalist Nan Javes that she commenced all magical rituals by burning incense to each of the deities involved, and that she placed a 'protective magical circle' around the ritual area where she was working.[29] Countering charges made by Anna Hoffmann and others, that Norton had conducted the Black Mass in her Kings Cross apartment, Norton told Dave Barnes in her December 1956 interview that she had never attended ceremonies at which there had been blood sacrifices. She then added, no doubt in jest, '...And I've never drunk bat's blood either...'

An insight into what a ritual gathering at Brougham Street may have been like, at least on some occasions, is provided by a short section of film footage in the 1964 television documentary on Kings Cross, *The Glittering Mile*, and by reference to one of the drawings in *The Art of Rosaleen Norton* (1952) titled *Rites of Baron Samedi* [Plate XIV]. In *The*

Glittering Mile, a robed Rosaleen Norton performs a banishing ritual by inscribing a pentagram in the air with her ceremonial *athame*, or dagger, thereby purifying and defining the 'sacred space' associated with the ritual. However we know that Norton was not always robed during her ceremonial performances because she confirmed in her interview with D.L. Thompson that 'ceremonial attire ranges from nakedness to full regalia – robes, hood, sandals and accessories...'[30] Norton appeared during her interview with Thompson clad only in her dark leather 'witch's apron',

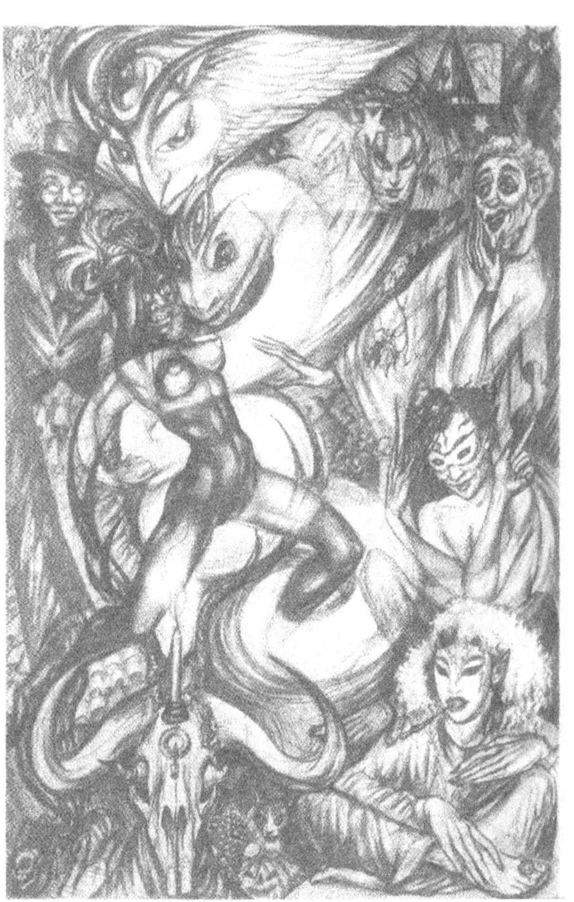

Norton's Rites of Baron Samedi *– a work which reflects Norton's keen interest in Voodoo. The figures in the lower right-hand corner are probably based on Norton and Greenlees*

naked from the waist up, although she later posed for a photograph wearing a cat's mask in addition to her apron. During Norton's interview with Thompson her fellow coven members wore ritual animal masks to disguise their identity and referred to each other by using code names like the Rat and the Toad, thereby remaining effectively anonymous. The exotic masks brought back into Australia by Sir Eugene Goossens were intended for ritual use in the coven.

Unpublished manuscript notes by Rosaleen Norton accompanying the draft manuscript for her book *The Art of Rosaleen Norton*, describe *Rites of Baron Samedi* as an 'impression of a personal experience... a ritual invocation' and Gavin Greenlees' accompanying poem portrays the scene as a 'saturnalia'. Norton acknowledges the influence of Voodoo in her magical rituals and confirms that 'the mantelpiece, the bison's skull, the candlelight, cats etc are part of the artist's living quarters'. In *Rites of Baron Samedi* we are shown a ritual performance where an exotic dark-skinned woman is dancing naked in a state of frenzy in the centre of a small room while a small gathering of ritual devotees look on enthusiastically. Some of these onlookers are wearing masks: one of them, who may be Norton herself, sits cross-legged wearing sandals and smoking a cigarette in a long cigarette-holder. Behind her sits a young man wearing a simple unadorned mask: this figure closely resembles Gavin Greenlees. A candle has been mounted atop the bison's skull – perhaps to honour Janicot, Norton's principal servitor and familiar-spirit – and magical forces throng through the room. The winged face of Baron Samedi and a coiled snake rise up around the dancer, suggesting that the ritual combines elements from Voodoo, Tantra and sex magic. The dancer meanwhile thrusts her naked body into full view as she embodies the frenzied lust of Erzulie. Erzulie is a Voodoo goddess known for her love and passion, an archetypal figure associated with the sensual magic of the Left-Hand Path, and here the dancer has become her Priestess as she is 'possessed' by the Voodoo deity's inspirational magical energies.[31]

* * *

Rosaleen Norton was undoubtedly a woman who embodied potent passions and primal desires, and as a close friend of hers has confirmed to me recently, 'she loved sex in all its various forms'. So it is hardly surprising that sex magic should have featured so prominently in her occult repertoire. As we have seen, invocations to Pan, Hecate, Lucifer and Lilith – and regular contact with her Spirit-in-Chief, Janicot – were key elements in her approach to ritual magic. However, they do not represent the full story. Norton was very much a visionary magician, and her astral plane ventures with a small group of inner-circle intimates were also crucial to her occult perspective. This particular dimension of Norton's magic – her quest for astral encounters – is the subject of the next chapter.

1 Grant's major publications on sex magic and the Western esoteric tradition (and which relate specifically to practices in the British branch of the Ordo Templi Orientis which he headed until his death in 2011) date from 1972 and for this reason cannot be said to have substantially influenced Norton, especially with regard to Norton's relationship with Gavin Greenlees and Sir Eugene Goossens: indeed, it is not known whether she was familiar with any of Grant's writings during the last seven years of her life when they were available. In any case, Grant was substantially influenced by Crowley and regarded himself as a Thelemite – a follower and spiritual disciple of the Great Beast 666. Much of Grant's sex magic practice derived directly from Crowley although Grant greatly

expanded its scope and range.

2 Literally 'Light in extension' , a reference to the alchemical light of consciousness projected into the darkness of matter – see *J. Symonds, The Great Beast: the Life and Magick of Aleister Crowley*, Granada, London 1973: 87 fn.

3 Crowley's *Konx Om Pax* was Item 187 in the catalogue issued by The Antique Bookshop & Curios, McMahons Point, Sydney, in October 1996. Items 188-193 were etchings and drawings by Norton. Two copies of the 1952 edition of *The Art of Rosaleen Norton* were also listed for sale – for $600 and $550 respectively – both volumes listed as 'very scarce'.

4 The image of *Fohat* (plate XIX) was published in the 1982 facsimile reprint edition of *The Art of Rosaleen Norton* without incurring any legal charges of alleged obscenity.

5 These notes were passed in manuscript form by Norton to the book's publisher, Walter Glover, who in turn passed them on to me c.1981, when we were working together on the re-release of *The Art of Rosaleen Norton* as a facsmile edition. These unpublished notes remain in my possession.

6 *Daily Mirror*, Sydney, 1 June 1956.

7 See N. Heseltine, *Capriol for Mother, a Memoir of Philip Heseltine (Peter Warlock),* Thames Publishing, London 1992: 75. Nigel Heseltine was Philip Heseltine's son.

8 Philip Heseltine is included in a list of O.T.O. members provided by O.T.O. practitioner Ithell Colquhoun in *Sword of Wisdom: MacGregor Mathers and the Golden Dawn*, Spearman, London 1975: 207-208.

9 Ibid.

10 Ibid.

11 Ibid.

12 Dr Marguerite Johnson of the University of Newcastle obtained copies of these letters from film-maker Geoff Burton in 2003; he in turn had obtained them from Trevenar. See M. Johnson 'The Witching Hour: Sex Magic in 1950s Australia', conference presentation, University of Melbourne, 2004.

13 The *djinn* or *genii* are daemons or spirits in the Islamic tradition and were traditionally considered to be a higher order of beings than humans, and composed of 'more subtle' matter. According to Islamic belief, the genii ruled the earth before the creation of Adam and were regarded as an intermediate race of spirit-beings between angels and humans. They were believed to have special architectural skills and, according to the *Qur'an*, were employed by King Solomon to assist in erecting his magnificent temple.

14 M. Johnson, 'The Witching Hour: Sex Magic in 1950s Australia', loc. cit.

15 D. Salter, 'The strange case of Sir Eugene and the witch', loc.cit.:21.

16 I. Shah, *The Secret Lore of Magic* [1957], Abacus, London 1972:11

17 There are several versions of the *Goetia* in the British Museum. The listing of spirits contained in the *Goetia* was first published by Johann Weyer, also known as Johannes Wier, or Wierius, (1515-1588) a German demonologist who chronicled the hierarchy of Hell in his *Pseudomonarchia Daemonum* (1577).

18 *Goetia: the Lesser Key of Solomon. The Book of Evil Spirits*, trans. S.L. MacGregor Mathers with an introduction by Aleister Crowley, [1904] De Laurence, Scott & Co., Chicago 1916:45-46 (re-issued by Weiser, Boston 1995).

19 Other than the *Goetia* (and putting aside Mathers' translation of *The Greater Key of Solomon* which contains the magical pentacles of planetary spirits but not 'seals') the only other publication of a similar nature, readily available to Goossens, would have been A.E. Waite's *The Book of Ceremonial Magic* (London: 1911) or its predecessor, *The Book of Black Magic and Pacts* (London 1898). *The Book of Ceremonial Magic*, which contains all the material from the earlier book, is a collection of grimoires and composite rituals rather than a single grimoire, and there was no connection between this publication and Aleister Crowley. Crowley was, in fact, very dismissive of Waite.

20 *Goetia: the Lesser Key of Solomon. The Book of Evil Spirits*, trans. S.L. MacGregor Mathers with an introduction by Aleister Crowley, loc cit.1916:31.

21 Ibid:46.

22 J. Symonds, *The Great Beast*, Rider, London 1951.

23 P-R. Koenig, 'Spermo-Gnostics and the O.T.O' , available at www.cyberlink.ch/-koenig/spermo.htm. According to Dave Robinson, a Wiccan practitioner who knew Norton well during the late 1950s and early 1960s and paid several visits to Brougham Street, Norton was very fond of anal sex – as was Gavin Greenlees. Robinson maintains that both Norton and Greenlees were bisexual and he also speculates that Norton's death from colon cancer in 1979 may have been either directly or indirectly connected with her practice of anal sex. Personal communication to the author, 10 October 2006.

24 D. Barnes, 'I am a Witch!', loc cit.: 8.

25 See R.E. Guiley, *The Encyclopedia of Witches and Witchcraft*, Facts on File, New York 1989: 8. North is the traditional location for the Witch's altar, although occasionally practitioners locate it in the East.

26 See D.L. Thompson, 'Devil Worship Here!' loc cit. 6 October 1955: 4.

27 See photograph in R. Norton 'Hitch-hiking Witch', *Australasian Post*, 7 February 1957: 11

28 See D.L. Thompson, 'Devil Worship Here!' loc cit. 6 October 1955: 37.

29 N. Javes, 'Witches of Sydney', *The Sun*, Sydney, 7 February 1969.

30 D.L. Thompson, 'Devil Worship Here!' loc cit. 6 October 1955: 37.

31 In Voodoo, Baron Samedi is a *loa*, or deity, whose role is lord and guardian of the cemetery. Baron Samedi is an aspect of Guede, 'god of the grave'. Erzulie is the *loa* of love, wealth, beauty and prosperity – and the lunar wife of the sun god, Legba.

10
Astral Transformations

In addition to their sex magic rituals and improvised forays into the realm of Tantra and Voodoo, members of Norton's inner circle attempted 'aerial' or 'out-of-the-body' journeys comparable to the flights which medieval witches claimed to undertake en route to the 'Witches Sabbath'. In the Middle Ages there was a common belief in Europe that witches could fly through the air,[1] transporting themselves by means of a broomstick, pitchfork or shovel. During the medieval witch-trials many witches were also accused of paying homage to the Devil by kissing his posterior. Occult historian Rosemary E. Guiley claims that the so-called osculum infame or 'kiss of shame' was mentioned in 'virtually every recorded account of a witches' sabbat, most confessions of which were extracted under torture'.[2]

Some medieval witches were believed to 'ride' in the company of demons that were able to transform themselves magically into such animals as goats, cows, horses or wolves. In a characteristic case from Simmenthal, near Bern, reported during the witch trials held there between 1395 and 1405, a number of people were convicted of witchcraft and subsequently burnt at the stake:

> The witches at Simmenthal were accused of constituting a sect that met at Church on Sunday morning, not for mass, but to worship Satan. There they performed rites including homage to the Devil. They stole children, killed them, and then cooked

> and ate them, or else they drained them of juice in order to make ointments. With the ointment, they changed themselves into animals, rendered themselves invisible, or rubbed their bodies in order to obtain the power of flying through the air. [3]

In another case, which occurred in 1587, Walpurga Hausmannin, a midwife, was tried and burnt at the stake in Dillingen:

> Arrested and tortured, she admitted to having intercourse with the Devil and making [a] pact with him, riding out at night on a pitchfork, trampling on the consecrated host, keeping a familiar named Federlin as a lover, manufacturing hailstorms, and committing a long list of maleficia...[4]

The notorious text *Malleus Maleficarum*, (*The Hammer of the Witches*), compiled as an instructional manual by the Inquisitors Jacob Sprenger and Heinrich Kramer and first published in Germany in 1486, also includes a chapter on witches' flight titled 'How they are transported from place to place'. Sprenger and Kramer write:

> Now the following is their method of being transported. They take the unguent ['flying ointment'] which...they make at the Devil's instruction from the limbs of children, particularly of those whom they have killed before baptism, and anoint with a chair or broomstick; whereupon they are immediately carried up into the air, either by day or by night, and either visibly or, if they wish, invisibly... at times [the Devil] transports the witches on animals, which are not true animals but devils in that form; and sometimes even without any exterior help they are visibly carried solely by the operation of the Devil's power.[5]

However, during the Renaissance some observers began to suspect that, at least in some cases, the phenomenon of 'aerial flight' ascribed to

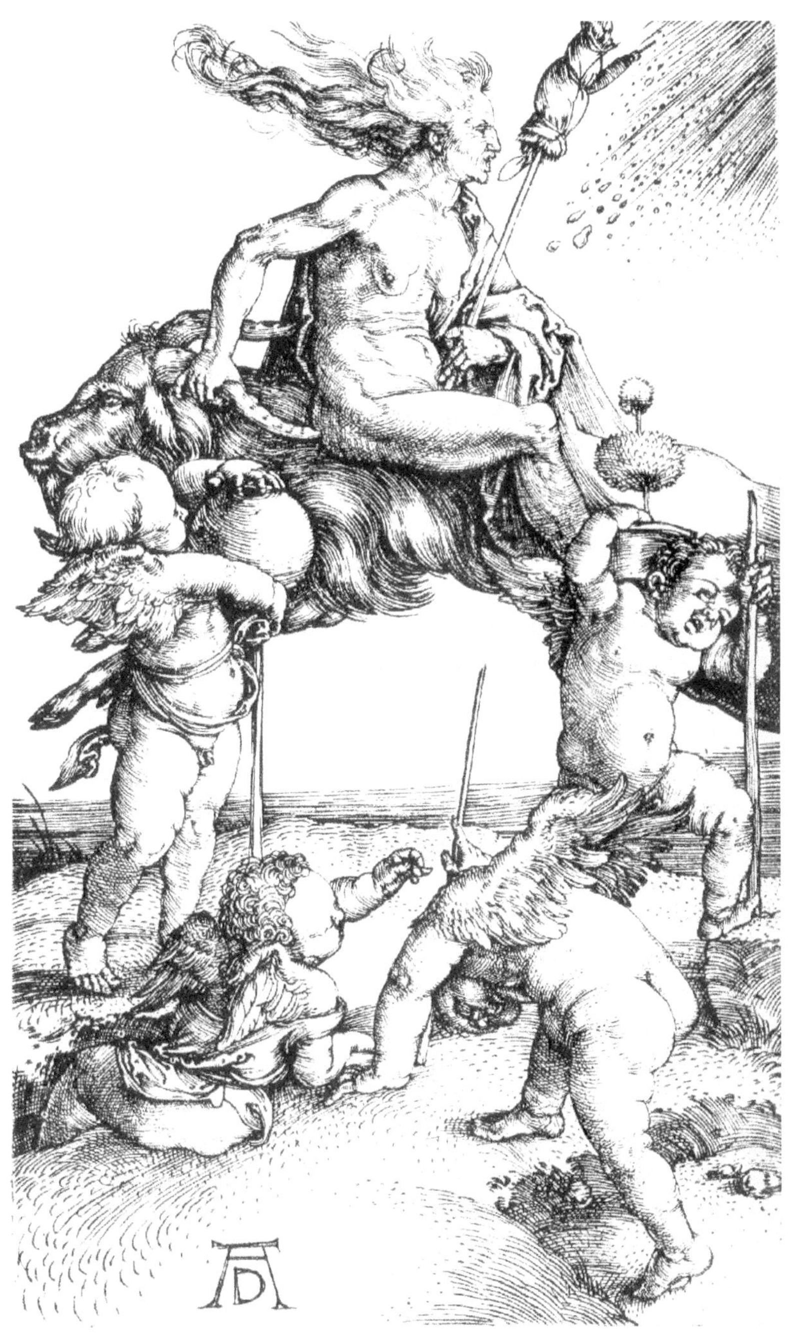

WITCH FLYING TO SABBATH, AN ETCHING OF A WITCH RIDING ON A GOAT TO THE SABBATH. ETCHING BY ALBRECHT DURER C.1501

the witches was an internal perception rather than an external reality. The 16th century scientist Giambattista della Porta, a colleague of Galileo, was one who entertained such doubts:

> ...An old woman came to my notice, [one of those] whom they call screech-owls [striges], from the resemblance between the night-owl [strix] and the witches [strigae], and who suck the blood of tiny children in their cradles; who promised of her own accord to bring me answers in a short while. She ordered all of us who were gathered there with me as witnesses to go outside. Then she stripped off all her rags and rubbed herself very thoroughly and heartily with some ointment (she was visible to us through the cracks in the door). Then she sank down from the force of the soporific juices and fell into a deep sleep. We then opened the doors and gave her quite a flogging; the force of her stupor was so great that it had taken away her senses. We returned to our place outside. Then the powers of the drug grew weak and feeble and she, called from her sleep, began to babble that she had crossed seas and mountains to fetch these false answers. We denied; she insisted; we showed her the black-and-blue marks; she insisted more tenaciously than before.[6]

Della Porta proposed a physiological explanation of the witches' ointment, noting that after the witches had concocted a brew which included such ingredients as aconite and 'sleep-inducing nightshade' [Solanum somniferum] and after they had anointed 'parts of the body, having rubbed them very thoroughly before' so that the 'flesh may be loose and the pores open', they then experienced a drug-induced aerial sensation which also included strong elements of fantasy:

> Thus, on some moonlit night they think that they are carried off to banquets, music, dances, and coupling with young men, which they desire most of all. So great is the force of the imagination and the appearance of the images, that the part of the brain called memory is almost full of this sort of thing; and since they themselves, by inclination of nature, are extremely prone to belief, they take hold of the images in such a way that the mind itself is changed and thinks of nothing else day or night.[7]

The contemporary American anthropologist Dr Michael J. Harner, has noted more recently, however, that it could be the potency of the psychotropic herbal ingredients within the witches' ointments, rather than 'the force of the imagination' referred to by Della Porta, that produced the aerial sensation reported by the medieval witches. Harner notes that when the German scholar Karl Kiesewetter, who had himself been inspired by the insights of Della Porta, created a witches' ointment and rubbed himself with it, he experienced a dream in which he felt he was flying in spirals.[8] And when Professor W.E. Peukert of Göttingen, Germany, employed a 17th century witches' formula and created a 'flying ointment' containing belladonna, henbane and datura, he too experienced a bizarre altered state of consciousness. Peukert and some of his colleagues rubbed the ointment onto their foreheads and into their armpits, and the result was dramatic: 'They fell into a twenty-four hour sleep in which they dreamed of wild rides, frenzied dancing, and other weird adventures of the type associated with medieval orgies.'[9] Jeffrey B. Russell similarly supports the view that the sensations of flight and ecstasy induced by the medieval witches' ointments could be induced by the innate chemical properties of herbal ingredients like aconite and nightshade [belladonna]: '... aconite depresses the cardiovascular system and produces sensory semi-paralysis, while...nightshade induces delirium, excitement, and sometimes unconsciousness.'[10]

In his correspondence with Rosaleen Norton, Eugene Goossens makes reference to astral encounters with mythic beings, to magical unguents, and also to the notorious osculum infame, or 'kiss of shame'. There are also references to 'familiars', or magical helper-spirits, and to the idea of transforming into animal forms. Collectively these references indicate a strong interest in the medieval witchcraft tradition. Based on the level of detail provided in the correspondence, it would appear that Goossens and Norton were seeking to validate aspects of medieval witchcraft practices in a personal, experiential way. In an undated letter which opens 'Roiewitch', Goossens writes that

> contemplating your hermaphroditic organs in the pictures nearly made me desert my evening's work and fly to you by first aerial coven. But, as promised, you came to me early this morning (about 1.45) and when a suddenly flapping window blind announced your arrival, I realised by a delicious orificial tingling that you were about to make your presence felt in a very real sense! [11]

Quite apart from the erotic content of this letter, which is intriguing, Goossens and Norton clearly had a prior arrangement for an 'astral' rendezvous because at the time this letter was written they were physically separated by a substantial distance: other details in the same letter suggest that Gossens posted this letter to Norton either from an interstate location or from Europe. Goossens' letter continues:

> Seriously, you were very definitely here, and you were doubt-

lessly enjoyably aware of what took place. I was in the middle of a rite to A and he had just asked for the 'osculum infame' (which I was about to administer) when you took advantage of my position and administered same to me. A strange hoofed creature was in the room with us – upper and middle parts female, lower centaur, and a pretty crustacean creature with milky breasts also appeared. I will draw it for you when I see you. All night I was in sheer s.m. [sex magic] delight and my offerings

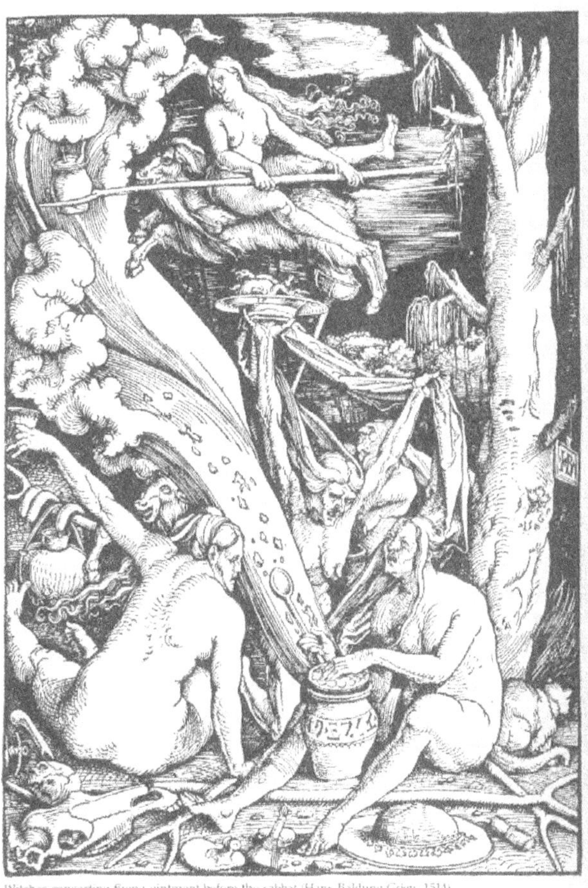

Witches concocting flying ointment before the sabbat (Hans Baldung Grien, 1514)

WITCHS' FLYING OINTMENT. ETCHING BY HANS BALDUNG GRIEN, 1514

were, by results, most acceptable to the beings... More of this later. [12]

Goossens goes on to remark that 'Your description of the triple S.M. Rite (you, G and me) was curious because I was aware of you both as female (G always comes to me as a female) and I was fully present, also in changing form.' This section of the correspondence shows Goossens comparing astral visions with Norton, almost like two enthusiasts comparing dreams, into order to confirm whether both parties (ie. Goossens and Norton) had experienced the same phenomena during the astral encounter. The figure identified as 'A' is clearly not a physical person but a metaphysical entity associated with the Devil because according to the correspondence, 'A' has requested the 'osculum infame', usually regarded as an act of demonic ritual homage, and Goossens has agreed to comply.

We know that Goossens is referring to inner-plane encounters because he uses the expression 'our astral meetings' in another letter when describing similar activities. In that particular letter Goossens also makes reference to 'Asmodeus' and to 'a succubus in the form of Astarte'.[13] Given these references, the metaphysical being referred to simply as 'A' in the first letter could theoretically be either one of these magical entities. Of the two, Astarte is the less likely alternative because she is an Assyrian-Babylonian mother goddess associated with love, battle, war, sex and fertility and there is no cultural connection between her and the notorious 'osculum infame'.[14] On the other hand, Asmodeus was well known to the compilers of medieval grimoires as the demon of lust and lechery, and Goossens' interest in such magical grimoires has already been established.

Possibly derived from the Persian Aeshma Daeva and otherwise known as a 'fiend of the wounding spear' and also as a storm spirit and the personification of rage, Asmodeus – who is sometimes known as Ashmedai – features in ancient Jewish literature as a demon who causes frustration in marriage.[15] Goossens may have become interested in Asmodeus because of his fascination with medieval grimoires like the Goetia. An entity known as Asmoday [a variant on Asmodeus / Ashmedai] is listed in the Goetia as one of the 72 'evil spirits' – here he is described as a three-headed demon with the tail of a serpent.[16] As historian Richard Cavendish notes, Asmoday's three heads are those of a ram, a bull and a man, 'all traditionally lecherous creatures', and in Jewish literature Asmodeus is a demon also associated with lechery: he has the feet of a cock, a bird noted for indiscriminate sexual vigour. Taking into consideration Goossens' magical name, Djinn, it is significant that Asmodeus also has a specific connection with the legendary King Solomon. According to Jewish tradition, Asmodeus was forced by King Solomon, along with other devils, to build his Temple in Jerusalem. However, in his characteristically lecherous manner, Asmodeus pursued one of King Solomon's wives and it was not until the archangel Michael intervened by offering King Solomon a magic ring that this mighty demon could be conquered.[17]

Goossens' 'Roiewitch' letter is of interest for other reasons as well. Goossens clearly conceives of the astral magical encounter referred to above as being one where both he and Norton will be able to jointly observe what is occurring, because he writes: '...you were doubtless enjoyably aware of what took place.' He also shares an implied understanding with Norton that the magical entities that appear in such visionary circumstances are both tangible and experientially real, even if they emanate from other planes of existence. Goossens writes in his letter that 'A strange hoofed creature was in the room with us – upper and middle parts female, lower centaur...' However, this is no fictional centaur from the literature of classical Greek legends but a magical 'god-form' experienced as real within the context of the visionary encounter. When Goossens writes that his offerings 'were, by results, most acceptable to the beings' he is acknowledging that these entities have their own, tangible reality, and that one can interact meaningfully with them, even if their presence can only be fully experienced on the 'inner planes'. Finally, in the same letter there is a notable reference to a triple S.M.[sex magic] rite involving Goossens, Norton and Greenlees. Goossens writes that 'G always comes to me as a female' which in itself is an interesting remark, given that Greenlees was openly bisexual.[18] The letter confirms that on some occasions, at least, the Brougham Street sex magic ritual workings involved a menage à trois – a detail later confirmed by Vice Squad detective Bert Trevenar in an interview with Sydney crime writer Ned McCann in 1999.[19]

Goossens' references to unguents similarly link his correspondence with Norton to the medieval magical tradition. In one of his letters,[20] as mentioned earlier, Goossens makes a passing reference to a substance called Ashtaroth cream which, he writes, is intended 'for you [ie Norton], and no-one else'. As previously noted, Ashtaroth is referred to in the Goetia but, in addition, he is also listed by the ceremonial magician and grimoire enthusiast, S.L. MacGregor Mathers, as one of the Qliphoth, or negative forces, on the obverse, evil face of the Kabbalistic Tree of

Life.[21] Unfortunately, we are not told what was actually contained in the Ashtaroth cream, or why it received its distinctive name.

In another letter Goossens tells Norton that she has begun 'to take almost concrete form' during their recent astral experiments and he says 'I will send you next week, on my return, a pleasant unguent, which applied to you, may perhaps be helpful in this matter' – that is to say, an unguent that would help produce the dissociative effects required for astral encounters. Once again we are not given details of what is contained in the unguent itself, but Goossens adds as an aside that he has been told about this unguent 'by one familiar with these things in Paris, where they are by no means uncommon...' However, Goossens does provide a much more detailed commentary on the use of a magical unguent in another letter which lists the specific procedures Norton should undertake in applying the ointment to her body. It reads: 'Use half level teaspoonful. Massage cream into skin over wide area on inner face of the thigh (between crotch and knee) or on abdomen. Use on unwashed skin. Don't bathe anointed area one hour before or three hours after. Don't use during menstrual period. No man must use this unguent. It would be more than dangerous.' Goossens signs the letter 'Djinn' and then adds some further details: 'Base Cream d'Egypte prepared by Anna (Paris). Herb ointment – blood base. Apply once a day for 3, 4 or 5 days.'

Finally, one needs to ask whether Goossens really believed that he could transform into an animal form on the astral plane, for this aspect of magical practice is clearly connected to the medieval European witchcraft tradition. It has to be conceded that sometimes Goossens adopts a light-hearted approach in referring to occult matters and this factor needs to be taken into consideration. In one letter to Norton,

Goossens mentions jokingly that he sometimes refers to London's Covent Garden as Coven Garden. In another he writes that a large package has arrived by 'daemonic angel carrier', obviously a metaphor for speedy airfreight, and later in the same letter he writes that after being stimulated by Norton's erotic artwork he felt he wanted to fly to her 'by first aerial coven'.

In light of such remarks it is not easy to decide whether Goossens takes seriously the notion of magical animal transformation, or lycanthropy. Is Goossens expressing himself literally or metaphorically when he writes in one of his letters to Norton: 'Even now my bat-wings envelop and lift you, as yours often enfold me, into Arimanic [sic] 22 spheres'? Just prior to making this particular remark Goossens writes: 'You don't know what your long letter means to me; understanding and eloquent they are and happily satisfying to my nature, occult, obscene, and of other worlds and beings. I am mastering many things; in all of which you figure and help.' The latter sentence suggests that Goossens is taking his magical practice seriously, and on the previous page of the same letter he advises Norton that 'the Master, in Paris, passed on a few months back. So no more unguent...' Harner's investigation of witches' ointments, referred to earlier, strongly suggests that in medieval witchcraft it is the unguent that facilitates the perception of animal transformation so it is especially significant that in another letter, when Goossens refers to his 'astral meetings' with Norton, he then goes on to refer to unguents in terms of their specific effects: 'I am however working on an unguent (with the one you have as basis) to bring about our physical transportation.' Goossens seems to be suggesting here that the innate properties of the magical unguent, that is to say, its capacity to produce dissociative effects, could bring about a projection of the 'astral body' onto the inner planes allowing 'transportation' and an ability to engage in visionary encounters ('astral meetings'), as if they were tangible and real. Goossens would surely not have believed that his actual physical body was transported through the effects of the unguent, but given the potency of the unguent he would have had good reason to believe that his 'astral vehicle' could be 'transported' by the flying ointment as it entered an altered state of consciousness. On balance, then, it seems reasonable to conclude that even though Goossens sometimes made whimsical remarks like 'daemonic angel carrier' and 'flying by first aerial coven' in his personal correspondence, he nevertheless believed in the fundamental validity of his magical explorations and 'astral meetings' with Norton.

DRUGS AND HEXINGS

Theoretically one might have expected that Norton would follow Aleister Crowley's well known example of frequently using mind-altering drugs to induce 'magical' states of consciousness. However, it has not been confirmed in any surviving documents that this was a substantial aspect of Norton's magical practice. Crowley was a habitual drug-user and kept meticulous records of his experiences with laudanum, opium, cocaine, hashish, alcohol, ether and heroin.[23] Furthermore, at the end of his life he was addicted to heroin and required regular injections to sustain him. Crowley was probably introduced to the magical use of drugs by his mentor Allan Bennett and when he was in Paris during the 1920s he experimented with *Anhalonium lewinii*, otherwise known as the mescaline-yielding cactus, peyote. However, apart from the use of the dissociative unguents described by Eugene Goossens in his letters, drug-use seems to have been a comparatively minor feature of Rosaleen

Norton's magical practices and may indeed have been more specifically associated with her creative, art-making processes than her ritual activities. It would also appear that, although Norton sometimes liked to present herself to the tabloid press as the 'wicked witch of Kings Cross', spells and hexes did not play a major role in her magical practice.

During legal hearings held at Sydney's Central Court in October 1955 in relation to the charges associated with the controversial Honer/Ager photographs, a psychiatrist, Dr S.J. Minogue, submitted a medical certificate on Norton's mental state. The certificate was dated 18 October 1955 and read as follows: 'This is to certify I examined Miss Norton today. In my opinion she is still suffering from the after-effects of drugs, chiefly Dexedrine and Methedrine, and is incapable of sustained concentration. At the present time I think that the court proceedings would impose too great a strain on her, but she should be much better in a month's time.'[24] Mr. A. Griffith, representing Norton, asked that his client be remanded to 2 December 1955. At the same time it was noted during court proceedings that the Lunacy Court had committed Gavin Greenlees to an institution and he was likely to be there 'for at least six months'.

In addition to using Dexedrine and Methedrine, Norton had also been taking Benzydrine pills. In one of the letters that found their way into Detective Trevenar's possession, Eugene Goossens expresses concern about 'heart attack' symptoms that Norton has referred to in earlier correspondence: Goossens warns her that the Benzedrine tablets she has been consuming are likely to produce such symptoms, 'especially when you've eaten nothing'.

Dexedrine, Methedrine and Benzedrine are all forms of

amphetamine, chemical stimulants that produce temporary states of euphoria, confidence and mental alertness but which are also associated with insomnia and mild irritability. Dexedrine and Benzedrine are both forms of dextroamphetamine, marketed under different brand names and in different strengths. Methedrine is a generic name for methamphetamine, a form of amphetamine associated with heightened sexual awareness. According to the *High Times Encyclopedia of Recreational Drugs* (1978), as amphetamine use continues, or the dose increases or periods of sleep grow less frequent,

> the adverse effects become more severe, the personality is definitely modified, most often afflicted with paranoia and delusions. Even though at first the user may view this development with a certain intellectual detachment, chronic heavy use typically destroys mental balance and the delusions become strikingly real. [25]

In addition to using various amphetamines, it was also reported in the *Sydney Morning Herald* in April 1972 that Norton had admitted to using LSD to gain inspiration for her art.[26] Regarded as an 'amplifier' of emotional states, aesthetic perceptions and sensory input from the subconscious mind, LSD remains one of the most potent psychoactive drugs ever discovered. Derived from ergot (*Claviceps purpurea*) and classified as a 'psychedelic', or 'mind-manifesting' drug, LSD was first synthesized by Dr Albert Hofmann at the Sandoz Laboratories in Basel, Switzerland in 1938 and became a hallmark of the American counter-culture during the late 1960s. LSD had some surprising and distinctive characteristics that would have made it especially attractive to Norton. In particular, she would have been aware that the states of heightened awareness accessed through LSD were often reflected in greater artistic and mystical sensitivity. As psychiatrist Dr Stanislav Grof has noted in *Realms of the Human Unconscious: Observations from LSD Research*:

> Many LSD subjects reported in their sessions unusual aesthetic experiences and insights into the nature of the creative process ...[and another] area in which the use of LSD appeared to be rather revolutionary was the psychology of religion....some LSD sessions had the form of profound religious and mystical experiences quite similar to those described in the holy scriptures of the great religions of the world...[27]

Norton's use of LSD may well be reflected in the intense and vibrant colours associated with some of Norton's artworks during the late 1960s and 1970s, but no substantial documentation has so far emerged regarding her magical, inspirational or artistic use of LSD. Nevertheless, from time to time Norton did seek to change her magical persona and soon she began referring to herself as a 'Coven Master'. During an interview with the noted journalist and writer Robert Drewe, published in the *Australian* newspaper,[28] Norton explained that as 'Coven Master of the Wicca branch of the witch cult' she was now presiding over major ritual meetings four times a year; Candlemas was the next ceremony that would be held in her coven. Perhaps sensing the drama of the occasion, Norton then went on to say:

> We feast, dance and drink. The sexual side of things is very important. We invoke deities and spirits and set to work to formulate whatever we mutually want through spells, and also things that we each want for ourselves. Black magic is a very personal thing. It is an integral part of our lives.[29]

If Norton truly saw herself at this time as 'Coven Master of the

Wicca branch of the witch cult', that is to say, as the Australian counterpart to the British 'King of the Witches', Gerald Gardner (to whom she had sent a copy of her book *The Art of Rosaleen Norton*), she would not have referred to herself as a practitioner of black magic. Gardner and his colleagues were adamant that the Wicca revival in Britain focused very much on fertility rites, the imagery of the Goddess, and the cycle of the seasons, and had nothing whatever to do with black magic, sorcery or Satanism. However, referring to her ritual practice as 'black magic' may have been part of Norton's strategy to impress Drewe during her meeting with him. 'Some of the things they [ie. the witches in Norton's coven] may mutually or individually want,' wrote Drewe in his article, 'include zapping some enemy with a hex or spell, and at this Rosaleen professes to be quite proficient.' Drewe then quotes Norton again: 'I took care of two policemen who were foolish enough to tangle with me...One was soon afterwards forced to resign from the [police] force, and the other, a detective-sergeant, soon found himself pounding the beat again.'[30] Apparently Norton did not provide Drewe with the details of her hexing spell against the policemen in question, and did not seek to validate the effectiveness, or otherwise, of her act of 'black magic'.

There is, indeed, a genuine question-mark over Norton's assertion that she was a practitioner of 'black magic'. As noted earlier, Norton certainly oriented towards the 'dark' side of magic and felt attracted to the Qliphoth or negative forces of the Kabbalistic Tree of Life. However, while she certainly undoubtedly practised Thelemic sex magic, and explored Left-Hand path Tantra and Voodoo-oriented ceremonial practices in addition to various forms of witchcraft, there is little, if any, evidence that she used her magical practices to wreak harm and injury on others.

Norton appears to have been preoccupied at this time with her need to generate her media persona as a 'witch'– a fact alluded to by Norton's publisher Wally Glover. As mentioned above, when Glover first met her Norton did not refer to herself as a witch: 'She resented being called a witch,' writes Glover, 'and had little respect for so-called witches and fortune tellers. Later, I believe, she found it convenient for business to go along with the media and openly declare herself to be a witch.'[31] Declaring oneself to be a 'black' witch may have seemed even more dramatic, and was apparently part of Norton's media strategy from the mid-1960s through to the early 1970s.

Approximately three years prior to her interview with Drewe, Norton had agreed to participate in a television programme titled *Seven Days*, screened on Channel Seven, Sydney, on 13 December 1967. Here she was shown in a pre-recorded filmed interview wearing a goat's head mask and casting a spell.[32] Norton had been interviewed at home by two journalists, Phil Crookes and Bryon Quigley, amidst 'all the paraphernalia of witchcraft, including an altar' and was attended by her pet cat, some salamanders, and a rat named Percy whom Norton said she was training to become a 'familiar'. Norton apparently sought to charm Crookes and Quigley by presenting the same 'witch-hexing' persona that she would emphasise in her media interview with Drewe three years later. Crookes describes what took place during the filmed interview at Norton's home:

> We found Miss Norton to be a charming person. She offered us a cup of tea and told us quite frankly that these days she was

> engaged mostly in hexing various people by request. She said it was the work she most preferred and added – with a mild degree of pride – that she performed it with some notable success. During the casting of the spell, Miss Norton wore a goat's head mask and rang bells, poured water and burnt incense, all the time chanting to summon the forces of the earth god. After it was all over – it took about three and a half minutes – we asked Miss Norton what spell she had cast. She told us she had cast a spell to assure the production success. The next day our camera broke down...'[33]

The facts associated with this particular media episode speak for themselves. Norton seems to have been far removed from being a master 'hexer'– a sorcerer renowned for casting dark and evil spells – but was clearly willing to oblige in projecting a particular media image when the television cameras were rolling.

1 This phenomenon is sometimes referred to in the literature of medieval witchcraft as 'transvection'. See R.H. Robbins, *The Encyclopedia of Witchcraft and Demonology*, Crown, New York 1959: 511 et seq.

2 R.E. Guiley, *The Encyclopedia of Witches and Witchcraft*, loc cit: 185.

3 J.B. Russell, *Witchcraft in the Middle Ages*, Cornell University Press, Ithaca, New York 1972: 216.

4 J.B. Russell, *A History of Witchcraft*, Thames & Hudson, London and New York 1980: 84. *Maleficia* are acts of 'low magic' or sorcery.

5 Chapter III , J. Sprenger and H. Kramer, in M. Summers (ed.), *Malleus Maleficarum, (The Hammer of the Witches)* , Folio Society, London 1968: 68-69.

6 G.B. Porta, *Magiae Naturalis siue de Miraculis Rerum Naturalium* [1562] , II xxvii, quoted in M.J. Harner (ed.) *Hallucinogens and Shamanism*, Oxford University Press, New York 1973: 138-139.

7 Ibid: 138.

8 Ibid: 139.

9 Ibid: 139, quoting M.B. Krieg, *Green Medicine: The Search for Plants that Heal*, Bantam, New York 1966:53.

10 J.B. Russell, *Witchcraft in the Middle Ages*, loc.cit 1972: 54.

11 Quoted in D. Salter, 'The strange case of Sir Eugene and the witch', loc.cit.:18.

12 Ibid.

13 In medieval demonology a succubus is a demon or discarnate spirit that takes the form of a woman and has sexual intercourse with a man. Her male counterpart is the incubus.

14 See P. Turner and C.R. Coulter, *Dictionary of Ancient Deities*, Oxford University Press, Oxford, UK 2000: 75.

15 R. Cavendish, 'Asmodeus' in *Man, Myth and Magic*, Marshall Cavendish, London, 1970: 141.

16 Asmoday is the 32nd. demon, or 'evil spirit', listed in the *Goetia*. See *Goetia: the Lesser Key of Solomon. The Book of Evil Spirits*, trans. S.L. MacGregor Mathers with an introduction by Aleister Crowley, loc cit.1916:32. See also A.E. Waite, *The Book of Ceremonial Magic* [1911], University Books, New York 1961: 204 and I. Shah, *The Secret Lore of Magic*, loc cit: 191.

17 Asmodeus is sometimes associated with Samael, a leading fallen angel and, in the Jewish religious tradition, one of the supreme sources of evil.

18 This has been confirmed by several commentators, most recently Dave Robinson who knew both Norton and Greenlees and was a frequent visitor to Brougham Street during the late 1950s and early 1960s. personal communication from Dave Robinson to the author, 10 October 2006.

19 McCann asked Trevenar whether the Honer/Ager photographs obtained by the Vice Squad showed 'Eugene buggering Greenlees as well as Roie', to which Trevenar replied 'Yeah' – although he added that the photographs he had were 'mainly between Roie and Greenlees'. Interview between McCann and Trevenar conducted

on 19 June 1999: see http://nedmccann.blogspot.com.

20 Johnson letter 1, loc cit.

21 Ashtaroth is the dark or 'evil' aspect of Chesed, associated with the Roman god Jupiter in the system of 'magical correspondences' drawn up in the Hermetic Order of the Golden Dawn (see Chapter Five). Interestingly, Mathers identifies Asmodeus as the Qliphotic counterpart to Mars, Roman god of war, who is associated with Geburah on the Kabbalistic Tree. See S.L. MacGregor Mathers (trs.) *The Kabbalah Unveiled*, George Redway, London 1887:30.

22 Given Norton's orientation towards the 'night' side of magic, the unusual reference to 'Arimanic spheres' may well be connected to a comment made by Goossens in aother letter in relation to Norton's amazing 'Arimanes dream episode'. Ahrimanes (old Persian) and Ahriman (Pavlavi) were names ascribed to the Zoroastrian deity Angra Mainyu, the 'wicked, evil prince of demons' who was 'the chief opponent of Ahura Mazda, the god of light'. See P. Turner and C.R. Coulter, *Dictionary of Ancient Deities*, Oxford University Press, Oxford, UK 2000: 53.

23 See A. Crowley, *Confessions of Aleister Crowley*, Hill and Wang, New York 1969, republished Arkana, London 1989; L. Sutin, *Do What Thou Wilt: A Life of Aleister Crowley*, St Martin's Press, New York 2000 and S. Skinner (ed.), *The Magical Diaries of Aleister Crowley*, Weiser, York Beach, Maine 2003.

24 Reported in both the Sydney *Sun* on 20 October 1955 and the Sydney *Daily Telegraph* on 21 October 1955.

25 See M. Aldrich, R. Ashley and M. Horowitz (ed.), *High Times Encyclopedia of Recreational Drugs*, Stonehill Publishing, New York 1978: 110.

26 See 'Two skulls for Rowie', *Sydney Morning Herald*, Sydney, 8 April 1972. Norton also offered LSD to me when I interviewed her in her Roslyn Gardens apartment in 1977. I declined this invitation, knowing from my own previous experiences that LSD is an amplifier of subconscious processes. Norton's flat was eerie and confining and would probably have resulted in a terrifying 'trip'.

27 S. Grof, *Realms of the Human Unconscious: Observations from LSD Research*, E.P.Dutton, New York 1976: 3.

28 R. Drewe, 'At last the law gives witches a spell', *The Australian*, 8 January 1971.

29 R. Drewe, 'At last the law gives witches a spell', loc cit., 8 January 1971.

30 Ibid.

31 W. Glover, unpublished written notes on Norton and her background given to the author c.1986 to assist the research for *Pan's Daughter* (Sydney 1988).

32 'Witch is so charming', television programme preview, *Sun*, Sydney, 5 December 1967.

33 Ibid.

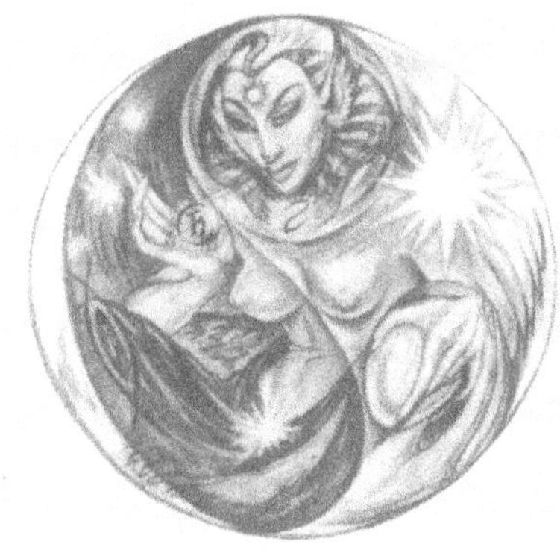

11 Pagans and Christians

Meanwhile, Roie was fully engaged in developing her persona as a practising witch. The British Witchcraft Act of 1735 had not yet been repealed in New South Wales – that would not happen until January 1971 – but Roie was earning a day-to-day living making charms and performing hexes for a small group of clients, as required. Now and then she would also dash off new occult paintings to sell. These would range in price from £5 for a small work to £100 for a large canvas. Alternatively, she would recycle her more familiar themes, such as portraits of Pan and Lucifer.

During this time Roie moved house several times. For a number of years she lived at 8 Hargrave Street, East Sydney, a house owned by Gavin Greenlees' parents. On 17 January 1964, Gavin returned on temporary release from hospital and caused havoc, threatening to kill Roie with a knife and hurling her furniture and ritual bric-a-brac into the street – it was one of his 'schizophrenic' attacks. Detective Sergeant Harry Giles, who was called to the house by anxious neighbours, found Gavin leaning over a sink running a knife across his throat.

'Did you harm anyone?' asked Giles anxiously. 'Not yet,' said

Greenlees, 'but it is time for me to kill her.' He then pointed to the basement. 'She is in there...'

Giles found Roie kneeling before an altar and muttering to herself, and he then arrested both Gavin and Roie as vagrants. Roie was also charged with 'offensive behaviour' and using 'indecent' language. Later she was acquitted of the vagrancy charge and fined £2 for using indecent language. Gavin was sentenced to a month's jail for carrying a knife with intent to harm - a ridiculous sentence in view of his mental condition.[1]

After this episode Roie moved in for a while with her sister Cecily [Boothman], who was living in a flat in Kirribilli, overlooking the Harbour. Cecily had always been close to Roie and made her feel welcome if ever she needed a 'retreat'. By now Cecily was Roie's only close surviving relative – Phyllis had died in 1946, having spent most of her married life in Armidale. So it was only natural that Roie would turn to Cecily in times of crisis. Roie stayed with Cecily for several months and to get her mind off the troubles in the Cross she liked to spend long sessions meditating beneath a large Moreton Bay Fig tree which grew in the garden and which is still there today. It is clearly visible despite new building developments in the area and is located reasonably close to the Sydney Harbour Bridge on the northern foreshore. This became a symbol in several of Roie's later paintings – a type of fairy-tale tree that reached up to the heavens and which was a secure haven for Nature-spirits as well as for Roie herself.

Roie did not stay in Kirribilli, however, and by June 1967, she had recovered from the trauma of Gavin's attack and was back again in the Cross, this time in rather squalid quarters in Bourke Street, between William Street and Woolloomooloo. Roie's new home was one of several derelict houses, most of them in total disrepair and likely candidates for a demolition order. Hers was one of the better ones – yellowish brown in colour with cracked stone and paint-peeled bricks at the front, a battered front door, and a bent iron railing.

Roie lived in a small room some ten feet by six, dimly illuminated by an oil lamp. She had constructed a new altar in the fireplace and had retained her familiar range of occult ornaments, various masks, portraits of Pan, trinkets, a metal gong and several small statuettes of cobras. She also still had her pets – a rat named Percy and his friend, Moonstone. A year or so later, she would also acquire a pet turtle while walking in Centennial Park. During this particular stroll she slipped into a pond and when she emerged she found she had a little turtle in her hand! She interpreted this as a gift from Pan.

When *Sun* journalist Nan Javes called on her in February 1969, Roie was still living in Bourke Street and continuing to refer to herself as a 'Coven Master'. Perhaps aware that her bohemian image was fading a little, and that she was fast becoming a figure from the past, she put on a more aggressive front, depicting herself and the unnamed members of her witchcraft as potentially hostile and dangerous.

'It's ridiculous to say we never do harm,' she told Javes. 'If we weren't capable of fighting people through hexes and charms we couldn't survive. But here we are in the twentieth century, stronger than ever. Of course, we sometimes do good turns too. The sort of people I might put a spell on are those who harm me or someone close to me. I mightn't do it immediately if the circumstances weren't propitious, but you can bet your life I'd get around to it in time - and it works!'

Roie then explained to Nan Javes that she was now conducting ceremonies in her home to honour each of the four major Witches' Sabbaths – Candlemas, May Eve, Lammas and Halloween – and taking her responsibilities very seriously. 'It's not easy to become a witch,' she emphasised, making signs in the air with her raven's claw cigarette holder. 'There are many people eager to join who would only be nuisances. Millions try to hinder us, but they'll never succeed in stamping us out.' [2]

According to Nan Javes, Roie was now claiming to have two hundred followers in Sydney and hundreds more throughout the country. Her efforts in recruiting neophytes to the pagan cause might have gone largely unnoticed, however, had it not been for rumblings from within the Anglican Church. A number of vocal fundamentalists within the ultra-conservative Sydney diocese had long been arguing that the occult was influencing school children and that there was an increasing and alarming interest in such pagan diversions as astrology, tarot cards and ouija boards. So in 1974 it came as no surprise when the Anglican Archbishop of Sydney, Marcus Loane, agreed to the establishment of a Commission of Inquiry into the Occult. It was only the second such enquiry in a Protestant country since the Middle Ages.

DEVILS EVERYWHERE

The whole area of the occult had really been opened up by the release of the film *The Exorcist* in 1974, for this had provoked great excitement in ecclesiastical circles, including a rush of candidates for Christian exorcism as well as widespread condemnation of the film as an incitement to diabolical evil. This was despite the fact that the film told of a girl who had become possessed as a result of playing with an ouija board, and presented the story with clear divisions between good and evil. 'Mention the Devil and he will appear' seems to have been the motto of those who rushed into print to condemn *The Exorcist*, and the film certainly did have the effect of focusing the attention of the press onto the occult revival which had burst onto the world scene in the early 1970s. Church ministers reported large numbers of people seeking exorcism or healing as a result of seeing the film, and the press in Australia continued its occult sensationalism with tales of witches and warlocks, Satanism in the suburbs, and the perils of playing with ouija boards. Headlines throughout 1974 continued to feed this hysteria: 'Church fears voodoo is rife', 'Black magic girl tells', 'Devil worship in Sydney', 'Students try black magic at age of 10', and 'Our kids are hooked on the occult'.

The Anglican Commission of Inquiry was chaired by the Dean of Sydney, Lance Shilton, and included four clergymen of the Anglican Church, several of whom had already expressed their fervent opposition to anything vaguely connected with the occult. One them, Rector Peter Hobson, had already acquired a reputation at St Michaels, Surry Hills, for exorcising the 'spirits' of the Hare Krishnas, tobacco smoking, Theosophy, homosexuality, spiritualism and many other 'deviant' practices. The Commission, meanwhile, was required to do three things:

– inquire into the current fascination with the occult, especially among young people
– examine the biblical basis of spiritualism and associated practices, as well as providing warnings against dabbling in the occult
– examine the various current expressions of the occult and its effects

The report of the Commission would then be published to provide guidelines 'about the attitudes Christian people ought to take and any action the Church as a whole ought to pursue'.

The Commission of Inquiry received widespread publicity and

submissions from all sorts of people – Christians, occultists, Christian occultists, academics, teachers and psychologists – and on 13 August 1975, the report was released. It began by stating that the 'most sinister' of all modern 'crazes' was occultism and Satanism, spread by the mass media; furthermore, it was quickly becoming respectable. The report suggested that interest in the occult was related to the increase in violence and pornography in literature since occultism could provide pornography 'with a religious base to work from'.[3]

The general conclusion of the Inquiry as to why there was such a current fascination with the occult reflected the opinions of several churchmen: the failure of organised religion, the loss of personal identity and meaning in life resulting from the sterility of modern technological society, and the fact that this in turn left a vacuum filled by alternative belief systems disapproved of by the Church. The Commission was especially interested in the opinion of its psychiatrist member, Dr David Collison, who had developed the concept of a 'possession syndrome'. This was characterised by mental disturbance following involvement in occult practices, but it was difficult to define in terms of conventional diagnostic labels. Furthermore, this 'possession syndrome' failed to respond to conventional medical treatment. In fact, conventional treatment was thought to make the condition worse. Dr Collison believed that exorcism could be effective, though, and he had begun to use it in working with patients afflicted by the syndrome. He also counselled his colleagues that psychiatric disturbances resulting from involvement in the occult were becoming much more common and could lead to great mental suffering and disturbance – and perhaps even suicide.

The Commission was also especially concerned with the

paraphernalia of the occult – Tarot cards, ouija boards and various 'alternative publications' – and suggested that if there was legislation to protect children against inflammable nightwear, the same legislation could perhaps be applied to protect them from the occult! It recommended that the media should present the occult in a realistic way, mentioning the harmful effects as well as the fascination. It also declared that there

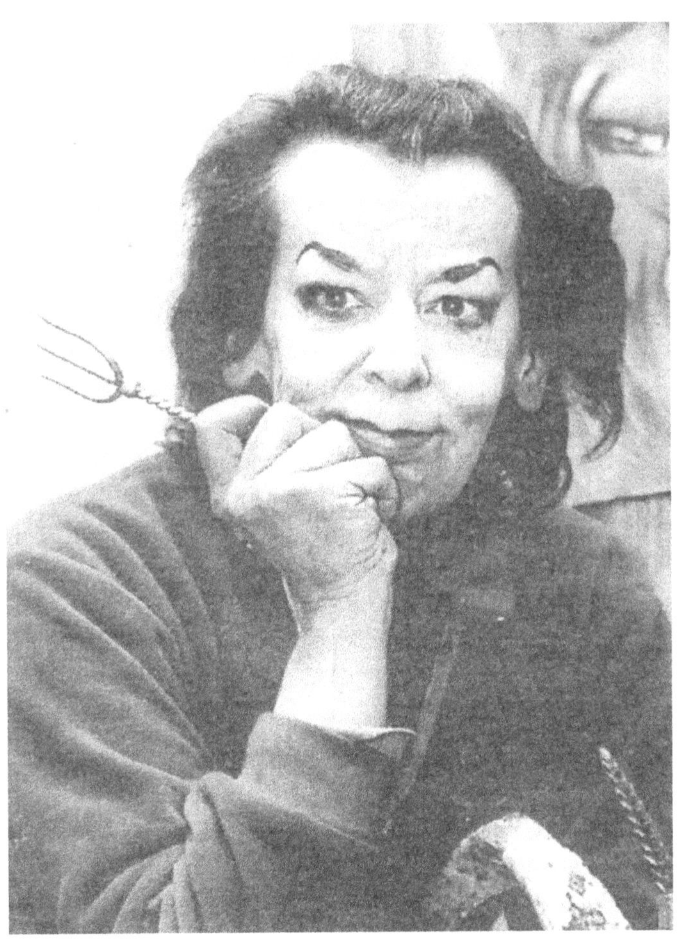

ROSALEEN NORTON – A PHOTOGRAPH TAKEN IN 1975

was a need for restrictions on occult literature and equipment, just as there were already restrictions on objects linked to violence or pornography. And the Commission also recommended that the space currently devoted to horoscopes and fortune-telling in popular magazines and newspapers should be replaced by articles on the Christian faith, since this was the religion 'nominally accepted by the majority'. The report produced spectacular results in the press. For weeks after its release, the tabloids featured dramatic headlines based on its findings. There were also numerous illustrations of medieval witches, images from *The Exorcist*, and sinister photographs of modern occult practitioners. Predictably, journalists were now especially keen to have a response from Rosaleen Norton.

When Gus de Brito of the *Sunday Mirror* tracked her down in August 1975, Roie was living in the basement of a block of flats in Roslyn Gardens, down the hill from the El Alamein fountain in the direction of Rushcutters Bay. Looking a little haggard, but as 'witchy' as ever and wearing an occult medallion around her neck, Roie stood in the doorway of her flat and pronounced on the Church's findings. Perhaps surprisingly, she agreed with Dean Shilton's view that amateurs meddling in the occult could get themselves into deep water. 'Magic can send you round the bend,' said Roie with a twinkle in her eye. 'It is as dangerous as drugs.' She then went on to explain that the real danger lay in people without any knowledge of magic or witchcraft attempting rituals that they had read about somewhere. 'They can release various entities that they don't know anything about,' said Roie, 'and such people have no idea how to handle these entities...' Roie did not agree, however, with the proposed ban on ouija boards. Theoretically, she conceded, school children could contact spirits using equipment like this, but she personally 'couldn't see any danger in it'.[4]

This appearance in the tabloid pages was one of Roie's last pronouncements to the media. She was now already withdrawing into obscurity and restricting her day-to-day contacts to just a few close friends and her sister Cecily, who now lived down the corridor in the same block of flats. It was an increasingly private existence, and that was the way Roie liked it. As Cecily told me later, Roie was quite happy by herself. Accompanied by her two pet cats, she lived among a litter of easels, paintings and books, and liked to watch the fish swimming gracefully in her aquarium. She also spent a lot of time listening to classical music – Mozart, Stravinsky, Beethoven, Bach and Sibelius being among her favourites. And although her flat had a dark and somewhat gloomy sitting room, it did open out onto a courtyard and a profusion of greenery – a secluded corner of Nature. During the summer months Roie loved sitting in the sun near her French windows, beside a red pot containing an umbrella plant, reading her books on magic and mysticism. She had also retained her youthful habit of spending long hours in the bath in the evenings. Ever a 'night' person, Roie loved lying in the soap suds sucking oranges, drinking endless cups of tea, or alternatively sipping Italian Strega liqueur – the ultimate witch's drink. These, for her, were the true luxuries of life.

Nevertheless, in recent years she had suffered from intermittent bouts of sickness. This hadn't alarmed her unduly, even though she sometimes felt down on her energy. But towards the end of 1978 she suddenly became sick, and required hospital tests. Her doctor subsequently told her that she had cancerous growths in her colon and there would have to be an operation. At first it was thought that the surgery was totally successful but this proved not to be so, and the cancer quickly recurred.

Late in November 1979 Roie was taken to the Roman Catholic Sacred Heart Hospice for the Dying at St Vincents Hospital, Darlinghurst, the end clearly in sight. Here she was attended during her final days by Sister Jacinta de Capo, who was apparently unaware of Norton's bohemian reputation. 'If she was a witch,' she told journalist Ned McCann many years later, 'she was a very nice one.'[5]

Rosaleen Norton was well aware that her situation was terminal. Shortly before she died she told her friend Victor Wain: 'I came into this world bravely; I'll go out bravely.' And she was true to her word. Unrepentant in her worship of Pan, unintimidated by the crucifixes all around her in the hospice, and a pagan to the end, she departed this life on 5 December 1979.

* * *

Roie was gone but certainly not forgotten. Moves were soon afoot to auction a large collection of her paintings, which until now had remained in storage and had been seen by very few people. The man behind the auction was Don Deaton, a printer who had also owned several pubs and hotels where Roie's works had been displayed over the years.

The link between Roie and Deaton went back several years. Deaton owned the Hotel Manly, the Prince of Wales in the Haymarket, and also a pub at Collector, on the Federal Highway north of Canberra. Roie used to drink regularly at the Prince of Wales and would pay for her gin and tonics with paintings. When the Apollyon cafe in Kings Cross was marked for demolition in 1970 to make way for the new Eastern suburbs freeway, Roie asked Deaton to take the paintings which had been on display there, and store them in the basement of the Prince of Wales instead. All of the paintings which would later be exhibited for auction

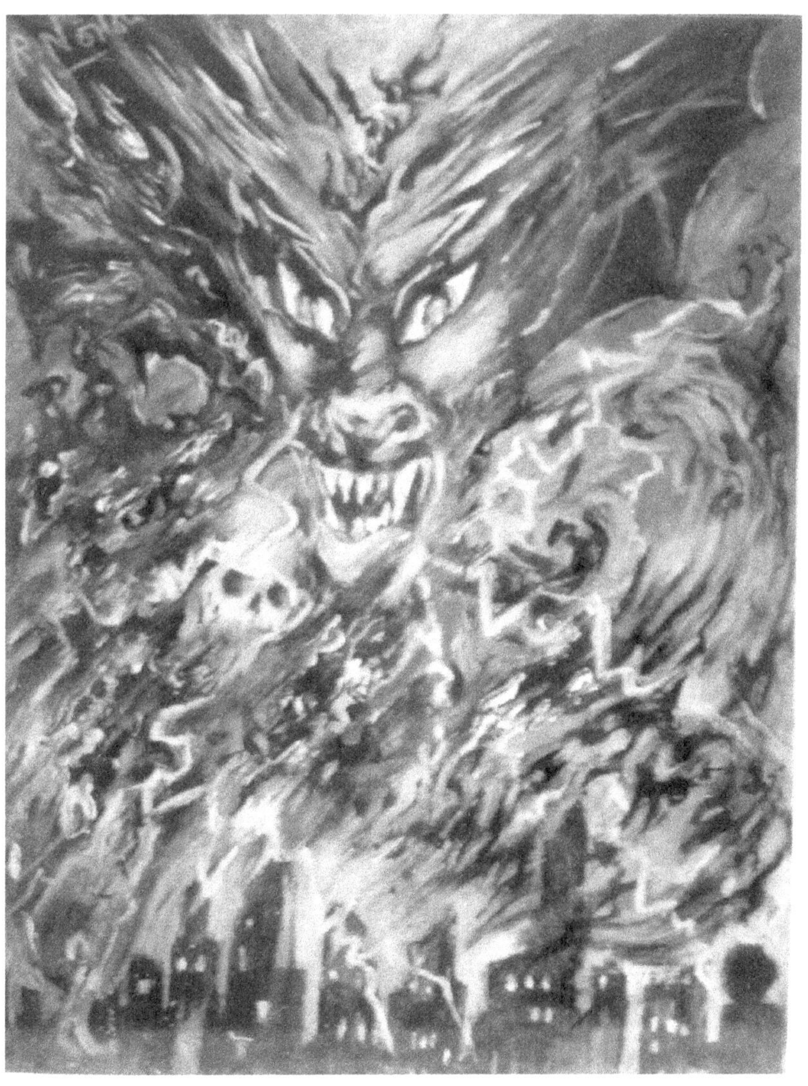

Fur Fur the Storm Demon – *one of Norton's less impressive later works*

were works from this collection. Deaton later maintained that by virtue of his agreement with Roie the paintings were his property, a point strongly disputed by Roie's sister Cecily, who believed that the paintings now belonged to her as next of kin.

In February 1981 advertisements appeared in several Sydney newspapers announcing a forthcoming art auction at the Wentworth Hotel. Scheduled to go under the hammer on 2 March were such works as *Changing Times* by Sali Herman, *Bomboro Castle* by Sir Arthur Streeton, *Wimmera Landscape* by Arthur Boyd – and twelve works by Rosaleen Norton. These included *Masque of Eidolons*, a drawing which had been published in *The Art of Rosaleen Norton*, a large and garish oil painting titled *Devil Worship*, and minor works like *The Rabbit* and *The Gomblins*. Few of these paintings were sold at the Wentworth and they would not have been seen again until Wally Glover's re-publication of *The Art of Rosaleen Norton* nearly two years later.

Wally had long since retired as editor of *The Pastrycook's Review*, but despite the obscenity charges which had caused his bankruptcy in the 1950s he still had a hankering to republish the book once again. This time fortune would smile on him. He was able to regain the copyright to Rosaleen's paintings from the Official Receiver in Bankruptcy in May 1981 and this coincided with an accident compensation payment to him of around $11,000. Wally realised he had enough money at his disposal to reissue the book as a facsimile edition.

Wally contacted me [Nevill Drury] around this time, following the publication of a book I had co-authored on the occult in Australia titled *Other Temples, Other Gods,* and he commissioned me to write a new introduction for the forthcoming publication. Apart from the addition of four colour plates and the new introduction, *The Art of Rosaleen Norton* would be republished in a format identical to the 1952 edition. This time there would be 1000 copies for general trade distribution and 50 limited edition copies bound in red leather for collectors. It seemed unlikely that there would be charges of obscenity this time, and hopefully no plates in the book would need to be blacked out! As it transpired, publication was able to proceed with a minimum of fuss.

Earlier, Wally Glover had suggested to Don Deaton that he display a selection of Rosaleen's works in a gallery to accompany the release of the facsimile edition. So from 1-7 October 1982, Deaton held a concurrent exhibition in the upstairs gallery at Exiles Bookshop near Taylor Square, this time for the specific purpose of selling off the remaining paintings by 'slow auction'. Intending purchasers were asked to indicate their choice of painting and to provide a maximum bid for the selected work. Deaton would later inform the successful bidders of their purchases.

Few of the exhibited works showed the skill of Roie's early paintings and drawings. Thirty-seven paintings were displayed, including *The Cauldrons*, *Asmodeus*, *Dionysus*, *The Bells*, a large work called *The Seance*, and an obscure and rather amateurish painting titled *Fur Fur the Storm Demon.*

As it turned out, the paintings did not go to individual buyers but to a single collector, Jack Parker, who purchased them *in toto* for $5000. Like Deaton, Parker was in the hotel business and he wanted Rosaleen's works for display in his Southern Cross Hotel at St Peters, in south Sydney. However the paintings did not go down well with patrons of Parker's hotel. Interviewed in the *Daily Telegraph* on 22 December 1984, Parker reported that two thirds of his patrons, most of them truckdrivers, made no bones about the fact that they hated them. Parker quickly sold the paintings to a private buyer.

While the Parker collection consisted mostly of minor or poorly executed works – the sort of paintings Roie dashed off quickly to make some extra money – a new publication released around the time of the Parker sale provided a clear indication of Roie's real ability as an artist. In 1984 Wally Glover issued a work which he titled *A Supplement to The Art of Rosaleen Norton*. This small book, with a spiral binding and colour prints individually mounted on cream art paper, was of considerable interest because it contained reproductions of nineteen works shown at the University of Melbourne in 1949.

At the time of the publication of the facsimile in 1982, many of these paintings had not yet come to light. However, following a radio interview, Wally Glover received a letter from Mrs Y. Raphael-Oeser, whose late husband had been Professor of Psychology at the University of Melbourne at the time of the exhibition. Fortunately, many of Roie's original works had been photographed as colour transparencies, thus making quality reproduction possible, and these works became the highlight of the new book.

It seemed that the story of Rosaleen Norton would conclude with the second of Wally Glover's publications. However, two other significant events were to occur after her death – the staging of a short two-act play based on her life, and the premature demise of Gavin Greenlees. In December 1982 I received a call from Wally Glover telling me that a play titled *Rosaleen – Wicked Witch of the Cross* would soon open at Sydney's Tom Mann Theatre. Written by Barry Lowe and directed by Roddie

Thomas for the Hullabaloo Theatre Company, the production starred Jane Parker as Rosaleen and Alan Archer as Pan.

An invitation to the opening night provided me with the opportunity to meet Gavin Greenlees for the first time. He had recently been allowed to leave the Alma Mater Nursing Home in Kensington and, with Wally, was able to watch himself portrayed on stage for the first time. Wally Glover's role was performed by Peter Laurence and Gavin's by Christopher Lyons.

Unfortunately the play itself had most of the weaknesses of an amateur production – it was unconvincingly acted and was not acclaimed a critical success. However it did attempt to portray Rosaleen sympathetically as 'a victim of an era in which her lifestyle had no hope of being understood'. The programme for the play also made it clear that while the script was based on the life and times of Rosaleen Norton 'poetic licence [had] been taken with some episodes in her life and there [was] no intention that the play be literally factual'.[6]

Wally Glover, always a jovial character, seemed greatly amused by the play, while for Gavin it all seemed to belong to the distant, and often painful, past. Frail and drawn from many years spent in hospitals and psychiatric institutions, Gavin had been devastated by Roie's death. He had been so upset that he hadn't been able to attend her funeral, and although he was still seeing Roie's sister Cecily quite frequently, the loss of Roie produced a great void in his life.

Fortunately, he did have other pursuits to distract him temporarily from his gloom. He told me his main interests now were writing a novel and pursuing his ongoing enthusiasm for European literature. He was also preparing for a trip to Germany with his language tutor. However, as events turned out, these interests were not enough to sustain him. I did not see Gavin again but learnt of his death later that year, like most people, by reading about it in a newspaper. Gavin had returned from Germany and was living in a flat in the Sydney suburb of Woollahra. His body was found slumped over a table next to a bowl of soup, and police investigating his death said there were no suspicious circumstances. Gavin was just fifty-four years old and the date was 5 December 1983 – four years to the day after the death of Rosaleen Norton.

1 *Daily Mirror*, Sydney, 23 February 1964.

2 Nan Javes, 'Witches of Sydney', *The Sun*, Sydney, 7 February 1969.

3 For an overview of the Anglican Commission of Inquiry into the Occult see N. Drury and G. Tillett, *Other Temples, Other Gods*, Methuen, Sydney 1980.

4 Gus de Brito, 'A Witch's Warning', *Sunday Mirror*, Sydney, 17 August 1975.

5 McCann, N., interview with Sister Jacinta de Capo, July 1998. See 'And Dangerous to Know' published on http://nedmccann.blogspot.com.au/2005/09/blog-post_1126598873608270086.html, 13 September 2005.

6 For reports of the play see *Campaign,* Sydney, January 1983 (pp.50-51) and February 1983 (p.40).

Appendix A
The rise of Thelemic Sex Magick

Aleister Crowley (1875-1947) remains the best known and most influential occultist of the 20th century and, perhaps predictably, was a major influence on Rosaleen Norton – *Magick in Theory and Practice* (1929) is listed in the bibliography in *The Art of Rosaleen Norton* alongside titles by Dion Fortune, Papus and Eliphas Lévi. And although Rosaleen Norton actively encouraged her controversial persona as a witch – a persona fed in turn by the tabloid media in Sydney during the 1950s – her rebellious libertine personality and practice of sex magic, inspired by Crowley and his teachings, align her as much with *Thelema* as with modern Wicca.

CROWLEY'S THELEMIC REVELATION

The Thelemic practice of sex magick derives specifically from a transformative spiritual event that occurred during Crowley's visit to Cairo in 1904. Crowley would come to believe that the revelatory communication itself emanated from the ancient Egyptian gods, via an entity named Aiwass (or Aiwaz) whom Crowley believed to be a messenger from Horus. Paradoxically Crowley's personal revelation would also come to acquire a quasi-biblical orientation for it led him to regard himself henceforth as the Beast 666 referred to in the *Book of Revelation*. Crowley's life and career as a ceremonial magician would subsequently focus on the ongoing personal quest to find the ideal Whore of Babalon – Crowley's variant spelling[1] – or Scarlet Woman, with whom to enact the philosophy of *Thelema*, or magical will. According to the doctrine of Thelema, Crowley's sex-magick encounters with his Scarlet Women – there would be many more than one – were sacramental acts confirming Crowley's role as Lord of the New Aeon. According to the revelation detailed in *Liber Al vel Legis* (*The Book of the Law*) Crowley's doctrine would supersede Christianity and all the other outmoded religions that had constructed barriers to spiritual freedom, and the way this would be achieved was through the power of sexuality.

Liber Al vel Legis summons the Scarlet Woman to 'raise herself in pride!' and calls for uninhibited sexual freedom:

> Let her work the work of wickedness! Let her kill her heart! Let her be loud and adulterous; let her be covered with jewels, and rich garments, and let her be shameless before all men. Then will I lift her to the pinnacles of power: then will I breed from her a child mightier than all the kings of the earth. I will fill her with joy...[2]

Crowley came to believe that the so-called Great Work – sacred union, or the attainment of Absolute Consciousness – would be achieved through the sexual union of the Great Beast with the Whore of Babalon. As the late Thelemic writer Kenneth Grant has written: 'The Beast, as the embodiment of the Logos (which is Thelema, Will) symbolically and actually incarnates his Word each time a sacramental act of sexual congress occurs, ie. each time love is made under Will.'[3] *Liber Al vel Legis* also contained instructions relating to ceremonial offerings associated with sacramental sex magic, specifically the preparation of what later came to be known as 'cakes of light'. Preparation of this ritual offering as specified by Ra-Hoor-Khuit, is outlined in III: 23-25 of *Liber Al vel Legis*:

For perfume mix meal and honey and thick leavings of red wine: then oil of Abramelin and olive oil, and afterward soften and smooth down with rich fresh blood. The best blood is of the moon, monthly: then the fresh blood of a child, or dropping from the host of heaven: then of enemies; then of the priest or of the worshippers; last of some beast, no matter what. This burn: of this make cakes and eat unto me.[4]

As one of Crowley's most recent biographers, Lawrence Sutin, has noted:

> There is no evidence that Crowley ever used the fresh blood of a child or an enemy in preparing the cakes. Indeed, in his comment on this verse, written during the period, Crowley was careful to specify that the 'child' was 'Babalon and the Beast conjoined'– that is, the elixir of sexual magic. [5]

The magical elixir itself consisted of the 'ingredients' of sexual congress itself: semen from the male, gluten from the woman's vagina, and preferably fresh menstrual blood, as specified in stanza 24 of Book III of *Liber Al vel Legis.* These ingredients were included in the preparation of the 'cakes of light' which were then consumed by participants as a ritual offering to Ra-Hoor-Khuit. It is clear that Crowley placed great emphasis on the magical elixir because it is later referred to as 'the germ of life' in *The Book of the Unveiling of Sangraal* – part of the 'Secret Instruction of the Ninth Degree' in the Ordo Templi Orientis, which Crowley was able to gradually transform into a Thelemite order after joining it in 1910. In the Ninth degree of the Ordo Templi Orientis, which employs veiled sexual references, the candidate is instructed as follows:

> Now then, entering the privy chapel [the vagina], do thou bestow at least one hour in adoration at the altar, exalting thyself in love toward God, and extolling Him in strophe and antistrophe [sexual lovemaking]. Then do thou perform the Sacrifice of the Mass [ejaculation of semen]. The Elixir [a mixture of semen and female sexual secretions] being then prepared solemnly and in silence, do thou consume it utterly.[6]

THE ARGENTEUM ASTRUM AND VICTOR NEUBURG

In 1907 Crowley established his own magical order, the Argenteum Astrum, or Silver Star. Two years later he commenced production of a semi-annual periodical titled *The Equinox*, as its official publishing arm. Some of the early issues of *The Equinox* contained Crowley's first writings on sex magic rituals. In these writings Crowley identified three types of sexual activity – autoerotic, heterosexual and homosexual – as a way of raising magical energy and he also formulated the notion that sex magic rituals could be dedicated to achieving specific results like financial gain, attaining personal creative success etc. His central idea was that sex magic could enable the practitioner to focus on a specific goal or outcome. The magician would dedicate the sexual activity to the goal of the magical ritual and would hold the image of that goal in his mind at the moment of sexual climax: at that very moment the energy raised during the ritual would be directed to the goal by the magical will. In this way the sex magic practitioner would be able to 'wed the image and the magical power'.

Initially the Argenteum Astrum drew primarily on borrowed sources from the Hermetic Order of the Golden Dawn – the influential late 19th century magical order that Crowley had belonged to at the beginning of his esoteric career. Crowley began rewriting the order's Kabbalistic rituals, employing an amended form of the Golden Dawn grades as well as including some yogic and oriental material of his own. He also published the secret rituals of S.L. MacGregor Mathers' Second Order, the Red Rose and Cross of Gold, in *The Equinox*. Interestingly, although Crowley had made a commitment to the sex magic proclaimed in *Liber Al vel Legis*, he did not initially include it within the grades of his new magical order. Nevertheless the Argenteum Astrum would gradually develop as a vehicle for Crowley's increasingly explicit bisexuality, thereby complicating the apparently clear sex-role distinction between the Beast and the Scarlet Woman delineated in *Liber Al vel Legis*.

One of the early members of the Argenteum Astrum was Victor Neuburg, a young poet who, like Crowley, had studied at Trinity College, Cambridge. Crowley heard about Neuburg from another A.A. member, Captain J.F.C. Fuller, and invited him to his magical retreat in Boleskine, Scotland. Crowley quickly recognised in Neuburg a kindred spirit, and they would soon enter into a homosexual magic liaison tinged with sado-masochistic tendencies, which would last until 1914. Following a painful divorce from his wife Rose in 1909, Crowley went with Neuburg to Algeria where they explored the Enochian magic of the sixteenth century Elizabethan occultists Dr John Dee and Edward Kelley.[7] This process involved the magical evocation of thirty so-called 'Aethyrs' or 'Aires' – a group of metaphysical spirit-entities that included Choronzon, the demon of Chaos. Deep in the Algerian desert, at such locations as Aumale, Ain El Hajel, Bou-Saada, Benshrur, Tolga and Biskra, Crowley summoned the different Aethyrs in turn. Crowley was carrying with him a large golden topaz set in a wooden rose-cross decorated with ritual symbols. Choosing a place of solitude, Crowley would recite the required Enochian conjuration and then use his topaz as a focusing glass to concentrate his attention on the visionary landscape as it unfolded before his gaze. As a result of his Enochian 'calls' Crowley had a number of visionary experiences which were then transcribed by Neuburg as they took place. These visionary transcripts would later form the basis for one of Crowley's most significant books, *The Vision and the Voice*.[8]

After Crowley returned to England the Argenteum Astrum began to grow modestly, building on its core membership which included Captain J.F.C. Fuller and Crowley's Golden Dawn teacher George Cecil Jones. The Argenteum Astrum would in due course initiate around a hundred of Crowley's followers, among them Neuburg's friend and fellow poet Pamela Hansford Johnson, Australian violinist Leila Waddell, mathematics lecturer Norman Mudd from Bloemfontein, and the visionary English artist Austin Osman Spare.[9] Events took a strange turn in London in May 1912 when Crowley was contacted one evening at his Fulham flat by a man named Theodor Reuss. Reuss identified himself as Brother Merlin, head of the German branch of the Ordo Templi Orientis. Crowley would already have been familiar with the O.T.O. because according to occult historian Francis King he had been admitted to its lower grades a year earlier.[10] What surprised the British occultist was Reuss's claim that Crowley had published a statement which revealed the most prized secret of the Order's ninth degree – the sacrament of sex magic.[11] Crowley was initially perplexed by Reuss's accusation and wondered which publication he was referring to. Reuss then reached across to Crowley's bookshelf and pulled down a copy of his recently published work *The Book of Lies*, a collection of magical commentaries and reflections. The offending lines were contained in Chapter XXXVI titled 'The Star Sapphire' which begins with the words: 'Let the Adept be armed with his Magick Rood and provided with his Mystic Rose.' Further on Crowley's text reads as follows: 'Let him drink of the Sacrament and let him communicate the same.'

Crowley pointed out to Reuss that he had not yet been admitted to the ninth degree of the O.T.O, so he was not in a position to reveal its secrets. In 'The Star Sapphire' Crowley had used the Old English word *rood* to mean a cross, and Reuss had assumed that he was referring to the phallus. Reuss had also assumed that the Mystic Rose was a reference to the vagina. Then there was the issue of what 'drinking the Sacrament' could actually be referring to. As they were speaking Crowley realised intuitively that sexual intercourse between priest and priestess must be a culminating event in the ritual of the O.T.O's ninth degree, and he now engaged Reuss in a discussion about sex magic which lasted for several hours. The outcome was that Crowley would in due course become the head of a new magical order to be called the Mysteria Mystica Maxima, effectively an English subsidiary of the German Ordo Templi Orientis.[12] Some time later – in 1922, following Reuss's retirement – Crowley would replace Reuss as the head of the O.T.O. itself, a position he held until his death in 1947.[13]

THE RISE OF THE ORDO TEMPLI ORIENTIS

Two key figures are associated with the early development of the O.T.O in Europe – Carl Kellner and Crowley's visitor, Brother Merlin, otherwise known as Theodor Reuss. Kellner was a wealthy Austrian chemist and industrialist and also a Freemason – he was a member of the Humanitas Lodge, established in Neuhäusl, Austria, in 1871 under the constitution of the Grand Lodge of Hungary. Reuss was an Anglo-German Freemason who specialized in buying and selling Masonic charters, even though he was not recognised by any authentic Lodges in Craft Masonry. According to occult historian Peter R. Koenig, Reuss invented an organization known as the 'Order of the Illuminati' as well as several Rosicrucian societies.[14] While it is evident that Kellner was a businessman and inventor of considerable integrity, Reuss's reputation was more dubious and some historians consider him a swindler. Nevertheless it was through their joint efforts that the organization known as the Ordo Templi Orientis (O.T.O.) would eventually emerge.

Around 1895 Kellner had the idea of forming a private group which could explore various 'Tantric' exercises within a Hatha Yoga circle. Kellner had a long-standing interest in both the Western esoteric tradition and also Eastern mysticism. Kellner is believed to have studied with three Eastern masters – a Sufi and two Hindu Tantrikers – and was also in touch with an American esoteric order known as the Hermetic Brotherhood of Light, which in turn drew on the sex magic ideas of the influential American occultist Paschal Beverly Randolph, whose work and ideas are discussed later in this chapter. Kellner and Reuss had in mind that they would form a new esoteric order that would fuse Craft Masonry, Rosicrucianism and Hindu Tantra. At the time Kellner was one of the few Western figures with a detailed knowledge of Yoga and he regarded 'white sexual magic' as a source of godlike power. Kellner performed Tantric rites with his wife and a small group of disciples in order to produce the so-called 'divine Elixir' – an amalgam of male and female sexual fluids.

Like Kellner, Reuss was also interested in phallic cults and Tantra and would later produce a treatise on sexual worship titled *Lingam-Yoni.*[15] Reuss believed that sexual congress mirrored the cosmic act of creation and that the *lingam*, or phallus, was a key symbol of the creator of the universe. He in turn was responsible for incorporating sexual magic into the upper grades of the O.T.O.[16] Unfortunately Kellner did not live to see the actual establishment of the new esoteric organisation – he became terminally ill in 1904 and died the following year. Reuss was forced to act on his own, recruiting a range of 'Oriental Freemasons' for the new Order and eventually naming it the 'Order of Oriental Templars' or Ordo Templi Orientis. With the assistance of Franz Hartmann and Heinrich Klein, Reuss prepared a constitution for the O.T.O. in 1906.[17]

It is unlikely that Reuss initially regarded the O.T.O as a potential vehicle for Crowley's doctrine of *Thelema* but he was sufficiently impressed by Crowley's ideas that he translated his sex magick ritual, the *Gnostic Mass* (composed in 1913), into German and had it recited at a special O.T.O congress at Monte Verità.[18] Reuss also announced at the same congress that he was translating Crowley's *Book of the Law* into German. Crowley reciprocated the gesture by publishing several major O.T.O. documents in *The Equinox*, among them *Liber LII: the Manifesto of the O.T.O.*[19]

In his *Confessions*, Crowley states that Reuss 'resigned the office [of the Outer Head of the Order] in 1922 in my favour' although even in the official O.T.O History it is conceded that that no evidence or letter from Reuss has ever been found confirming this claim.[20] Nevertheless, Crowley succeeded Reuss as O.H.O. (Outer Head of the Order) in 1922 and would hold this position until his death in 1947. Under Crowley, the

O.T.O.'s original nine degrees were expanded to eleven. The eighth, ninth and eleventh degrees focused on non-reproductive sexual acts including masturbation, the consumption of sexual fluids – referred to earlier as the 'magical elixir' – and homosexual intercourse.[21] According to Peter Koenig other elements of Crowleyan sex magic, in addition to the ritual consumption of semen and vaginal fluids, were also incorporated into the rites of the O.T.O. at this time. They included various forms of sexual visualisation and the act of masturbating on magical sigils:

> Crowley's VIIIth degree unveiled...that masturbating on a sigil of a demon or meditating upon the image of a phallus would bring power or communication with a [or one's own] divine being... The IXth degree was labelled heterosexual intercourse where the sexual secrets were sucked out of the vagina and when not consumed...put on a sigil to attract this or that demon to fulfil the pertinent wish... In the X1th degree, the mostly homosexual degree, one identifies oneself with an ejaculating penis. The blood (or excrements) from anal intercourse attract the spirits/demons while the sperm keeps them alive.[22]

CROWLEY'S WRITINGS ON SEX MAGIC

Crowley produced several short texts on sex magic, some of which are written in veiled symbolic language. These texts include *De Arte Magica* (written in 1914 and also translated and published in Reuss's German-language O.T.O. magazine, *Oriflamme*, in the same year); *Liber Agape*; *Energized Enthusiasm: a Note on Theurgy*, and the notorious, but blandly titled *Emblems and Modes of Use*. Crowley's *Gnostic Mass* and the *Mass of the Phoenix* also contain sex magic references. Despite their often discursive language and veiled symbolism these texts provide intriguing insights into Crowley's philosophy and practice of sex magic.

De Arte Magica was intended as a document for IX° O.T.O candidates. After reminding the reader that 'the Phallus is the physiological basis of the Oversoul'[23] – a statement with which Reuss would surely have agreed – Crowley goes on to describe sex magic methods drawn from both the Jewish Kabbalah and the Hindu spiritual tradition. With regard to the former, Crowley states that 'in the semen itself…lies a creative life which cannot be baulked'. According to Jewish teachings, says Crowley, conjugal love should be a holy act, preceded by ablutions and prayer: 'All lustful thoughts must be rigidly excluded, the purpose must be solely that of procreation [and] the blessing of God must be most earnestly invoked.' However Crowley was also interested in the magical consequences of other types of sexual act:

> All other sexual acts involving emission of semen…attract other spirits, incomplete and therefore evil…nocturnal pollutions bring succubi, which are capable of separate existence and of vampirising their creator. But voluntary sterile acts create demons, and (if done with concentration and magical intention) such demons…may subserve that intention. [24]

Crowley also makes reference to the Hindu concept that *prana* or life-force 'resides in the *Bindu*, or semen'. Certain yogic practitioners, writes Crowley, are able to

> stimulate to the maximum its [ie. sperm's] generation, and at the same time vigorously withhold by will. After some little exercise they claim that they can deflower as many as eighty virgins in a night without losing a single drop of the Bindu. Nor is

> this ever to be lost, but reabsorbed through the tissues of the body. The organs thus act as a siphon to draw constantly fresh supplies of life from the cosmic reservoir, and flood the body with their fructifying virtue … in the semen itself exists a physical force which can be turned to [the] magical or mystical ends of the Adept. [25]

Here we have a clear expression of the concept that the individual human will can harness the life-force in semen and direct it to a specific magical purpose. Writings like *Liber Agape* and *Energized Enthusiasm: a Note on Theurgy*, on the other hand, are much more obscure: they contain veiled symbolism and require more detailed scrutiny. *Liber Agape* is also known as *The Book of the Unveiling of the Sangraal* and was intended as 'a secret instruction of the Ninth degree' in the O.T.O.[26]

Liber Agape begins with a prayer, a salutation to Baphomet[27] and a statement inferring that the Ninth degree of the O.T.O. will reveal occult secrets hitherto associated with the Knights of the Temple (Knights Templar) and the 'Brethren of the Rose Crosse'. The rite itself is described as a 'High Mass to be celebrated in the Temple of the Holy Ghost'. Crowley also employs alchemical imagery in his text, making reference to the 'Medicine of Metals', 'the Philosopher's Stone', 'Tinctures White and Red' and 'the Elixir of Life'. The latter are clearly intended as sexual images. As mentioned earlier, the Elixir of Life refers to the sexual fluids produced and co-mingled in the vagina through sexual intercourse. The white tincture is also described elsewhere in Crowley's sex magic writings as the 'Gluten of the White Eagle'[28] and is a reference to the sexual fluids (and sometimes also the menstrual blood) of the female participant in sex magic. The red tincture is the 'Blood of the Red Lion', a reference to the semen generated by the male participant (Crowley often linked blood symbolically with semen).[29]

Interestingly, *Liber Agape* incorporates within its structure the text of *The Star Sapphire*, previously published as Chapter 36 of *The Book of Lies* – the short work which Theodor Reuss believed betrayed the innermost secret of the Ninth degree of the O.T.O. We are fortunate that a commentary on *The Star Sapphire* has recently been made available by American ceremonial magician Frater Osiris, a former member of the O.T.O., who was privy to the inner-Order *Thelemic* interpretation of the text.[30]

While it is clear at the outset that *The Star Sapphire* is intended as a sex-magic tract, and it comes as no surprise that the *Magick Rood* is the phallus, and the *Mystic Rose* is the vagina, it is perhaps less obvious that the reference to 'make the Holy Hexagram' is an instruction that the man and woman should interlock their heads and bodies in a mutual oral sex position to form the shape of a hexagram.[31] Crowley provides a clue in the aptly numbered Chapter 69 of *The Book of Lies* where he refers to the Holy Hexagram and the 'Double Gift of Tongues'. According to Frater Osiris, 'Making the Rosy Cross' is also a reference to sexual intercourse and the participants should utter the magical exclamation *'Ararita'* three times at the moment of orgasm. The instruction 'Let him drink of the Sacrament and let him communicate the same' is an instruction that the 'sacrament' – the 'elixir' or fluids arising from sexual intercourse – should be consumed by both participants, each providing this elixir to the other. As Frater Osiris notes, 'It is suggested elsewhere in Crowley's writings that the Sacrament be dissolved and absorbed in the mouth to obtain the fullest effect.'[32]

Energized Enthusiasm: a Note on Theurgy (Liber DCCCLX) – a work dedicated to 'IAO, the supreme One of the Gnostics, the true God'[33] – is one of Crowley's most interesting writings on sex magic, combining didactic content with a seemingly autobiographical, yet highly symbolic, narrative written in the first person. Crowley begins by introducing the reader to the idea that divine consciousness is 'reflected and refracted' in works of Genius and in turn feeds on 'a certain secretion… analogous to semen, but not identical to it.'[34] Later Crowley claims that he can always trace a connection between his sexual state and 'the condition of [his] artistic creation' and that what he calls 'energized enthusiasm' is 'the lever that moves God'.[35] In other words, there is a technique of ecstasy, heightened by sexuality, which is directly related to artistic creativity and Genius, and this is a technique that subjects God to the artistic intent and human will. In *Energized Enthusiasm* Crowley writes quite specifically that through 'the sacramental and ceremonial use of the sexual act, the divine consciousness may be attained'.

Later in the same work (which consists of sixteen short chapters) Crowley describes a sex-magick ceremony of the Rose Croix. The ceremony – which is presented in Crowley's text as taking place in a mystical vision – is a High Mass and is conducted in a private chapel. The altar is covered by a cloth which displays the symbols of the Rose and Cross, and at the entrance of the chapel stand a young man and woman 'dressed in simple robes of white silk embroidered with gold, red and blue'. The High Priest presiding over the ceremony is a man of about sixty, with a white beard, and he is accompanied by a High Priestess. Both wear richly ornamented robes, have a 'stately' presence, and embrace each other. Knights and Dames make up the congregation. The chapel is consecrated, the litany begins, and the High Priest takes from the altar a flask which resembles a phallus – an indication that the ceremony about to be performed has a sexual orientation. The High Priestess then kneels and presents a boat-shaped cup of gold (the cup, as a receptive vessel, being traditionally perceived in the Western esoteric tradition as a 'female' symbol, especially in the sexual sense). The High Priest's flask contains wine that looks like fire but which is cool to drink. Crowley somehow receives this as a sacrament – he is an onlooker at the ceremony and feels he is experiencing this sacred rite while in a mystical out-of-the-body state. Crowley writes that he 'trembles' as he consumes this sacred drink, as do other members of the congregation – for the ritual is charged with sacred meaning. In due course the celebrants move down the chapel aisle and the Knights and Dames rise up and give the secret sign of the Rose Croix. The High Priestess discards her robe, stands naked before the congregation, and begins to sing: 'Io Paian! Io Pan!'... A sacred mist now rises up around the participants, heightening the sense of mystery as organ music wafts through the chapel, and the High Priest joins his partner at the altar of the Rose Croix where they both lie down. The celebrants, meanwhile, stretch forth their arms in the shape of a cross...

Presumably the 'Great Rite' is about to be performed by the High Priest and High Priestess – Crowley does not provide us with the details of what happens next. However, given that in the O.T.O. 'Making the Rosy Cross' is a reference to ritual sexual intercourse, it would seem that Crowley's High Mass of the Rose Croix is analogous to the mystic marriage of the alchemical King Sol and Queen Luna who consummate their sacred union and thereby create the 'Elixir of Life'.[36]

Crowley's Thelemic sex-magick ritual, the *Gnostic Mass* (*Liber XV*,

Ecclesiae Gnosticae Catholicae Canon Missae), composed in 1913, is linked thematically to *Energized Enthusiasm* and was written around the same time. The *Gnostic Mass* – Crowley's *Thelemic* (and perhaps also blasphemous) response to the Roman Catholic Eucharist – employs specific sexual motifs and draws on the theme of transubstantiation. Although other minor characters play a part, the Mass focuses on two central figures, the Priest, who bears the Sacred Lance (a symbol of the phallus) and the Priestess, who in this ritual context is deemed to be 'Virgo Intacta' and is identified symbolically with the Holy Graal (the sacred Cup). During the 'Consecration of the Elements', the Priest gives a blessing and oversees the transubstantiation of the 'cakes of light' ('By the virtue of the Rod / Be this bread the Body of God!') and wine ('By the virtue of the Rod / Be this wine the Blood of God'), and during the 'Mystic Marriage and Consummation' the Priest and Priestess jointly lower the Sacred Lance into Cup in a symbolic expression of sexual union. All congregants then partake of the consecrated 'cakes of light' which contain the sexual elixir and which are said to embody 'the essence of the life of the Sun'.

The Mass of the Phoenix (Liber XLIV), by way of contrast, is a simplified form of the Eucharist intended for daily life by the practising Thelemic magician. Despite its simpler form Crowley nevertheless considered it to be just as significant as the *Gnostic Mass*.[37] *The Mass of the Phoenix* derives its name from the mythical phoenix, an alchemical symbol of transmutation and resurrection. The phoenix was said to feed its young on blood drawn from its own breast. First published as Chapter 44 of *The Book of Lies*, the Mass is performed only at sunset and is undertaken as a solitary ceremonial activity. At the climax of the ritual the magician makes the Mark of the Beast [38] on his (or her) breast, either drawing blood directly with a burin (a small sharp knife) or by cutting a finger and inscribing the sign in blood. A cake of light is used to staunch the blood and is then ritually consumed.[39]

Crowley's most controversial work on sex magic, however, is a short four-page article titled *Emblems and Modes of Use*, which was intended as a 'secret' text for the Ninth degree of the O.T.O.[40] Once again, Crowley utilises alchemical imagery, writing that the 'Egg' (Emblem 1) is borne by the 'menstruum [that] the Alchemists call the Gluten [capitals in Crowley's text]. The Egg will be fertilized by the 'Serpent' (Emblem 2). Crowley says that the Serpent is 'the principle of immortality, the self renewal through incarnation, of persistent will, inherent in the "Red Lion" *who is, of course, the operator'* [* *note* – Crowley generally presents his magickal texts from the viewpoint of the male practitioner, even when a woman is involved]. Crowley writes that 'both Lion and Eagle must be robust, in good health…overflowing with energy, magnetically attracted to one another, and in absolute understanding [and] harmony about the object of the operation'. According to Crowley the sex magick operation has to be sufficiently intense that it creates a state of 'Black-Out' where 'the Ego-consciousness itself is abolished'.[41] At this stage, according to Crowley,

> the Will should still continue to create, stopping only when 'the blood of the Red Lion' [ie. semen] is one with the 'Gluten of the White Eagle' and the 'Serpent' and the 'Egg' have fused completely. The result of this fusion is called the Elixir – and numerous other names, eg. The Stone of the Philosophers, the Medicine of the Metals etc., especially the Quintessence.[42]

It would seem from this statement that Crowley believes the symbolism of medieval Alchemy – a key branch of the Western esoteric tradition – should be interpreted primarily in sexual terms. For him the elixir itself has innate magical potency. From a purely pragmatic point of view, it can be used to achieve specific magical outcomes and therefore becomes useful in the practice of sorcery:

> The Lion must collect it – the best method is by suction [ie., sucking it out of his partner's vagina] so as to avoid waste, and share it with the Eagle. It should be absorbed by the mucous membrane [ie through the upper palate of the mouth, rather than swallowed]. A portion is reserved and placed in physical contact with the magickal link, or with a talisman specially prepared for the Operation, and consecrated accordingly. At the very least, some suitable symbol, eg. if you are making an opus for $$ smear the Elixir on a gold coin, or ring; if for health, touch the bare earth, or the patient with it. In any case, be careful to consume it by absorption for it restores with interest any virtue that may have been expended in the work itself. [43]

This is not the only occasion where Crowley refers to the idea of the elixir, or semen, being used to achieve specific magical outcomes. In another short text, *Liber A'Aash vel Capricorni Pneumatici (Liber CCCLXX)* – which is specified as a major (Class A) sex magic document by members of the O.T.O.[44] – Crowley makes a veiled reference to masturbating on demonic sigils by using the magical utterance as a metaphor for ejaculation:

> Let him sit and conjure; let him draw back the hood from his head and fix his basilisk eye upon the sigil of the demon. Then let him sway the force of him to and fro like a satyr in silence, until the Word burst from his throat… that which floodeth

> him is the infinite mercy of the Genitor-Genitrix of the Universe, whereof he is the Vessel.[45]

Crowley's idea that the elixir could be used to activate magical talismans and demonic sigils must have become known to a select number of magical practitioners within the O.T.O. because the same technique surfaces again many years later in the relationship between Eugene Goossens and Rosaleen Norton: this time it is Goossens who wishes to instruct Norton in the sex-magic practice of masturbating on demonic magical seals from the *Goetia.* Goossens presumably learned this technique of sorcery from his close friend Philip Heseltine, who was a member of the O.T.O.[46] and first met Crowley around 1914, during the period when these sex-magick teachings were first being formulated. As far as we know, Goossens himself was not a member of the O.T.O. but his Thelemic orientation strongly influenced Rosaleen Norton, as we have seen.

SEX MAGIC PRIOR TO THE O.T.O.

Sex magic in the Western esoteric tradition did not begin with Carl Kellner, Theodor Reuss and the establishment of the O.T.O. Several researchers have drawn attention to the unique contribution made by the influential 19th century American occultist Paschal Beverly Randolph. Randolph is significant because, as religious scholar J. Gordon Melton puts it: 'Like Crowley, Randolph discovered the essential aspect of sex magick by suddenly combining long-term interests in sexuality and the occult.'[47] The bridging link between Randolph and the O.T.O. is provided by two other esoteric orders, the Hermetic Brotherhood of Luxor, and Randolph's Brotherhood of Eulis.

Born in New York in 1825, Paschal Beverly Randolph was the son of a wealthy Virginian named William Randolph, and a slave woman named Flora Beverly who was of mixed East Indian, European and Madagascan descent. Flora raised her son by herself in a gloomy house on Manhattan Island but when Randolph was five, his mother died during an epidemic and he was placed in an orphanage. Essentially growing up on his own, Randolph taught himself to read and write by copying letters from printed posters and billboards. Classified as a 'free man of colour', he trained as a natural physician and also studied spiritualism and Franz Anton Mesmer's theory of 'animal magnetism', a precursor of modern hypnosis. Randolph worked for the Abolitionist cause before the Civil War and helped raise money for the Black Militias of Louisiana. He also gained a reputation as a trance speaker and spiritualist medium. During the late 1840s he travelled widely in Europe, visiting England, Scotland, Ireland, France and Malta as well as also visiting Egypt, Turkey and Palestine. Intent on seeking out the sources of esoteric wisdom wherever he could find them, Randolph maintained that he received many high initiations while he was in Europe. During his travels he met the famous French Kabbalist and magician, Eliphas Lévi, whose writings and occult ideas would later greatly influence the Hermetic Order of the Golden Dawn. He also met the notable Rosicrucian occultists Kenneth R.H. Mackenzie and Edward Bulwer-Lytton and the eccentric cleric and Rosicrucian historian Hargrave Jennings, who was interested in ancient phallic worship. After returning to the United States, Randolph founded the Fraternitas Rosae Crucis in 1858, the oldest Rosicrucian organization in North America – currently headquartered in Beverly Hall, Quakertown, Pennsylvania. In 1861, after returning to Europe, Randolph was initiated into the Order of the Rose, a group headed by Hargrave Jennings. He then travelled on to Syria where he was inducted as a Hierarch of the Ansaireh before returning to the United States in 1863.

Randolph explored clairvoyant scrying with magic mirrors and also wrote a treatise on the use of hashish as an aid to trance possession. However he became a controversial figure largely because of his ideas on occult sexuality, expressed publicly at a time when such issues were largely a taboo subject. Randolph's Rosicrucian activities were interrupted during the Civil War period but in 1870 he re-established his Rosicrucian organisation in Boston, calling it the Brotherhood of Eulis and using it as a vehicle to explore sex magic.[48] Three years later Randolph published one of his best-known and most controversial books, *Eulis! The History of Love: Its Wondrous Magic, Chemistry, Rules, Laws, Modes, Moods and Rationale, Being the Third Revelation of Soul and Sex*.[49] In *Eulis!* – which derives its title ultimately from the Greek *eos*, meaning 'the dawn, the gate of light' – Randolph provides an account of how he was first initiated into the mysteries of sex magic while travelling in the Middle East:

> One night – it was in far-off Jerusalem or Bethlehem, I really forget which – I made love to… a dusky maiden of Arabic blood. I of her and that experience learned… the fundamental principle of the White Magic of Love; subsequently I became affiliated with some dervishes and fakirs by whom… I found the road to other knowledges… I am became practically… a mystic and in time chief of the lofty brethren… discovering the ELIXIR OF LIFE, the universal Solvent…and the philosopher's stone.[50]

Basing his ideas substantially on the ritual sex practices of the Islamic Nusairi sect in Syria, Randolph came to believe that the sexual instinct was a fundamental force in the cosmos. Randolph maintained that 'the pellucid aroma of divinity' suffuses the sex act but he also believed that sexual union could become a metaphysical and sacred ritual *only* between married loving couples and *only* when it resulted in full and complete orgasms for both partners. Many years before Aleister Crowley, Randolph proposed that the sexual orgasm could be used to gain practical and tangible outcomes, that is to say, *subject to willed intent, the power of sexuality could be harnessed to produce specific magical results*:

> It follows that as are the people at *that moment* [orgasm] so will be that which enters into them from the regions above, beneath, and round about; wherefore, whatsoever male or female shall truly will for, hopefully pray for, and earnestly yearn for, when love, pure and holy, is in the nuptive ascendent, in form, passional, affectional, divine and volitional, that prayer will be granted, and the boon given. *But the prayer must precede* [the moment of orgasm].[51]

In another text, *The Ansairetic Mystery: A New Revelation Concerning Sex!* (*circa* 1873-74), which was circulated privately to his Rosicrucian followers, Randolph lists over a hundred outcomes that he believed could be achieved or resolved through this type of sex magic. They include topics and issues relating to money matters, marital discord, prolonging life, eliminating disease and charging amulets with life-force. Randolph was unstinting in proclaiming the potency of sexuality but warned that it could lead to both highs and lows in the quest for spiritual awakening:

> The ejective moment…is the most divine and tremendously important one in the human career as an independent entity, for not only may we launch Genius, Power, Beauty, Deformity, Crime, Idiocy, Shame or Glory on the world's great sea of Life, in the person of the children we may then produce, but we may

> plunge our own souls neck-deep in Hell's horrid slime, or else mount the Azure as coequal associate Gods; for then the mystic Soul swings wide its Golden gates, opens its portals to the whole vast Universe and through them come trooping either Angels of Light or the Grizzly Presence from the dark corners of the Spaces. Therefore, human copulation is either ascentive and ennobling, or descensive and degrading...'[52]

Superficially, Randolph's theories of sex magic and tangible outcomes mirror those of Aleister Crowley. However, Randolph's interpretation of sex magic was actually very different from Crowley's. Randolph deplored masturbation and homosexuality and other forms of non-reproductive sexuality and believed that sacred sex could only occur between a loving heterosexual husband and wife. Randolph's approach essentially involved love among *equals*, whereas Crowley sometimes employed prostitutes or other available women who were not personally committed to his magical purpose and who were used purely for sex. Crowley's magical adventure with Victor Neuburg in Algeria, which involved homosexual anal sex, was also an act of ritual sexual *submission* by Crowley and would therefore have failed Randolph's criteria on at least two counts.

Randolph seems to have been far more averse than Crowley to the negative, or *Qliphothic*, realms of primal consciousness that could be unleashed through what Randolph regarded as misplaced acts of sex magic. Nevertheless, Randolph and Crowley would certainly have agreed that the orgasm itself was among the most powerful and profound of all human experiences, and Randolph would also have agreed with Crowley's statement in *Energized Enthusiasm* that through 'the sacramental...use of the sexual act, the divine consciousness may be attained'.[53] For both men, sexuality was a vital key to potency and transcendence.

Robert North, who contributed an introduction to the 1988 edition of Randolph's *Sexual Magic*, maintains that Carl Kellner derived many of the O.T.O. teachings directly from Randolph's instructions for the Brotherhood of Eulis. However, it now appears more likely that the Hermetic Brotherhood of Luxor – which in turn drew on Randolph's sex magic teachings – was probably the specific link connecting Randolph, Kellner and Reuss.

The Hermetic Brotherhood of Luxor was founded in 1870 by the Polish mystic Max Théon who was interested in Hermeticism and looked to ancient Egypt as the source of the Western esoteric tradition. However he was also highly eclectic, embracing the Kabbalah, the Rig-Veda, Tantrism, and elements of Freemasonry. For a time he lived in Algeria, where he formulated what he referred to as the Cosmic Tradition and took the mystical name Aia Aziz ('the beloved'). In 1873 Théon recruited the Scottish occultist and Freemason Peter Davidson, a close friend and colleague of Dr Gerard Encausse (also known as Papus), to join him in administering the Brotherhood. As an initiatory organisation the Hermetic Brotherhood of Luxor first became public in London in 1884, even though it had been in existence since 1870 [54] and its initiations – based on Rosicrucian and Masonic principles – resembled those of the Hermetic Order of the Golden Dawn, established several years later. Théon took the role of Grand Master of the Exterior Circle of the Order while Davidson was appointed Provincial Grand Master of the North (Scotland) and later also the Eastern Section (America). Together, Théon and Davidson made extensive use of ancient Egyptian symbolism in their magical ceremonies. This symbolic emphasis was further developed by Thomas H. Burgoyne, who joined the Hermetic Brotherhood of Luxor in 1883 and helped Théon and Davidson run the organisation from this time on. The early curriculum of the Hermetic Brotherhood also included selections from the writings of the Rosicrucian author Hargrave Jennings as well as Paschal Beverly Randolph. During the 1880s and 1890s Davidson and Burgoyne adapted Randolph's *The Mysteries of Eros* and *Eulis!*, placing more emphasis on practical sex magic in the Brotherhood's curriculum. It seems likely that it is through the reworking of Randolph's sex magic concepts in the Hermetic Brotherhood of Luxor, and in particular through Davidson's close association with Papus in Europe, that Randolph's sex magic teachings eventually attracted the attention of Reuss and Kellner. According to Peter Koenig, Reuss first made contact with Papus in 1901.[55]

Nevertheless, as indicated earlier, there is something of a gulf between Randolph's version of sex magic as the 'White Magic of Love' and the homo-erotic approach to sex magic advocated by Reuss and Crowley in the O.T.O. Clearly, Randolph cannot be considered the only major precursor of Crowley's Thelemic sex magick since there are major aspects of Crowley's occult doctrine that are entirely absent in Randolph's writings and philosophy. It is necessary to explore other sources entirely – sources much closer to the origins of the Western esoteric tradition itself – and it comes as no surprise that some of Crowley's libertine mystical and sex-magick ideas are mirrored quite specifically in the ritual practices of certain heretical Gnostic sects whose origins date back to the early centuries of the Christian era.[56] These include the Gnostic sects that religious scholar Mircea Eliade refers to as *Pneumatikoi* and O.T.O. historian P-R.Koenig calls 'Spermo-Gnostics'.[57]

One of the most intriguing elements in the rise of Gnosticism during the early Christian era was the concept that spiritual redemption could be attained by collecting, salvaging, and carrying to heaven the sparks of divine light that were buried in living matter – primarily within the human body. Mircea Eliade notes that

> the equation divine light = *pneuma* [Greek: 'spirit'] = semen plays a central role only among the Phibionites (and sects related to them) and among the Manichaeans. But while the latter, on the ground of this very equation, scorned the sexual act and exalted a severe asceticism, the Phibionites extolled the most abject sexual orgies and practised the sacramental absorption of *semen virile* and menstrual fluids, careful only to avoid pregnancy.[58]

Despite the overt sensuality of their sexual rituals, the Syrian Phibionites regarded themselves as Christian Gnostics: they believed that the divine power of the crucified Son had been trapped within the physical confines of the material world. The Phibionites also believed they were giving true expression to their Christian beliefs by releasing this spiritual power during their sacred rituals without creating more children in the process – from their perspective, pregnancy and the act of giving birth would trap more souls within the painful constrictions of physical existence. For them, consuming semen and menstrual blood during the Eucharist was a purer form of ritual communion than the more conventional symbolism of blood and wine. The practices of the Phibionites are described in the *Panarion*, written by the 4th century Christian writer, Epiphanius:

> The power, which is in menstruation and in the sperm they called *psyche*, which would be gathered and eaten. And whatever we eat, flesh or vegetables or bread or anything else, we do a favour to the creatures because we gather the psyche from everything…And they say that it is the same psyche which is dispersed in animals and beasts, fishes, snakes, men, vegetables, trees and anything that is produced.[59]

Epiphanius was clearly horrified by what he describes as the 'shameless' sexual practices of the Phibionites:

> …they serve rich food, meat and wine even if they are poor. When they thus ate together and so to speak filled up their veins, from the surplus of their strength they turn to excitements. The man, leaving his wife, says to his own wife: 'Stand up and make love with the brother ('Perform the *agapē* with the brother'). Then the unfortunates unite with each other, and as I am truly ashamed to say the shameful things that are being done by them… nevertheless I will not be ashamed to say those things which they are not ashamed to do, in order that I may cause in every way a horror in those who hear about their shameful practices. After they have intercourse in the passion of fornication they raise their own blasphemy toward heaven. The woman and the man take the fluid of emission of the man into their hands, they stand, turn toward heaven, their hands besmeared with the uncleanness, and pray as the people called *Stratiotikoi* and *Gnostikoi*, bringing to the Father of the Nature of All, that which they have on their hands, and they say: 'We offer to thee this gift, the body of Christ.' And then they eat it, their own ignominy, and say: 'This is the body of Christ and this is the Passover for the sake of which our bodies suffer and

> are forced to confess the suffering of Christ.' Similarly also with the woman: when she happens to be in the flowing of the blood they gather the blood of menstruation of her uncleanness and eat it together and say: 'This is the blood of Christ.'[60]

The Phibionite ritual of consuming menstrual blood and semen is mirrored in Crowley's sex magick practice of consuming 'cakes of light', which contained precisely the same key ingredients (based on the instructions conveyed to Crowley by Aiwass in 1904, as recorded in *The Book of the Law*). As with the Phibionites, Crowley included the consumption of sacramental 'cakes of light' in both his *Gnostic Mass* and also in the *Mass of the Phoenix*, and it is clear that Crowley intended that in these magickal ceremonies the 'cakes of light' should serve as an alternative to the Body of Christ consumed by congregants during Christian communion. Although Crowley does not mention the Phibionites specifically in his writings, he nevertheless believed he was perpetuating the Gnostic tradition through such ceremonies, and for him the ritual consumption of blood and semen was a sacred act. According to the text of the *Gnostic Mass*, consecrated 'cakes of light' contain the sexual elixir and therefore embody 'the essence of the life of the Sun'.

TANTRA AND KUNDALINI YOGA

An important element in Rosaleen Norton's magical practice – and a theme also reflected in some of her artworks – was her interest in Kundalini Yoga and Tantra. Both of these are highly significant in Thelemic sex magick practice and, interestingly, even prior to meeting Eugene Goossens, the relationship between magick and Tantra was something that Rosaleen Norton seems to have understood intuitively, acting independently and drawing on her practical knowledge of Kundalini Yoga and magical consciousness. The word 'yoga' derives from the Sanskrit *yuj*, meaning 'to bind' or 'to yoke' and the essential aim of yoga is union with the Godhead, Brahman. The Sanskrit word *kundalini* translates literally as 'of spiral nature', while the Sanskrit word *tantra* ('weft, context, continuum') refers to the nature of energy and power in the universe. In *Tantra: The Yoga of Sex*, Omar Garrison provides a concise overview of the philosophy associated with Tantra:

> The broad, underlying foundation of Tantra philosophy may be summarised briefly as follows: The universe and everything in it is permeated by a secret energy or power, emanating from the single Source of all being. This power, although singular in essence, manifests in three ways, namely, as static inertia, dynamic inertia or mental energy, and as harmonious union of these reacting opposites. The universe or macrocosm through which these modalities of cosmic force function is exactly duplicated by the human form as microcosm. The Tantrik [sic] seeks, therefore, by mystic formularies, rites and symbols, to identify the corresponding centres of his own body with those of the macrocosm. Ultimately, he seeks union with God Himself.[61]

Agehananda Bharati, an authority on the different branches of Tantra, distinguishes between guru-oriented, meditative yoga and Tantra *per se*, by drawing attention to the focus on a sexual partner in the Tantric tradition:

> Orthodox yoga, that is the system of Patanjali and his protagonists, teaches the ascent of the dormant, coiled-up force as a process induced in the individual adept after due instruction by

> his own guru, and as a procedure in which the adept practises in solitude. The tantric's practice, however, is undertaken in conjunction with a partner of the other sex. She is considered as the embodiment of Sakti [Shakti], the active principle conceived as female, by the Hindus.[62]

In the Tantric tradition of Kundalini Yoga this sexual partnership is expressed as the merging of two opposites – Shiva and Shakti – who represent the male and female polarities of existence respectively. While the Higher Self (Atman) is represented in Kundalini Yoga as male, all created forms, all manifestations of life energy, intelligence, will, thoughts and feelings, are considered to be female, and as such are aspects of Shakti. As the Great Goddess, Shakti encompasses three *gunas*, or characteristics of creation, known as *sattva* (purity), *rajas* (activity) and *tamas* (inertia) as well as the five elements from which the universe is formed. Swami Sivananda Sarasvati provides an eloquent summation:

> She [Shakti] is the primal force of life that underlies all existence. She vitalises the body through her energy. She is the energy in the Sun, the fragrance in the flowers, the beauty in the landscape… the whole world is her body. Mountains are her bones. Rivers are her veins. Ocean is her bladder. Sun and Moon are her eyes. Wind is her breath. Agni is her mouth.[63]

Kundalini Yoga encompasses many different techniques, including the use of mantras, visualisation and breath control, in order to activate specific chakras [*chakra*: Sanskrit,'wheel'] or spiritual centres, in the body. These chakras can be listed as follows:

First chakra: Muladhara, located at the base of the spine, near the coccyx

Second chakra: Svadisthana, located
below the navel in the sacral region
Third chakra: Manipura, located
above the navel in the lumbar region
Fourth chakra: Anahata, located near the heart
Fifth chakra: Visuddha, located in the throat
Sixth chakra: Ajna, located between the eyebrows
Seventh chakra: Sahasrara, located above the crown of the head

Kundalini Yoga identifies a potentially cosmic process within every yogic practitioner: manifestations of the Hindu gods and goddesses are said to lie within the energy matrices of the human organism and the purpose of Kundalini Yoga is to bring them to life, unleashing their energy through the nadis [*nadi*: Sanskrit: 'tube', 'vessel'], or spiritual channels in the body. The principal channel through which the Shakti energy can be awakened is via a nadi which passes through each of the seven chakras referred to above, extending from Muladhara at the base of the spine to Sahasrara located just above the crown of the head. This energy-channel is known in Kundalini Yoga as *Sushumna* and corresponds to the central nervous system in the human body. Around the Sushumna are coiled two other major channels: Pingala – which is symbolically masculine and associated with the heat of the Sun – and Ida, which is symbolically feminine and is represented by the cool, reflected light of the Moon. As Ida and Pingala coil themselves around the Sushumna, they meet in the lowest chakra energy centre in the body, Muladhara, and again in the sixth centre, Ajna. The essential meditative task in Kundalini Yoga is to 'raise' the energy of the Goddess Shakti so she may once again be united with her consort Lord Shiva in the supreme bliss of *Samadhi*. This occurs in the supreme chakra, Sahasrara, which is considered Shiva's domain. This chakra is associated with the experience of Brahman or the bliss of 'One-ness'.

The Tantric practice of Kundalini Yoga focuses on the mystical properties of energy and this in turn is reflected in the ritual use of mantras (energy as sound) and in meditations employing specific colours in relation to each chakra (energy as light). It is also demonstrated by the symbolic dance of Shiva and Shakti as they unite one with the other, dissolving old forms and creating the universe anew (energy as movement). The chakras themselves are conceived as sources of subtle energy depicted as 'wheels' (the literal meaning of the Sanskrit word *chakra*) or as lotuses (*padma*). The meditative process in Kundalini Yoga involves 'flowing' from one chakra to the next by visualising each Tattva (or element) in turn, dissolving it in the associated mantra vibration, and then merging it with the next Tattva in sequence. The five Tattva elements – Earth, Water, Fire, Air and Spirit – are associated with the first five chakras. No element is ascribed to the transcendent sixth chakra, Ajna, which is considered the seat of all spiritual knowledge. Shakti is united with her consort, Lord Shiva, in the seventh chakra, Sahasrara, which is located above the crown of the head, just outside the physical body and beyond the realm of human awareness. This is a sacred union represented by the symbolism of mystical androgyny for, as Swami Sivananda Radha notes: 'In the Kundalini symbolism, the union of Siva [Shiva] and Sakti [Shakti] is presented in one body, not as two bodies united. Lord Siva ultimately becomes half-man and half-woman indicating that power and its manifestations are inseparable.'[64] The sacred union of Shiva and Shakti within the One-ness of Brahman can also be considered a mystery for, according to the Tantric tradition, at this point all aspects of form and creative manifestation are transcended. As the psychologist C.G. Jung has written, Sahasrara represents a 'philosophical concept with no substance whatever for us – it is beyond any possible experience'.[65]

MAGIC AND THE LEFT-HAND PATH IN TANTRA

In *The Art of Rosaleen Norton*, Norton defines the Kundalini as the 'undifferentiated elemental and potential creative power of the Self, generally symbolised as a Serpent, and traditionally associated with the spinal cord'. Norton was well aware of its potency: 'When latent it manifests only sporadically and partially in the sex force and sometimes as artistic or inventive creativity. Active, it confers supernormal powers in various directions.'[66] Given Norton's reference to 'supernormal powers' it is reasonable to assume that her interest in Kundalini Yoga would have been associated with awakening heightened occult, sexual and creative sources of energy and inspiration. Indeed, in the text which accompanies her drawing *At Home* Norton refers to the Kundalini in a specifically magical context. Here she writes that Kundalini 'sometimes assumes the shape of a serpent' and is 'my most powerful Familiar'.[67]

We know that Norton had access to rare and relatively obscure works that Aleister Crowley published in England and in this context it is useful to consider Crowley's perspective on the magical applications of Tantra, especially in relation to sex magic. Lawrence Sutin believes that Crowley's first reference to sex magic is recorded in a diary titled *The Writings of Truth* which was later published in a modified form in his *Temple of Solomon the King*.[68] It was while visiting his friend and former Golden Dawn colleague Allan Bennett (*Frater Iehi Aour*) in Ceylon in 1901 that Crowley was tutored for the first time in yoga. Bennett had left the world of ceremonial magic behind in England and had come to Ceylon to become a Buddhist monk. Bennett was willing to share his practical knowledge of yoga with his friend and together they rented a furnished bungalow in the hills near Kandy for a period of several months so Crowley could be shown the yogic techniques.[69] Crowley's diary entries in *The Writings of Truth* record that during his stay in Kandy he practised yogic *pranayama* (control of prana, or life-energy, utilising breathing techniques) and that he had also been exploring *vamacharya*, a form of 'left-hand path' Tantra devoted to licentious rites and sexual debauchery.[70] Sutin writes:

> This reference to *vamacharya* is most important, as it documents his [ie.Crowley's] first known foray into ritual sexual magic. This Sanskrit term refers to a Hindu tantric practice of sexual intercourse that could – if the spiritual aspirations were untainted by lust – re-enact the cosmic coupling of Shiva and Shakti... In tantric tradition *vamacharya* is the 'left-hand path' that involves physical intercourse with a woman (*vama*) as partner, while the 'right-hand path' of *dakshinachara* enacts a symbolic intercourse.'[71]

In *Tantra: The Way of Action*, occult historian and ceremonial magician Francis King describes the ritual procedure adopted in left-handed Tantra:

The rite proper begins with the worshippers gathered in a circle, seated on the ground, man alternating with woman, the woman on the left of each man being his intended sexual partner – hence, of course, the term left-handed Tantra. At the centre of the circle stands the male adept who will conduct the ceremony, the 'priest', and near him sits or lies a naked woman, or 'priestess'. For tantrics all women are holy – as one text has it 'every woman is your image, O Shakti, you reside in the forms of all women in this world' – but for the duration of the rite the priestess, the woman at the centre of the circle who is to be the sexual partner of the officiating adept, is considered especially holy, a particular manifestation of Shakti. As such her vulva is peculiarly sacred, a symbol of her creative power which sustains the universe, and it is displayed as fully as possible to the assembled congregation, the priestess lying or sitting with her legs held wide apart.[72]

Before the Tantric rite itself can commence, however, certain purificatory procedures have to take place:

> ...the body of the priestess is ritually cleansed by being sprinkled with wine and consecrated 'holy water', and then Shakti is invoked into that body by the priest. This latter is done by the priest gently caressing her head, trunk and limbs while muttering or chanting invocations. Almost every part of the body receives these caresses but particular attention is paid to the vulva, which has an aromatic sandalwood paste applied to it, is lightly kissed, and is then, as the supreme expression of the nature of the Goddess, the recipient of symbolic sacrifice – that is to say libations of water, wine, or coconut milk are poured over it or on the ground beneath it.... The priestess is now looked upon as being deified, for the time being an avatar of Shakti.[73]

Within this ritual context the Shakti priestess is venerated by the entire assembled group but the priest himself has a specific sexual role:

> The ritual worship of the priestess is often immediately followed by her copulation with the priest, the assembled worshippers devoutly observing what is regarded as a sacred action, a physical expression of the eternal embrace of Shiva and Shakti. The sexual coupling is regarded as holy and so are the partici-

pants, *but only as manifestations of Shiva and Shakti.*[74]

King also comments further on the distinction between left-handed and right-handed Tantra, noting that in the first instance the ritual sexual coupling actually takes place, whereas in the latter case it is symbolic. Left-handed Tantra is also more exuberant and spontaneous:

> In right-handed Tantra the woman sits to the right side of the man; if the rite is left-handed, one which culminates in physical sexuality, the opposite is the case....In either case the practitioners now endeavour to think of each other as the God and Goddess, Shiva and Shakti. In right-handed worship this 'divine identification' remains on a fairly abstract level, but in left-handed rites it is very specific, the woman regarding her partner as 'the phallus of Shiva', while she is thought of as being not only Shakti but the living altar on which sacrifice is offered to herself – in the words of one text, held in high regard by many schools of Tantra, 'Her belly is the sacrificial altar, her pubic hairs the sacred grass-mat... the lips of her vagina are the sacrificial fire...'
>
> In left-handed working... fervour and spontaneity are the essence of the rite. The participants not only identify themselves with the God and Goddess, but they give the divine forces full play, letting themselves improvise, as the divine polarities inspire them, the feasting, the love play and the copulation of Shiva and Shakti. Within the boundaries of the Temple there are no hard and fast rules – 'Exceed, exceed' are the key words, and the Road to Excess leads to the Palace of Wisdom and Understanding and to that Greater Palace which subsumes them.[75]

King maintains that Hindu tantrics allow the ritual ejaculation of semen, whereas Buddhist tantrics try to avoid it.[76] However, on this point he is contradicted by Agehananda Bharati:

> The central rule behind the left-handed rites, both Hindu and Buddhist, is the retention of semen during the sexual act [ie. during *maithuna*, ritualistic copulation].The man who discharges semen is a *pasu*, an 'animal' in the Mahanirvana and the Yogini Tantra, whereas he who retains it during maithuna is *divya*, 'divine'.[77]

Because of Crowley's fascination with the magical potency of semen and his emphasis in Thelemic magical practice on the ritual consumption of sexual secretions as part of the 'magical elixir', it is possible that even if he was following a practice of retaining semen during his exploration of *vamacharya* in 1901 he was prepared to abandon this aspect of Tantra after his transformative revelations in Cairo, just three years later. Kenneth Grant meanwhile provides an important insight into the connection between the practice of left-hand path sex magic and the image of the Kundalini serpent – or 'fire-snake'. This is significant because it was the connection between the serpent (as spirit-familiar) and Kundalini (as a source of potent energy within the human organism) which fascinated Rosaleen Norton, especially with regard to exploring the so-called 'astral planes' while in a state of magical trance:

> The ability to function on the inner, or astral planes, and to travel freely in the realms of light or inner space, derived from a special purification and storage of vital force. This force in its densest form is identical with sexual energy. In order to transform sexual energy into magical energy (*ojas*), the dominant Fire Snake at the base of the spine is awakened. It then purges the vitality of all dross by the purifying virtue of its intense heat.

> Thus the function of the semen – in the tantras is to build up the body of light [the astral body], the inner body of man. As the vital fluid accumulates in the testicles it is consumed by the heat of the Fire Snake, and the subtle fumes or 'perfumes' of this molten semen go to strengthen the inner body. The worship of *shakti* means in effect the exercise of the Fire Snake, which not only fortifies the body of light but gradually burns away all impurities in the physical body and rejuvenates it. [78]

Grant supports Norton's contention that arousing the Kundalini can stimulate 'artistic or inventive creativity', referring to it as 'the serpentine or spiral power of creative consciousness'.[79] According to Grant, Tantric magicians utilising the Kundalini in this way 'will become as gods, because the power of creation (the prerogative of gods) will be wielded by them through the direction of forces at present termed 'occult' or hidden.'[80] As we have seen, Rosaleen Norton's entire magical career was all about unleashing heightened sources of creativity and exploring the visionary potentials of sex magic. It was in just such a way that she paid homage to the Great God Pan.[81]

1 Crowley's unique spelling for the Scarlet Woman of the Apocalypse, as revealed in *The Book of the Law*. The spelling 'Babalon' has a Kabbalistic numerical value of 156 which, according to Crowley's disciple Kenneth Grant, equates with the number of shrines in the City of Pyramids. Grant maintains that the name 'Babalon' means 'Gateway of the Sun, or solar-phallic power' (see *Nightside of Eden*, London 1977: 259) – thereby revealing its symbolic significance to practitioners of sex-magick.

2 Ibid: stanzas III: 44-45: 314.

3 K. Grant, *The Magical Revival*, Muller, London, 1972:.45. Grant elaborates on this point later in the same book :'In sexual congress

each coition is a sacrament of peculiar virtue since it effects a transformation of consciousness through annihilation of apparent duality. To be radically effective the transformation must be also an initiation. Because of the sacramental nature of the act, each union must be magically directed... the ritual must be directed to the transfinite and non-individualised consciousness represented by Egyptian Nuit... The earthly Nuit is Isis, the Scarlet Woman.' (loc cit.:145).

4 See appendix containing the text of *Liber Al vel Legis* in *The Magical Record of the Beast 666,* ed. J.. Symonds and K. Grant, Duckworth, London 1972:311-312.

5 L. Sutin, *Do What Thou Wilt: A Life of Aleister Crowley*, St Martin's Press, New York 2000: 292.

6 F. King (ed.), *The Secret Rituals of the O.T.O.*, C.W. Daniel, London 1973: 225.

7 Enochian magic derives historically from the work of Elizabethan occultists Dr. John Dee (1527-1608) and Edward Kelley (1555-15950, who met in 1581. Dee and Kelley made use of wax tablets called almadels, engraved with magical symbols,and also used a large number of 49-inch squares filled with letters of the alphabet. Nearby, on his table, Kelley had a large crystal stone upon which he focused his concentration and entered a state of trance reverie. Kelley maintained that while he was in a state of trance 'angels' would appear, and they in turn would point to various letters on the squares. These letters were written down by Dee as Kelley called them out. When these invocations were completely transcribed, Kelley then reversed their order, believing that the angels had communicated them backwards to avoid unleashing the magical power which they contained. Dee and Kelley considered that the communications formed the basis of a new language known as Enochian. These magical conjurations were subsequently incorporated into magical practice by the ritual magicians of the Hermetic Order of the Golden Dawn, who used them to induce trance visions on the 'astral plane'.

8 A. Crowley, *The Vision and the Voice* [1929], Sangreal Foundation,

Dallas, Texas 1972.

9 Spare was briefly a member of the O.T.O. *circa* 1910 but soon quarrelled with Crowley and thereafter sought to avoid him. Even though Spare became friendly with Thelemite Kenneth Grant in the late 1940s, Spare and Crowley were never reconciled. See also K. and S. Grant, *Zos Speaks !: Encounters with Austin Osman Spare*, Fulgur, London 1998.

10 F. King (ed.), *The Secret Rituals of the O.T.O.*, loc.cit: 28.

11 Crowley writes in *The Confessions*: 'I protested that I knew no such secret. He said, "But you have printed it in the plainest language." I said that I could not have done so because I did not know it. He went to the bookshelves and, taking out a copy of *The Book of Lies*, pointed to a passage in the despised chapter.' See A. Crowley, *The Confessions of Aleister Crowley*, ed. J. Symonds and K. Grant, Hill and Wang, New York 1970: 710.

12 Crowley later visited Berlin where he received instructional documents from the German O.T.O. He was also granted the grandiose title 'King of Ireland, Iona and all the Britains within the Sanctuary of the Gnosis" and took *Baphomet* as his new magical name. Later Crowley adapted the Ninth degree of the O.T.O so that it identified the priest and priestess as Osiris and Isis, 'seeking Nuit and Hadit through the vagina and the penis'. He also developed a series of homosexual magical rituals with Victor Neuburg featuring invocations to Thoth-Hermes. At one point in these rituals, which became known collectively as the *Paris Working*, Crowley scourged Neuburg on the buttocks and cut a cross on his chest For details see J.O.Fuller, *The Magical Dilemma of Victor Neuburg*, W.H.Allen, London 1965:203-216.

13 See F. King (ed.), *The Secret Rituals of the O.T.O.*, loc.cit: 29. King points out that Crowley was not accepted by a majority of German O.T.O. members until 1925. The Order was suppressed by the Nazis in 1937.

14 P-R. Koenig, 'Introduction to the Ordo Templi Orientis', published on-line at www.user.cyberlink.ch/~koenig/intro.htm.

15 T. Reuss, *Lingam-Yoni*, Verlag Willsson, Berlin and London 1906.

16 H. Urban, *Magia Sexualis: Sex, Magic and Liberation in Modern Western Esotericism*, University of California Press, Berkeley, California 2006: 101.

17 Sabazius X° and AMT IX°, *History of Ordo Templi Orientis*, U.S. Grand Lodge, 2006: 12-13. available on-line at www.oto-usa.org/history.html.

18 Sabazius X° and AMT IX°, *History of Ordo Templi Orientis*, loc cit.:17.

19 Published in *The Equinox* Vol.III:1, March 1919 – the so called *'Blue Equinox'*.

20 Sabazius X° and AMT IX°, *History of Ordo Templi Orientis*, loc cit.:17.

21 H. Urban, 'Magia Sexualis: Sex, Secrecy and Liberation in Modern Western Esotericism,' *Journal of the American Academy of Religion*, September 2004, Vol.72, No.3: 711.

22 P-R.Koenig, 'Spermo-Gnostics and the O.T.O' , available at www.cyberlink.ch/-koenig/spermo.htm.

23 A. Crowley, *De Arte Magica*, Ch.XII , available on-line at www.skepticfiles.org.

24 Ibid.

25 Ibid, Ch.XVI.

26 See See F. King (ed.), *The Secret Rituals of the O.T.O.*, loc.cit: 207.

27 Baphomet was Crowley's magical name after he assumed leadership of the British branch of the O.T.O. in 1912. It is also the name of a demonic deity represented graphically by Eliphas Lévi as a goat-headed god with wings, breasts and an illuminated torch between his horns. The Knights Templar were accused by King Philip IV of France of worshipping Baphomet although few members of the Order admitted to this ritual practice. It has been suggested that the name Baphomet may be a corruption of Mohammed.

28 See A. Crowley, 'Emblems and Modes of Use', private text intended for the Ninth degree O.T.O. Available on-line at www.aethyria.com.

29 See Frater Osiris, 'Analysis of the Mass of the Phoenix', Seattle 2003, published on-line at www.hermetic.com/osiris and also A. Rhadon, 'Sex, Religion and Magick: a concise overview', 2004,

published on-line at www.baymoon.com.

30 Frater Osiris, 'Analysis of the Mass of the Phoenix', loc cit.

31 See Frater Osiris, 'Analysis of Liber XXXVI, *The Star Sapphire*', Seattle 2004, published on-line at www.hermetic.com/osiris.

32 Frater Osiris, 'Analysis of Liber XXXVI, *The Star Sapphire*', loc cit. Frater Osiris is probably referring to Crowley's sex magic text *Emblems and Modes of Use*, where it is suggested that the 'elixir' should be consumed in this way.

33 This is Crowley's expression. IAO was one of the sacred names ascribed to the archon Abraxas, a planetary deity associated with Basilides, a Gnostic philosopher who lived and taught in Alexandria c.125-140 CE. The name Abraxas in Greek letters has a numerical value of 365, thereby linking the deity to the number of days in a year. Abraxas was said to rule over 365 heavens and was depicted on numerous charms, amulets and talismans in order to attract good luck.

34 A. Crowley, *Energized Enthusiasm: A Note on Theurgy*, available on-line at www.luckymojo.com/esoteric/occultism/magic/ceremonial/crowley. htm. This text was first published in *The Equinox*, vol.1 No.9, March 1913, and was republished by Weiser, New York 1976.

35 Ibid.

36 See L. Abraham, entry for the 'Chemical Wedding' of King Sol and Queen Luna, *A Dictionary of Alchemical Imagery*, Cambridge University Press, 1998:36.

37 In *Liber Aleph*, Crowley writes: 'Neglect not the daily Miracle of the Mass, either by the Rite of the Gnostic Catholic Church, or that of the Phoenix.' Quoted in Frater Osiris, *On the Mass of the Phoenix: An Analysis,* Seattle 2003. Published on-line at www.hermetic.com/osiris.

38 The Mark of the Beast is 'the sign of the Sun and Moon or Cross and Circle conjoined'. See www.thelemicgoldendawn.org/rituals/phoenix.htm.

39 Frater Osiris, *On the Mass of the Phoenix: An Analysis,* loc cit.

40 First published in the Thelemite journal *Mezla*, Vol.1:111, 1, Ithaca, New York 1985.

41 This is remarkably similar to Austin Spare's notion of the 'Void moment' which is described in Chapter Seven.

42 *Mezla*, Vol.1:111, 1.

43 Ibid.

44 See listing of key Crowley texts on sex magic published on-line at www.hollyfeld.org. *Liber A'ash_vel Capricorni Pneumatici* heads the list. A 'Class A' document in the Argenteum Astrum was one that could not be altered or modified in the slightest way and had to be adhered to by members strictly as presented by Crowley.

45 A. Crowley, *Liber A'Aash vel Capricorni Pneumatici (Liber CCCLXX)*, first published in *The Equinox*, vol.1 No.6.

46 See listing of O.T.O. members provided by O.T.O.practitioner Ithell Colquhoun in *Sword of Wisdom: MacGregor Mathers and the Golden Dawn*, Spearman, London 1975: 207-208.

47 J.G. Melton, 'The Origins of Modern Sex Magick', Institute for the Study of American Religion, Evanston, Illinois, June 1985

48 See R. North, Introduction to P.B.Randolph, *Sexual Magic*, Magickal Childe, New York 1988 (original French-language text: *Magia Sexualis*, Paris 1931) published on-line at www.supoervirtual.com.br.

49 P.B. Randolph, *Eulis!,* Randolph, Toledo, Ohio 1873, republished 1896.

50 P.B. Randolph, *Eulis!,* loc cit.: 48, 218.

51 P.B. Randolph, *Eulis!,* quoted in C.Yronwode, 'Paschal Beverly Randolph and the Ansairetic Mysteries', loc cit.

52 P.B. Randolph, *The Ansairetic Mystery: A New Revelation Concerning Sex!*, Toledo, Ohio, c.1973-74, republished in J.P.Deveney, *Paschal Beverly Randolph: A Nineteenth-Century American Spiritualist, Rosicrucian and Sex Magician*, State University of New York Press, Albany, New York 1997

53 A. Crowley, *Energized Enthusiasm: A Note on Theurgy*, loc.cit.

54 J. Godwin, C. Chanel and J.P. Deveney, *The Hermetic Brotherhood of Luxor*, Weiser, Maine 1995: 92-97.

55 P-R. Koenig, 'Correct Gnosticism', loc cit.

56 These Gnostic sects include the Carpocratians, the Ophites and the

Phibionites and they are of interest because of their libertine tendencies, chthonic snake-imagery, and ritual consumption of blood and semen respectively. The Phibionites provide arguably the most intriguing parallel to Thelema in relation to Crowley's sacramental sex-magick practices.

57 P-R. Koenig, 'Spermo-Gnostics and the Ordo Templi Orientis', www.user.cyberlink.ch/~koenig/spermo.htm
58 M. Eliade, *Occultism. Witchcraft and Cultural Fashions*, University of Chicago Press, Chicago 1976: 113.
59 Epiphanius, *Panarion* 26: 9, 3-4.
60 Ibid: 26: 17, 1 ff. quoted in M. Eliade, *Occultism. Witchcraft and Cultural Fashions*, loc cit: 110.
61 O.V. Garrison, *Tantra: The Yoga of Sex*, Julian Press, New York 1964: xxi-xxii.
62 A. Bharati *The Tantric Tradition*, Rider, London 1965: 293.
63 Quoted in S. Radha, *Kundalini Yoga for the West*, Shambhala, Boulder, Colorado 1981: 25-28.
64 S. Radha, *Kundalini Yoga for the West*, loc cit:336.
65 C.G. Jung, 'Psychological Commentary in Kundalini Yoga' (lecture given on 26 October 1932), *Spring*, New York 1976: 17.
66 Ibid
67 Ibid: 74.
68 L. Sutin, *Do What Thou Wilt: A Life of Aleister Crowley*, loc cit: 92.
69 Ibid: 91.
70 I. Fischer-Schreiber et al. (ed.) *The Encyclopedia of Eastern Philosophy and Religion*, Shambhala, Boston 1994: 355.
71 Sutin adds the pertinent observation that 'There is, in this tradition, no moral judgment attached to the use of "left" and "right", although Western interpreters have frequently interposed a negative connotation to "left" that is native to their own, but not Hindu, cultures.' See L.Sutin, *Do What Thou Wilt : A Life of Aleister Crowley*, loc cit: 92-93.
72 F. King, *Tantra: The Way of Action*, Destiny Books, Rochester, Vermont 1990: 89.

73 Ibid: 89-90.
74 Ibid: 90.
75 Ibid: 126-27.
76 Ibid: 92.
77 A. Bharati, *The Tantric Tradition*, Rider, London 1965: 179.
78 K. Grant, 'Cults of the Shadow' in J.White (ed.), *Kundalini: Evolution and Enlightenment*, Paragon House, St Paul, Minnesota 1990:400-401.
79 K. Grant, *The Magical Revival*, Muller, London 1972: 21.
80 Ibid.

Appendix B Modern Magic and Women's Mysteries

Much of the current interest in magic and the occult traditions is directly related to the rise and importance of feminism as a contemporary movement. Wicca, or witchcraft, and the broader-based concept of 'Goddess worship', both focus on the veneration of a female deity – usually Mother Nature or the Goddess of the Moon. The act of invoking feminine archetypes – each in turn representing different dimensions of the Universal Goddess – is central to Wiccan and Goddess worshippers' spiritual orientation and ritual practice. Nevertheless, while Rosaleen Norton was popularly labelled as a witch and one would like to present her, perhaps, as a forerunner of the modern Wicca movement, there is little evidence that she fits neatly into this framework.[1] Apart from the fact that she was a woman, and a very remarkable woman at that, her magical influences do not appear to have been shaped by the literature of women's spirituality. Even so, Rosaleen Norton's thinking as a whole was very much in line with the current directions of contemporary Neopaganism and although her original sources were different, one can argue that she arrived at much the same viewpoint as present-day feminist practitioners of witchcraft and Goddess-worship. It was simply that she came onto the scene too early to be appreciated on her own terms, and her frameworks were not ones that the public at large could understand or relate to.

The bibliography in the 1952 edition of *The Art of Rosaleen Norton* is a good place to start in understanding Rosaleen's sources and it lists various categories of books under the headings of psychology, esotericism, folklore and comparative religion, and witchcraft and demonology. Although Freud was mentioned as an influence during the obscenity trials, Rosaleen does not list him in her bibliography. Instead, pride of place is given to Carl Jung – especially his works *Psychological Types*, *The Integration of the Personality*, *Studies in Psychology* and *The Secret of the Golden Flower*. Also included are William James' classical work *The Varieties of Religious Experience* and H.G. Baynes' *Mythology of the Soul*, incorrectly listed as *Psychology of the Soul*.

Rosaleen was conversant with Sir James Frazer's *The Golden Bough*, highlighting 'the Egyptian, Chaldean [and]Babylonian sections in particular', and was also widely read in occult fiction. Her list included Gustav Meyrinck's *The Golem*, Charles Williams' *All Hallows*, C.S. Lewis's *That Hideous Strength*, Joan Grant's *Winged Pharoah* and Dion Fortune's *The Goat-foot God*. However it is her esoteric listings which are, perhaps, of greatest interest because they reveal that Rosaleen's main occult influences – as one would expect of person researching esoteric themes in the 1940s and '50s – were primarily works associated with Theosophy and Western Kabbalistic Magic. Rosaleen had obviously consulted the works of Madame Blavatsky – she lists *Isis Unveiled* and *The Stanzas of Dzyan* and refers to her in her Introduction – and she was also conversant with Alice Bailey's *A Treatise on White Magic*. Her major occult listings included Dion Fortune's *The Mystical Qabalah*, Papus's *The Tarot of the*

Bohemians, Aleister Crowley's *Magick in Theory and Practice* and Eliphas Lévi's *A Treatise on Magic* (the latter mistitled – a reference to either *The Key of the Mysteries*, *The History of Magic* or *Transcendental Magic*).

The latter works were all key tracts in the magical tradition emanating from the Hermetic Order of the Golden Dawn, or European figures who had influenced this magical organisation. The Golden Dawn itself had been founded in London in 1888 by a group of Freemasons. Both Aleister Crowley and Dion Fortune had been members of this Order (the latter, a Jungian therapist, had also been a member of the Theosophical Society and would later establish the Society of Inner Light). Eliphas Lévi and Papus were in turn important influences on both Crowley and the noted Golden Dawn occultist Arthur Edward Waite. The only listings for witchcraft in Rosaleen's bibliography were Montague Summers' *A History of Witchcraft*, a hostile and critical work, and Margaret Murray's controversial *Witchcraft in Western Europe*, a purely theoretical academic treatise and not the sort of work from which one could derive a practical system of magic.

One is left to conclude that Rosaleen's main occult sources, books she could actually *use*, were the occult manuals prepared by writers like Dion Fortune and Aleister Crowley. And in fact there is evidence to support this. In her interview with L.J. Murphy at the University of Melbourne, when Rosaleen was describing her magical trance techniques, she referred – albeit slightly inaccurately – to Crowley's dictum that magic is the art of changing consciousness at will. As we saw in Chapter Eight in the present book there also exists an especially relevant photograph showing Rosaleen engaged in ceremonial rituals using Hebrew 'words of power' derived from the Kabbalah (Qabalah). Published in *Australasian*

Post on 7 February 1957, the photograph shows Rosaleen at her altar with the name 'Uriel' clearly inscribed on the wall behind it. Uriel is the name of the Archangel of Earth, and is one of the words of power intoned during the Banishing Ritual of the Pentagram, an important preparatory ritual in the Golden Dawn system of magic. Rosaleen also titled her drawing of the archetypal war-god *Geburah* – a reference to the sphere of power and strength on the Kabbalistic Tree of Life. So even if Rosaleen did introduce witchcraft elements into her rituals – the lunar crescent is also visible on her altar and of course Pan would always occupy a central position in her worship – there is no doubting her Kabbalistic influences.

It is understandable that Rosaleen could not have been conversant with modern witchcraft practices because when she was formulating her occult concepts, witchcraft *per se* was still a forbidden practice. It was not until 1951 that the British Witchcraft Act was finally repealed and books advocating the use of witchcraft rituals allowed to be published. One of the early forerunners of the movement, Gerald Brosseau Gardner, had published *High Magic's Aid* in 1949 but it had been portrayed as a work of fiction. It was not until 1954 that Gardner's *Witchcraft Today* was released, followed by *The Meaning of Witchcraft* in 1959.

Following the controversial obscenity trials associated with Rosaleen Norton's art, Sydney-based *People* magazine continued to stir the media cauldron by periodically publishing articles on witchcraft and Satanism. One of these was an interview with Gerald Gardner, then seventy-four years old, who was living at the time in a flat in London's Shepherd's Bush. Published on 5 March 1958, the article described Gardner as the 'boss of the witches' and revealed that Rosaleen had been corresponding with him. 'During her trial – for obscenity I think they called it – Witch Norton wrote and implored me to keep her from prison,' Gardner was reported to have said. 'Through magical means, witches all over Britain came to her aid. Prayers and dances were held almost nightly. Finally the trial verdict was known. Witch Norton escaped from prison.' [2]

The tendency now is to broaden the notion of witchcraft to encompass the many different forms of goddess worship and 'women's mysteries'. Part of the reason for this is that, as with Rosaleen Norton, modern witches have attracted sensational, and frequently inaccurate, media coverage. This is certainly the case in the United States, especially in regions where Christian fundamentalism is strong. As American witch and practising attorney Phyllis Curott has noted, former United States president, George W. Bush went on record comparing witchcraft to satanism. Such responses seem to be based on a simplistic approach to alternative belief systems which are perceived as evil. As Wisconsin-based Neopagans Selena Fox and Jim Alan explained in an interview with *The Chicago Tribune*, 'Folks hear about witchcraft and witches and they cling to the old stereotypes about witches doing evil. That's totally out of our sphere.' [3]

FEMINISM AND GODDESS SPIRITUALITY

During the late 1960s – especially around the Bay Area of California – the psychedelic counterculture fuelled a fascination with diverse wisdom traditions and esoteric teachings from around the world. The psychedelic era of hippies and pranksters itself was short-lived, fizzling out in a just a couple of years, but in its wake an eclectic fusion of Eastern mysticism, Western esoterica, indigenous spirituality, metaphysics and popular self-help psychology became entrenched as part of the American subculture and would later give rise to the New Age movement.

Within this context of a burgeoning 'alternative spirituality', variations on imported Gardnerian witchcraft began to emerge in the United States from the late 1960s onwards. In particular, the blending of feminism and modern witchcraft gave rise to a more broad-based spiritual movement known as Goddess worship or Goddess spirituality. As theologian Mary Farrell Bednarowski has observed, this was a movement that rejected traditional Christianity and Judaism, seeking 'truth in the depths of the female psyche and [finding] its energy in the worship of the "the goddess".' According to Bednarowski the primary task of feminist spirituality involved 'the resacralization of the cosmos and the reimaging of the sacred.' Resacralization in turn required the 'reinfusion of the sacred into the universe' and for this to occur there had to be a 'redefining of the very nature of the sacred'.... It could not be 'contained solely within the transcendent being of the God of the Bible.'[4]

In her book *Changing of the Gods: Feminism and the End of Traditional Religions*, released in 1979, Naomi Goldenberg proposed that feminist witchcraft could create a 'powerful new religion' focused on the worship of the Goddess and that this new religion would encourage feminist witches to reject 'a civilization in which males in high places imitate a male god in heaven'. Influential thinker Mary Daly similarly claimed that the new feminist witchcraft was an appropriate alternative to a model of the universe in which a male God ruled the cosmos and thereby controlled social institutions to the detriment of women:

> The symbol of the Father God, spawned in the human imagination and sustained as plausible by patriarchy, has in turn

> rendered service to this type of society by making its mechanisms for the oppression of women appear right and fitting.[5]

In the United States, Goddess worship expanded the structure of Gardnerian coven-based witchcraft, adopting rituals that were broader in scope, more diverse, and less bound by Wiccan concepts. Although some Goddess-worshippers continued to refer to themselves as witches, others abandoned the term altogether, preferring to regard their neo-pagan practice as a universal feminist religion, drawing on mythologies from many different ancient cultures. Among the most notable figures in the new movement were Zsuzsanna Budapest and Starhawk who, between them, would redefine the very nature of feminist Neo-paganism in the United States.

In a lengthy interview with journalist Cheri Lesh, published in 1975, Budapest expressed her belief that Wicca was not an inverted form of Christianity but represented the remnants of a much older, matriarchal system of worship that recognized the feminine as the creative force in Nature. Budapest spoke of the bloody transition from a matriarchal society to a patriarchal form, in which roaming bands of warriors ravaged the great Queendoms of Anatolia, Sumer and Thrace and fragmented the 'Great Goddess' into a number of minor deities. This led to a much diminished status for the goddesses, who then had confined and restricted roles as a consequence. In Greek mythology, Aphrodite became simply a goddess of love and sexuality, while Artemis represented hunting, and Athena wisdom. Hera, Amphitrite and Persephone, meanwhile, became adjuncts to Zeus, Poseidon and Hades. According to Budapest, this transition was a major cultural disaster:

> Mythology is the mother of religions, and grandmother of history. Mythology is human-made, by the artists, storytellers and entertainers of the times. In short, culture-makers are the soldiers of history, more effective than guns and bombers. Revolutions are really won on the cultural battlefields...Women understand this very well, since we became aware of how women's culture had been ripped off by the ruling class. This resulted in a stunted self-image of women which resulted in insecurities, internalizing the cultural expectations of us created by male culture-makers. Most of the women in the world still suffer from this spiritual poverty.[6]

In order to eliminate any male influence, Budapest's Dianic witchcraft excludes men altogether. According to Budapest, women's mysteries must be kept pure and strong, and men have no place in them: 'We have *women's* circles. You don't put men in women's circles – they wouldn't be women's circles any more. Our Goddess is Life, and women should be free to worship from their ovaries.'[7]

The other key figure in the Goddess movement, Miriam Simos – otherwise known as Starhawk – has published several highly influential books since the late 1970s, including *The Spiral Dance*, *Dreaming the Dark* and *The Pagan Book of Living and Dying*, all widely regarded as key works in the revival of Goddess worship and neopaganism. Starhawk was a founding member of Reclaiming, a feminist network of women and men working within the Goddess tradition to unify spirituality and politics through progressive activism. Starhawk maintains that her Goddess perspective involves a process of re-sacralizing the world:

> What's important about witchcraft and about the pagan movement is, essentially, that it's not so much a way of seeing

> reality, as it's a different way of valuing the reality around us. We say that what is sacred, in the sense of what we are most committed to, what determines all our other values, is this living Earth, this world, the life systems of the earth, the cycles of birth and growth and death and regeneration; the air, the fire, the water, the land... [8]

In her writings Starhawk also refers specifically to the nurturing and revitalising power of the Goddess-energy:

> The symbolism of the Goddess has taken on an electrifying power for modern women. The rediscovery of the ancient matrifocal civilizations has given us a deep sense of pride in woman's ability to create and sustain culture. It has exposed the falsehoods of patriarchal history, and given us models of female strength and authority. The Goddess – ancient and primeval; the first of deities; patroness of the Stone Age hunt and of the first sowers of seeds; under whose guidance the herds were tamed, the healing herbs first discovered; in whose image the first works of art were created; for whom the standing stones were raised; who was the inspiration of song and poetry – is recognized once again in today's world. She is the bridge, on which we can cross the chasms within ourselves, which were created by our social conditioning, and reconnect with our lost potentials. She is the ship, on which we sail the waters of the deep self, exploring the uncharted seas within. She is the door, through which we pass to the future. She is the cauldron, in which we who have been wrenched apart simmer until we again become whole. She is the vaginal passage, through which we are reborn... [9]

Starhawk's *The Spiral Dance* and Z. Budapest's *Holy Book of Women's*

Mysteries have influenced the rise of American Goddess spirituality in much the same way that Gerald Gardner and Doreen Valiente's writings helped establish the foundations of British Wicca in the 1950s. According to Starhawk, the sacred presence of the Goddess remains at the very heart of all forms of feminist witchcraft: 'The Goddess is around us and within us. She is immanent and transcendent ... the Goddess represents the divine embodied in Nature, in human beings, in the flesh.'[10] Starhawk regards the Goddess as the source of all life, the ground of all being: 'The Goddess is first of all earth,' she writes, 'the dark, nurturing mother who brings forth all life. She is the power of fertility and generation; the womb, and also the receptive tomb, the power of death. All proceeds from Her, all returns to Her.'[11]

Starhawk's views are echoed by American feminist writer Carol P. Christ, who offers a similarly all-encompassing view of the Goddess:

> The earth is the body of the Goddess. All beings are interdependent in the web of life. Nature is intelligent, alive and aware. As part of nature, human beings are relational, embodied, and interdependent...The symbols and rituals of Goddess religion bring these values to consciousness and help us build communities in which we can create a more just, peaceful, and harmonious world.[12]

The Gardnerian high priestess, Margot Adler, also holds a similar view. In an interview published in *East West*, [13] she told journalist Victoria Williams that Wicca involved 'seeing the earth as sacred, seeing human beings and everything else as part of that creation, seeing divinity as immanent and not transcendent, and seeing people as basically good'. She also told me much the same thing when I interviewed her in New

York for a television documentary in the mid-1980s: 'I think that one of the reasons that so many people in the United States have come to paganism is that they see in it a way of re-sacralizing the world, of making it animated, of making it vivid again, of having a relationship to it that allows for harmony and wholeness. Perhaps this can help create a world that is more harmonious with Nature and can end the despoilation of the planet.'[14] However she also emphasised that one of the areas where Wicca differed from more organised religions was in its conviction that the divine principle could be found, potentially, within every living person – a formal structure or belief system was not required : 'The fundamental thing about the magical and pagan religions is that ultimately they say that within yourself *you* are the god, *you* are the goddess – you can actualise within yourself and create whatever you need on this earth and beyond. And therefore, what is so subversive about the pagan religions, in a very powerful and beautiful way, is that women can realise: "You too are god." And that's a powerful message. Go into a feminist bookshop anywhere and you will find a whole shelf devoted to feminist spirituality – books, many of them, trying to reinterpret Christianity, reinterpret Judaism. There again is the creative, feminine energy. And it's brought many, many women into the pagan religions.'[15]

There is no doubt in my mind that Rosaleen Norton would have flourished in the company of Starhawk, Z. Budapest and Margot Adler if she were alive today, but sadly she was ahead of her time. Such frameworks of thinking simply did not exist in her day. While Rosaleen emphasized Pan as the universal life-principle, rather than worshipping the Mother Goddess as a giver of life and sustenance, there was nevertheless a comparable feeling in her approach to life. As Rosaleen told me in 1977, Pan was very much a deity for the present day, not simply an archetypal figure from antiquity. For her, Pan was the creative force in the universe who protected the natural beauty of the planet and conserved the resources of the environment. And like Starhawk, Rosaleen believed that magic had political consequences – Pan was alive and well in the anti-pollution lobbies, and among the Friends of the Earth!

Like her contemporary counterparts, Rosaleen shared the vision of magic as a way of re-sacralizing the world, of finding divinity in Nature. In a sense we can say that Rosaleen was a feminist in a time when there were no feminists, a witch at a time when witchcraft was still widely misunderstood. But more than anything else, she was a free spirit – an independent venturer in the magical cosmos. Her visions of the night, those eerie phantasms which haunted her imagination and opened doorways to other realms of mythic consciousness, serve as a reminder that there are always greater realities in the universe which we can acknowledge and explore. This, I feel sure, is the single message she would have wished to leave behind, for others to pursue.

* * *

1 Readers interested in the origins and development of modern Wicca and related magical movements may wish to refer to my recent book *Stealing Fire from Heaven: The Rise of Modern Western Magic* (Oxford University Press, 2011), or Ronald Hutton's *The Triumph of the Moon* (Oxford University Press, 1999).

2 Peter Lucas, 'Witches in the Nude', *People*, Sydney, 5 March 1958:54.

3 *The Chicago Tribune*, 13 April 1980.

4 See M.F. Bednarowski,' The New Age Movement and Feminist Spirituality: Overlapping Conversations at the End of the Century' in J.R. Lewis and J.G. Melton (ed.) *Perspectives on the New Age*, State

University of New York Press, Albany, New York 1992:169. Feminist writer Carol P. Christ goes even further, arguing that the re-sacralization of the earth is part of the process of individual transformation: 'When the earth is the body of the Goddess, the radical implications of the image are more fully realized. The female body and the earth, which have been devalued and dominated together, are resacralized. Our understanding of divine power is transformed as it is clearly recognized as present within the finite and changing world. The image of earth as the body of the Goddess can inspire us to repair the damage that has been done to the earth, to women, and to other beings in dominator cultures.' See C.P. Christ, *Rebirth of the Goddess: Finding Meaning in Feminist Spirituality*, Routledge, New York 1997: 91.

5 M. Daly, *Beyond God the Father*, Beacon Press, Boston 1973:13.

6 C. Lesh, 'Goddess Worship: the Subversive Religion", *Twelve Together*, Los Angeles, May 1975.

7 Personal communication to the author, Berkeley, California, December 1984, during filming of the television documentary *The Occult Experience*, released in the United States on Sony Home Video.

8 See A. Blair-Ewart, *Mindfire:Dialogues in the Other Future* , Somerville House, Toronto 1995:128.

9 Starhawk, 'The Goddess' in Roger S. Gottlieb (ed.) *A New Creation: America's Contemporary Spiritual Voices*, Crossroad, New York 1990:213.

10 Starhawk, *Dreaming the Dark*, Beacon Press, Boston 1982:.8-9.

11 Ibid: 214.

12 C.P. Christ, *Rebirth of the Goddess: Finding Meaning in Feminist Spirituality*, Routledge, New York 1997: xv.

13 Victoria Williams, 'The Sacred Craft', *East West*, October 1984.

14 See my earlier book, *The Occult Experience*, London 1987: 43.

15 Ibid: 44.

Bibliography

Adler, M., *Drawing Down the Moon*, Beacon Press, Boston 1981

Agrippa, H.C., *Fourth Book of Occult Philosophy*, Askin Publishers, London 1978

______ *Three Books of Occult Philosophy or Magic* [1533], ed. W.F. Whitehead , Aquarian Press, London 1971

Aldrich, M, Ashley, R., and Horowitz, M. (ed.), *High Times Encyclopedia of Recreational Drugs*, Stonehill Publishing, New York 1978

Anon., 'Candid Reflections on Art', *Truth*, Melbourne, 27 August 1949

Anon., 'Inside Rosaleen Norton', *Squire*, Sydney, April 1965

Anon., 'More from the Folios of Miss Rosaleen Norton's Art', *Pertinent* 1(5) December 1941

Anon., 'More Occult Fantasy from the Portfolio of Rosaleen Norton', *Pertinent* 1 (4) November 1941

Anon., 'Rosaleen Norton, the Witch', *Daily Mirror*, Sydney, 24 March 1980

Anon., 'Rosaleen Norton's Art', *Pertinent* 1 (3) October 1941

Anon., 'She Hates Figleaf Morality', *People*, Sydney, 29 March 1950

Baddeley, G., *Lucifer Rising*, Plexus, London 1999

Bailey, M.D., 'The Meanings of Magic', *Magic, Ritual and Witchcraft*, University of Pennsylvania Press, Summer 2006: 1.

Bardon, F., *The Practice of Magical Evocation*, Rudolf Pravica, Graz-Puntigam, Austria 1967

Barnes, D., 'Rosaleen says she could be a Witch', *Australasian Post*, Sydney, 9 October 1952

______ 'I am a Witch', *Australasian Post*, Sydney, 20 December 1956

______ Confessions of a Witch', *Australasian Post*, 15 June 1967

Bednarowski, M.F., 'Women in Occult America' in H. Kerr and C.L. Crow (ed.), *The Occult in America: New Historical Perspectives*, University of Illinois Press, Urbana and Chicago 1983

______ ' The New Age Movement and Feminist Spirituality: Overlapping Conversations at the End of the Century' in J.R. Lewis and J.G. Melton (ed.) *Perspectives on the New Age*, State University of New York Press, Albany, New York 1992

Bharati, A., *The Tantric Tradition*, Rider, London 1965

Blaikie, G., *Remember Smith's Weekly?*, Rigby, Adelaide 1966
Blair-Ewart, A. (ed.), *Mindfire: Dialogues in the Other Future*, Somerville House, Toronto 1995
Blavatsky, H.P., *The Secret Doctrine*, fifth edition, Theosophical Publishing House, Madras 1962
Bogdan, H., 'Kenneth Grant: Marriage between the West and the East', extract from 'Challenging the Morals of Western Society: the Use of Ritualised Sex in Contemporary Occultism,' *The Pomegranate*, 8, 2, Equinox Publishing, London 2006, www.fulgur.co.uk
Bonner, J., *Qabalah*, Skoob Publishing, London 1995
Bracelin, J.L., *Gerald Gardner: Witch*, Octagon Press, London 1960
Broughton, O.M., 'The art of Rosaleen Norton', *Arna*, Sydney 1948
Budapest, Z., *The Holy Book of Women's Mysteries*, Wingbow Press, Los Angeles, 1989
Butler, W.E., *Magic: Its Ritual Power and Purpose*, second edition, Aquarian Press, London 1958
______ *The Magician: His Training and Work*, Aquarian Press, London 1959
______ *Apprenticed to Magic*, Aquarian Press, London 1962
______ *Magic and the Qabalah*, Aquarian Press, London 1964
Chaudhuri, H., 'Yoga Psychology' in C. Tart (ed.) *Transpersonal Psychologies*, Harper & Row, New York 1975
Choucha, N., *Surrealism and the Occult*, Mandrake, Oxford 1991
Christ, C.P., and Plaskow, J., (ed.), *Womanspirit Rising*, Harper & Row, San Francisco 1979
______ *Rebirth of the Goddess: Finding Meaning in Feminist Spirituality*, Routledge, New York 1997
Crabtree, V., 'Left Hand Path Practices in the West', 2002, www.dpjs.co.uk/lefthandpath.html
Crowley, A., 'Emblems and Modes of Use', www.aethyria.com, n.d.
______ *De Arte Magica*, www.skepticfiles.org, n.d.
______ *Liber A'ash vel Capricorni Pneumatici*, *Equinox* 1:6, September 1911
______ *Liber Cheth*, *Equinox* 1:6, September 1911
______ *Liber Stellae Rubae*, *Equinox* 1:7, March 1912
______ *Liber XVIV, The Mass of the Phoenix*, 1912, www.thelemicgoldendawn.org/rituals/phoenix.htm
______ *Energized Enthusiasm: A Note on Theurgy*, *Equinox*, vol.1 No.9, March 1913
(republished by Weiser, New York 1976)
______ *Magick in Theory and Practice* [1929], Castle Books, New York 1964; Routledge & Kegan Paul, London 1973
______ *The Book of Lies*, Haydn Press, Ilfracombe, Devon 1962
______ *The Confessions of Aleister Crowley* (ed.J. Symonds and K.Grant), Hill and Wang, New York 1970
______ *The Magical Record of the Beast 666*, ed. J..Symonds and K.Grant, Duckworth, London 1972
______ *Liber Al vel Legis* in *The Magical Record of the Beast 666*, ed. J..Symonds and K. Grant, Duckworth, London 1972
______ *Book Four*, Sangreal Foundation, Dallas 1972
______ *The Vision and the Voice*, Sangreal Foundation, Dallas 1972
______ *The Qabalah of Aleister Crowley*, Weiser, New York 1973
______ 'Talismans: The Lamen: The Pantacle' in *Magick Without Tears*, New Falcon Publications, Tempe, Arizona 1982
Crowley, V., *Wicca: the Old Religion in the New Millennium*, Thorsons, London 1996
______ 'Wicca as Modern-Day Mystery Religion' in G. Harvey and C. Hardman (ed.), *Pagan Pathways*, Thorsons, London 2000
______ *A Woman's Guide to the Earth Traditions*, Thorsons, London 2001
Crowther, P., *Lid off the Cauldron: A Handbook for Witches*, Muller, London 1981

Deren, M., *Divine Horsemen: the Voodoo Gods of Haiti*, Thames and Hudson, London 1953

Deveney, J.P., *Paschal Beverly Randolph: A Nineteenth-Century American Spiritualist, Rosicrucian and Sex Magician*, State University of New York Press, Albany, New York 1997

Drury, N., *Inner Visions: Explorations in Magical Consciousness*, Routledge & Kegan Paul, London 1979

______ *Stealing Fire from Heaven: The Rise of Modern Western Magic*, Oxford University Press, New York and Oxford, 2011

______ *Dark Spirits: The Magical Art of Rosaleen Norton and Austin Osman Spare*, Salamander and Sons, Chiang Mai, Thailand and Brisbane, Australia, 2012

Drury, N., and Tillett, G., *Other Temples, Other Gods: the Occult in Australia*, Methuen, Sydney 1980

Eliade, M., *Yoga, Immortality and Freedom*, Princeton University Press, New Jersey 1970

______ *Shamanism, Archaic Techniques of Ecstasy*, Princeton University Press, New Jersey 1972

______ *Occultism, Witchcraft and Cultural Fashions*, University of Chicago Press, Chicago 1976

Ellwood, R., *The Sixties Spiritual Revival*, Rutgers University Press, New Brunswick, New Jersey 1996

Evans, D., *The History of British Magick After Crowley*, Hidden Publishing, London 2007

Farrar, J. and S., *Eight Sabbats for Witches*, Hale, London 1981

______ *The Witches' Way: Principles, Rituals and Beliefs of Modern Witchcraft*, Hale,
London 1984

______ *The Witches' Bible*, Magickal Childe, New York 1985

______ *The Witches' Goddess*, Hale, London 1987

Farrar, S., *What Witches Do*, revised edition, Phoenix Publishing, Custer, Washington 1983

Feldman, D.H., *Qabalah: The Mystical Heritage of the Children of Abraham*, Work of the Chariot, Santa Cruz, California 2001

Fischer-Schreiber, I., et al. (ed.) *The Encyclopedia of Eastern Philosophy and Religion*, Shambhala, Boston 1994

Fisdel, S.A., *The Practice of Kabbalah: Meditation in Judaism*, Jason Aronson Inc., Northvale, New Jersey 1996

Folkard, F.C., *The Rare Sex*, Murray, Sydney 1965

Fortune, D., *Psychic Self-Defence*, Rider, London 1930

______ *The Goat-Foot God*, Williams and Norgate, London 1936

______ *The Mystical Qabalah*, Benn, London 1957

______ *Applied Magic*, Aquarian Press, London 1962

Fuller, J.O., *The Magical Dilemma of Victor Neuburg*, W.H.Allen, London 1965

Gardner, G.B., *High Magic's Aid*, Michael Houghton, London 1949

______ *Witchcraft Today*, Rider, London 1954

______ *The Meaning of Witchcraft*, Aquarian Press, London 1959

______ *Witchcraft Today*, Rider, London 1954

Garrison, O.V., *Tantra: The Yoga of Sex*, Julian Press, New York 1964

Ginsburg, C., *The Kabbalah: Its Doctrines, Development and Literature*, Routledge & Kegan Paul, London 1956

Godwin, J., Chanel, C., and Deveney J.P., *The Hermetic Brotherhood of Luxor*, Weiser, York Beach,Maine 1995

Goldberg, N., *Changing of the Gods: Feminism and the end of Traditional Religions*, Beacon Press, Boston 1979

Gottlieb, R.S. (ed.), *A New Creation: America's Contemporary Spiritual Voices*, Crossroad, New York 1990

Grant, K., *Cults of the Shadow*, Muller, London 1975

______ *Nightside of Eden*, Muller, London 1977

______ *Outside the Circles of Time*, Muller, London 1980

______ 'Cults of the Shadow' in J. White (ed.), *Kundalini: Evolution and Enlightenment*, Paragon House, St Paul, Minnesota 1990

______ *Hecate's Fountain*, Skoob, London 1992

Grant, R. (ed.), *Gnosticism -- an Anthology*, Collins, London

1961

Greenfield, T.A., 'Peter Davidson, Occultist', *Agape*, 2 May 2003

Grof, S., *Realms of the Human Unconscious: Observations from LSD Research*, E.P.Dutton, New York 1976

Guiley, R.E., *The Encyclopedia of Witches and Witchcraft*, Facts on File, New York and Oxford, 1989

Harner, M.J., (ed.) *Hallucinogens and Shamanism*, Oxford University Press, New York 1973

Harrison, P., *The Elements of Pantheism*, Element, Shaftesbury, Dorset 1999

Harvey, G., *Listening People, Speaking Earth: Contemporary Paganism*, Hurst, London 1997

Harvey, G., and Hardman, C. (ed.), *Pagan Pathways*, Thorsons, London 2000

Heseltine, N., *Capriol for Mother, a Memoir of Philip Heseltine (Peter Warlock)*, Thames Publishing, London 1992

Heselton, P., *Wiccan Roots: Gerald Gardner and the Modern Witchcraft Revival*, Capall Bann Publishing, Milverton, Somerset UK 2000

Howard, M., 'Gerald Gardner: the Man, the Myth & the Magick', *The Cauldron* ,

Beltane/Midsummer 1997

Howe, E., *The Magicians of the Golden Dawn,* Routledge & Kegan Paul, London 1972

Hume, L., *Witchcraft and Paganism in Australia*, Melbourne University Press, Melbourne 1997

Hutton, R., *The Triumph of the Moon: a History of Modern Pagan Witchcraft*, Oxford University Press, Oxford 1999

Huxley, A., *Moksha*, ed. M. Horowitz and C. Palmer, Stonehill Publishing, New York 1977

Idel, M, *Kabbalah: New Perspectives*, Yale University Press, New Haven 1988

Jacobi, J., *The Psychology of C.G. Jung,* Routledge & Kegan Paul, London 1942

Javes, N., 'Witches of Sydney', *The Sun*, Sydney, 7 February 1969

Johns, J., *King of the Witches: the World of Alex Sanders*, Coward-McCann, New York 1969

Johnson, M., 'The Witch of Kings Cross: Rosaleen Norton and the Australian Media', conference presentation, Symbiosis: Institute for Comparative Studies in Science, Myth, Magic and Folklore, University of Newcastle, 2002

______ 'The Witching Hour: Sex Magic in 1950s Australia', conference presentation, University of Melbourne, 2004

Jonas, H., *The Gnostic Religion*, Boston 1958

Jung, C.G., *Psychology of the Unconscious*, Kegan Paul, Trench, Trubner, London 1919

______ *Symbols of Transformation*, Bollingen Foundation / Princeton University Press, New Jersey 1956

______ *The Archetypes of the Collective Unconscious*, Routledge & Kegan Paul, London 1959

______ *Memories, Dreams, Reflections*, Collins/Routledge & Kegan Paul, London 1963

______ *Man and his Symbols*, Dell, New York 1968

______ 'Psychological Commentary on Kundalini Yoga', lecture given on 26 October 1932, *Spring*, New York 1976

Kazlev, M.A., 'The Teachings of Max Théon', www.kheper.net/topics/Theon/Theon.htm

King, F., ed.) *The Secret Rituals of the O.T.O.*, C.W. Daniel, London 1973

______ *Tantra: The Way of Action*, Destiny Books, Rochester, Vermont 1990

Koenig, P-R, 'Introduction to the Ordo Templi Orientis', www.user.cyberlink.ch/~koenig/intro.htm

______ 'Spermo-Gnostics and the Ordo Templi Orientis', www.user.cyberlink.ch/~koenig/spermo.htm

Kaczynski, R., *Perdurabo: The Life of Aleister Crowley*, North Atlantic Books, Berkeley, California 2010

Lesh, C., 'Goddess Worship: the Subversive Religion", *Twelve Together*, Los Angeles, May 1975

Levi, E., *The History of Magic*, Rider, London 1913

______ *The Key of the Mysteries,* Rider, London 1959

Lewis, J.R., (ed.), *Magical Religion and Modern Witchcraft*, State University of New York Press, Albany, 1996

Lucas,P., 'Witches in the Nude', *People*, Sydney, 5 March 1958

Marquardt, P.A., 'A Portrait of Hecate', *The American Journal of Philology*, 102, 3, Autumn 1981

Mathers, S.L. MacGregor, (ed.) *The Kabbalah Unveiled*, Redway, London 1887

______ (ed.) *The Greater Key of Solomon*, De Laurence, Chicago 1914

______ (ed.) *The Lesser Key of Solomon*, De Laurence, Chicago 1916

______ (ed.), *The Goetia: The Lesser Key of Solomon the King* [1889], revised edition, Weiser,Boston 1997

Matt, D.C., *The Essential Kabbalah*, HarperCollins, New York 1995

McCann, N., 'And Dangerous to Know' published on http://nedmccann.blogspot.com.au/2005/09/blog-post_112659887360827086.html, 13 September 2005.

McGlynn, K., 'Going to the Devil', *Sunday Telegraph*, Sydney, 16 July 1972

Melton, J.G., 'The Origins of Modern Sex Magick', Institute for the Study of American Religion,Evanston, Illinois, June 1985

Murray, M.A., *The Witch-cult in Western Europe*, Oxford University Press, Oxford 1921

______ *The God of the Witches*, Sampson Low, London 1931; second edition, Oxford University Press, Oxford 1970.

North, R., Introduction to P.B. Randolph, *Sexual Magic*, Magickal Childe, New York 1988 (original French-language text: *Magia Sexualis*, Paris 1931)

Norton, R., exhibition catalogue essay, *The Art of Rosaleen Norton*, Rowden White Library, University of Melbourne, 1-23 August 1949

______ *The Art of Rosaleen Norton*, Walter Glover, Sydney 1952 (republished 1982)

______ 'I was born a Witch', *Australasian Post*, Sydney, 3 January 1957

______ 'Hitch-hiking Witch', *Australasian Post*, Sydney 7 February 1957

______ 'Witches want no Recruits', *Australasian Post*, Sydney, 10 January 1957

______ 'Witch Was No Class At School', *Australasian Post*, Sydney, 24 January 1957

______ 'Inside Rosaleen Norton', interview, *Squire*, Sydney, April 1965

______ *Supplement to The Art of Rosaleen Norton*, Walter Glover, Sydney 1984

______ *Thorn in the Flesh: A Grim-memoire*, ed. Keith Richmond, Teitan Press, York Beach, Maine 2009

Osiris, Frater, 'Analysis of Liber XXXVI, *The Star Sapphire*', Seattle 2004, www.hermetic.com/osiris

______ 'Analysis of the Mass of the Phoenix', www.hermetic.com/osiris

Pandit, M.P., *Kundalini Yoga*, Ganesh, Madras 1968

Patai, R., *The Hebrew Goddess*, third edition, Wayne State University Press, Detroit 1990

Plaskow, J., 'Women's Liberation and the Liberation of God' in R.S.Gottlieb (ed.) *A New Creation: America's Contemporary Spiritual Voices*, Crossroad, New York 1990

Rabinowitz, J., *The Rotting Goddess: The Origin of the Witch in Classical Antiquity*, Autonomedia, New York 1998

Radha, S., *Kundalini Yoga for the West*, Shambhala, Boulder, Colorado 1981

Randolph, P.B., *Eulis!*, Toledo, Ohio 1873, republished 1896.

______ *Sexual Magic*, Magickal Childe, New York 1988 (original French-language text: *Magia Sexualis*, Paris 1931)

______ *The Ansairetic Mystery: A New Revelation Concerning Sex!*, Toledo, Ohio, c.1973-74, republished in J.P. Deveney, *Paschal Beverly Randolph: A Nineteenth-Century American Spiritualist, Rosicrucian and Sex Magician*, State University of New York Press, Albany, New York 1997

Reuss, T., *Lingam-Yoni*, Verlag Willsson, Berlin and London 1906

Rhadon, A., 'Sex, Religion and Magick: a concise overview', 2004, www.baymoon.com

Richmond, K., *The Occult Visions of Rosaleen Norton*, Oceania Lodge of the Ordo Templi Orientis/ Kings Cross Arts Guild, Sydney 2000

(ed.), *Thorn in the Flesh: A Grim-memoire*, Teitan Press, York Beach, Maine 2009

Robbins, R.H., *The Encyclopedia of Witchcraft and Demonology*, Crown, New York 1959

Rosen, C., *The Goossens: A Musical Century*, Andre Deutsch, London 1993

Russell, J.B., *Witchcraft in the Middle Ages*, Cornell University Press, Ithaca, New York 1972

______ *The Devil: Perceptions of Evil from Antiquity to Primitive Christianity*, Cornell

University Press, Ithaca, New York 1977

______ *A History of Witchcraft :Sorcerers, Heretics and Pagans*, Thames & Hudson,

London 1980

______ *Satan: the Early Christian Tradition*, Cornell University Press, Ithaca, New York 1981

Sabazius X° and AMT IX°, *History of Ordo Templi Orientis*, U.S. Grand Lodge, 2006

Salter, D., 'The Strange Case of Sir Eugene and the Witch', *Good Weekend / Sydney Morning Herald*, Sydney, 3 July 1999

Sarmiala-Berger, K., 'Rosaleen Norton – a Painter of Occult and Mystical Pictures', *Overland*, 162, Autumn 2001

Seabrook, W.B., *Magic Island,* Harcourt, Brace, New York, 1929

Seligmann, K., *Magic, Supernaturalism and Religion*, Pantheon, New York 1971

Shah, I., *The Secret Lore of Magic*, Abacus, London 1972

Souter, G., and Molnar, G., *Sydney Observed,* Angus & Robertson, Sydney 1968

Sprenger, J., and Kramer, H. (tr. M. Summers), *Malleus Maleficarum, (The Hammer of the Witches)*, Folio Society, London 1968

Springett, B.H., *Secret Sects of Syria and Lebanon*, Allen & Unwin, London 1922

Starhawk, *Dreaming the Dark*, Beacon Press, Boston 1982

______ 'The Goddess' in R.S. Gottlieb (ed.), *A New Creation : America's Contemporary Spiritual Voices*, Crossroad, New York 1990

______ *The Spiral Dance* [1979], revised edition, Harper San Francisco 1999

______ *Webs of Power: Notes from the Global Uprising*, New Society Publishers, Victoria, Canada 2002

Sutcliffe, R., 'Left-Hand Path Ritual Magick' in G. Harvey and C. Hardman (ed.), *Pagan Pathways: A Guide to the Ancient Earth Traditions*, Thorsons, London 2000

Sutin, L., *Do What Thou Wilt: A Life of Aleister Crowley*, St Martins Press New York 2000

Urban, H.B., *Magia Sexualis: Sex, Magic and Liberation in Modern Western Esotericism*,

University of California Press, Berkeley, California 2006

Valiente, D., *The Rebirth of Witchcraft*, Hale, London 1989

Van Lommel, P., 'About the Continuity of our Consciousness', in C. Machado and D.A. Shewmon (ed.), *Brain Death and Disorders of Consciousness*, Kluwer Academic/ Plenum, New York 2004: 115-132

Von Rudloff, R., *Hekate in Ancient Greek Religion*, Horned Owl Publishing, Victoria, Canada 1999

Walker, B., and Neville, R., 'Deliver us to E-Ville', *Tharunka*, University of New South Wales, Sydney, 3 July 1962

Walker, D.P., *Spiritual and Demonic Magic from Ficino to Campanella*, Sutton Publishing, Stroud, UK 2000

White, J. (ed.), *Kundalini: Evolution and Enlightenment*, Paragon House, St Paul, Minnesota 1990

Wright, L., 'Sympathy for the Devil', *Rolling Stone*, 5 September, 1991

Yronwode, C., 'Paschal Beverly Randolph and the

Ansairetic Mysteries', www.luckymojo.com
______ *The Reverend Hargrave Jennings and Phallism*, www.luckymojo.com
Zephyros, Frater, 'The Ophidian Current', www.groups.msn.com/TheMage/theophidiancurrent.msnw

Index

Q

R

S

T

U

Ithell Colquhoun :
pioneer surrealist artist, occultist, writer, and poet
by Eric Ratcliffe

£19.99/$35 ISBN 978-1869928-98-8 - 314pp -
90 ills (25 in colour)

The skills of Ithell Colquhoun in her main practice, that of artist and pioneer in this country of surrealistic art, have been long recognised. Additionally, other interests - alchemy, Earth-magic, active occultism, poetry, druidism, the pre-Christian Pagan calendar, the history and membership of the Golden Dawn - and writing of and involvement in these interests by book publication and in a widely scattered field of correspondence, have created a miscellany of truly gargantuan proportion. Eric Ratcliffe considered it was time to get together some of these pieces, to add something of what is known of Colquhoun's early life and family history and to take the opportunity of listing a comprehensive calendar of her work and exhibitions. The result is neither strictly biographical nor a treatise on any one subject, but it is a first gathering of the roots, passions and multi-directions of this artist.

Surrealism & the Occult, By Nadia Choucha

£9.99 / $20 ,164 pps ISBN 9781906958749

Many people associate Surrealism with politics, but it was also permeated by occult ideas, a fact often overlooked by art historians. This occult influence goes beyond general themes to the movement's very heart.

This occult influence goes beyond general themes to the movement's very heart. The antinomian stance of Surrealism can be traced directly to the influence of radical nineteenth century magi such as Eliphas Lévi, whose Dogma and Ritual of High Magic was widely read by Surrealism's ideologues. Amongst these we find its progenitor André Breton. Surrealism did not establish itself in Britain until the 1930s but a select few felt something in the air. Almost ten years before the Surrealist experiments with automatic drawing, an obscure English artist, Austin Osman Spare had perfected the technique.

Nadia Choucha shows, convincingly, that occult and surrealist philosophies were often interchangeable. Surrealism and the Occult is seminal reading for art historians and occultists alike, while artists will find it a vital guide to the unlocking of the imagination.

Praise for Nadia Choucha's Surrealism & the Occult
"Highly readable…seminal… fascinating" – Francis X. King
"alive, with the heady mixture of occult and pictorial symbolism treated with laudable lucidity."- Art Book Newswith laudable lucidity."- Art Book News

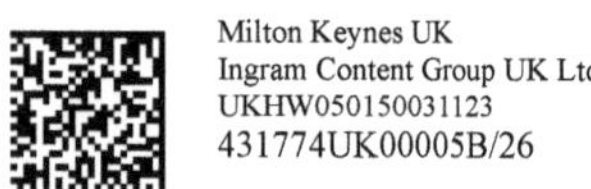

Milton Keynes UK
Ingram Content Group UK Ltd.
UKHW050150031123
431774UK00005B/26